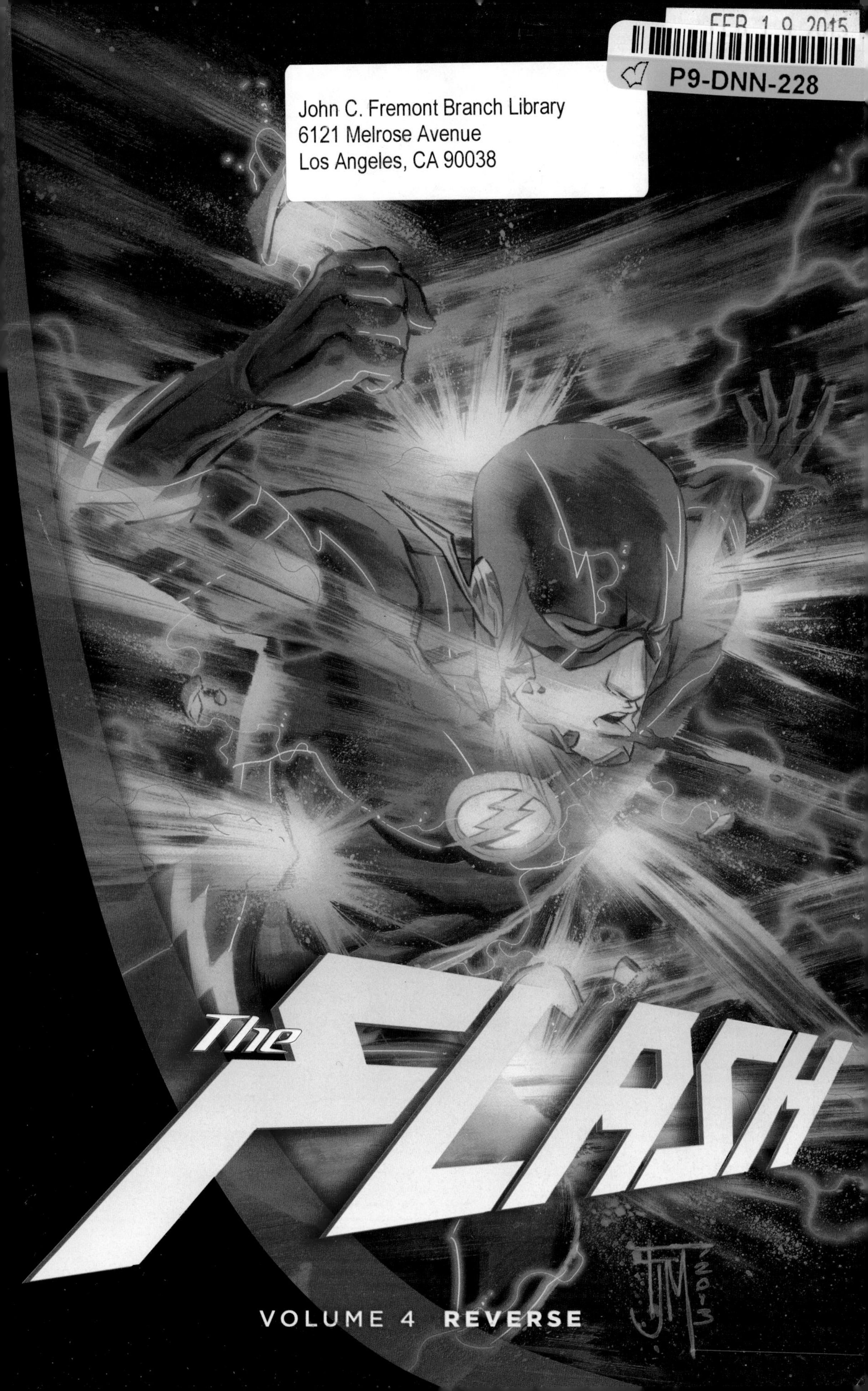
The FLASH
VOLUME 4 REVERSE

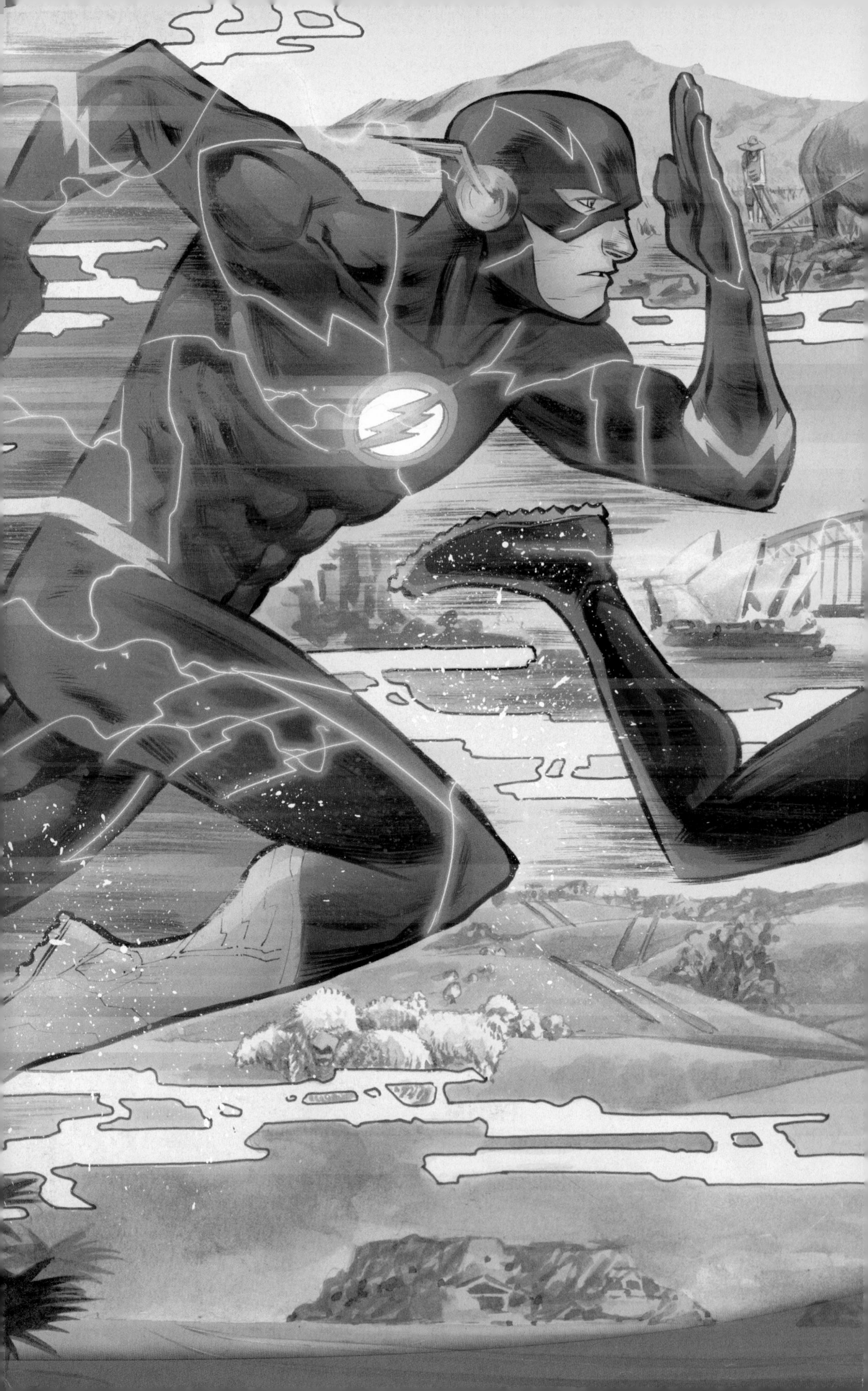

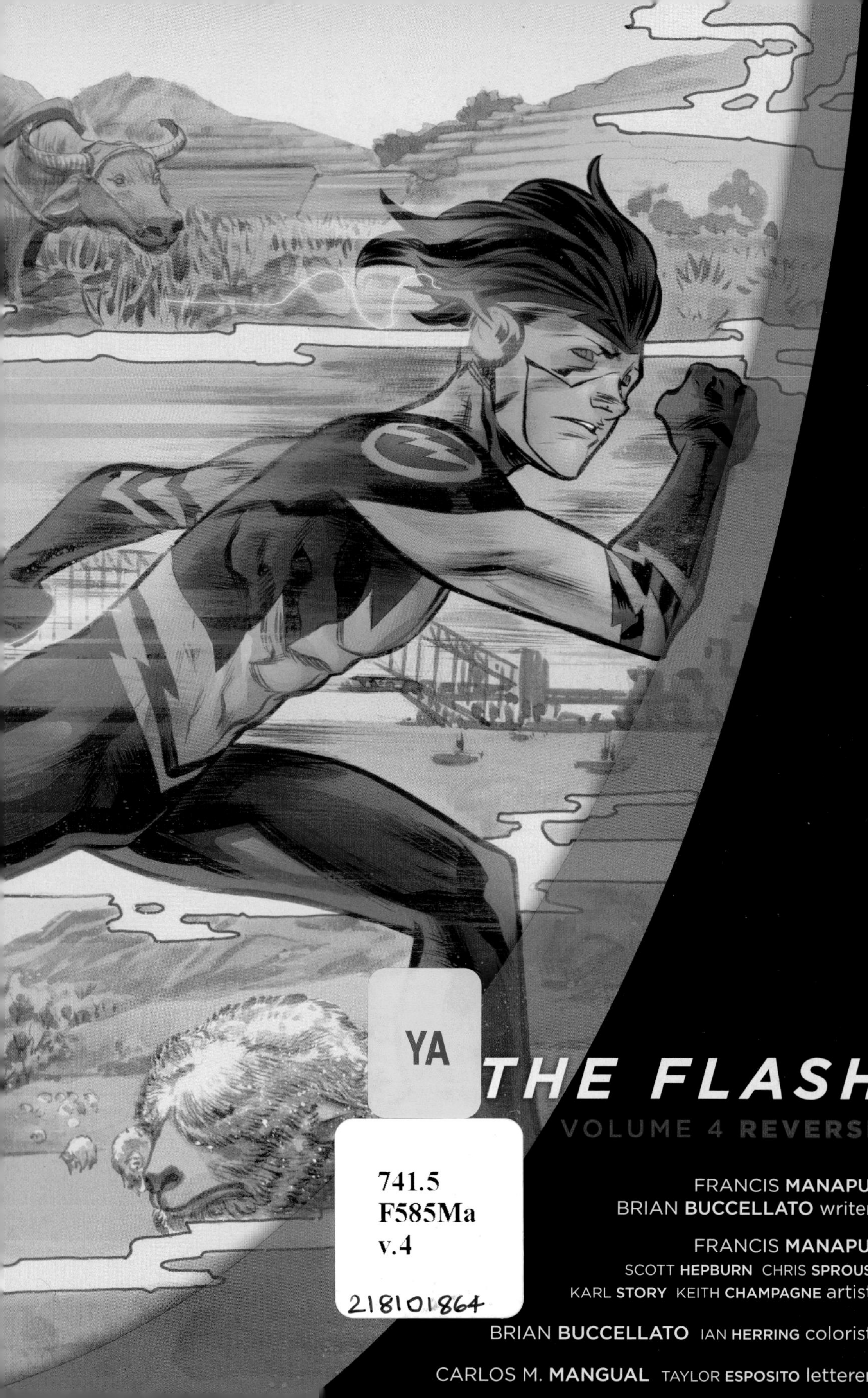

THE FLASH

VOLUME 4 REVERSE

FRANCIS **MANAPUL**
BRIAN **BUCCELLATO** writers

FRANCIS **MANAPUL**
SCOTT **HEPBURN** CHRIS **SPROUSE**
KARL **STORY** KEITH **CHAMPAGNE** artists

BRIAN **BUCCELLATO** IAN **HERRING** colorists

CARLOS M. **MANGUAL** TAYLOR **ESPOSITO** letterers

WIL MOSS Editor – Original Series HARVEY RICHARDS Associate Editor – Original Series
ROBIN WILDMAN Editor ROBBIN BROSTERMAN Design Director – Books
ROBBIE BIEDERMAN Publication Design

BOB HARRAS Senior VP – Editor-in-Chief, DC Comics

DIANE NELSON President DAN DIDIO and JIM LEE Co-Publishers GEOFF JOHNS Chief Creative Officer
AMIT DESAI Senior VP – Marketing and Franchise Management
AMY GENKINS Senior VP – Business and Legal Affairs NAIRI GARDINER Senior VP – Finance
JEFF BOISON VP – Publishing Planning MARK CHIARELLO VP – Art Direction and Design
JOHN CUNNINGHAM VP – Marketing TERRI CUNNINGHAM VP – Editorial Administration
LARRY GANEM VP – Talent Relations and Services ALISON GILL Senior VP – Manufacturing and Operations
HANK KANALZ Senior VP – Vertigo and Integrated Publishing JAY KOGAN VP – Business and Legal Affairs, Publishing
JACK MAHAN VP – Business Affairs, Talent NICK NAPOLITANO VP – Manufacturing Administration SUE POHJA VP – Book Sales
FRED RUIZ VP – Manufacturing Operations COURTNEY SIMMONS Senior VP – Publicity BOB WAYNE Senior VP – Sales

THE FLASH VOLUME 4: REVERSE

Originally published in single magazine form as THE FLASH 20-25, 23.2 © 2013, 2014 DC Comics. All Rights Reserved.
All characters, their distinctive likenesses and related elements featured in this publication are trademarks of DC Comics.
The stories, characters and incidents featured in this publication are entirely fictional. DC Comics does not read or
accept unsolicited ideas, stories or artwork.

DC Comics, 1700 Broadway, New York, NY 10019
A Warner Bros. Entertainment Company.
Printed by RR Donnelley, Owensville, MO, USA. 12/26/14. First Printing.

ISBN: 978-1-4012-4949-6

Library of Congress Cataloging-in-Publication Data

Manapul, Francis, author.
The Flash. Volume 4, Reverse / Francis Manapul, Brian Buccellato.
pages cm. — (The New 52!)
ISBN 978-1-4012-4949-6
1. Graphic novels. I. Buccellato, Brian, illustrator. II. Title. III. Title: Reverse.
PN6728.F53M39 2014
741.5'973—dc23
                2014011627

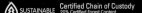

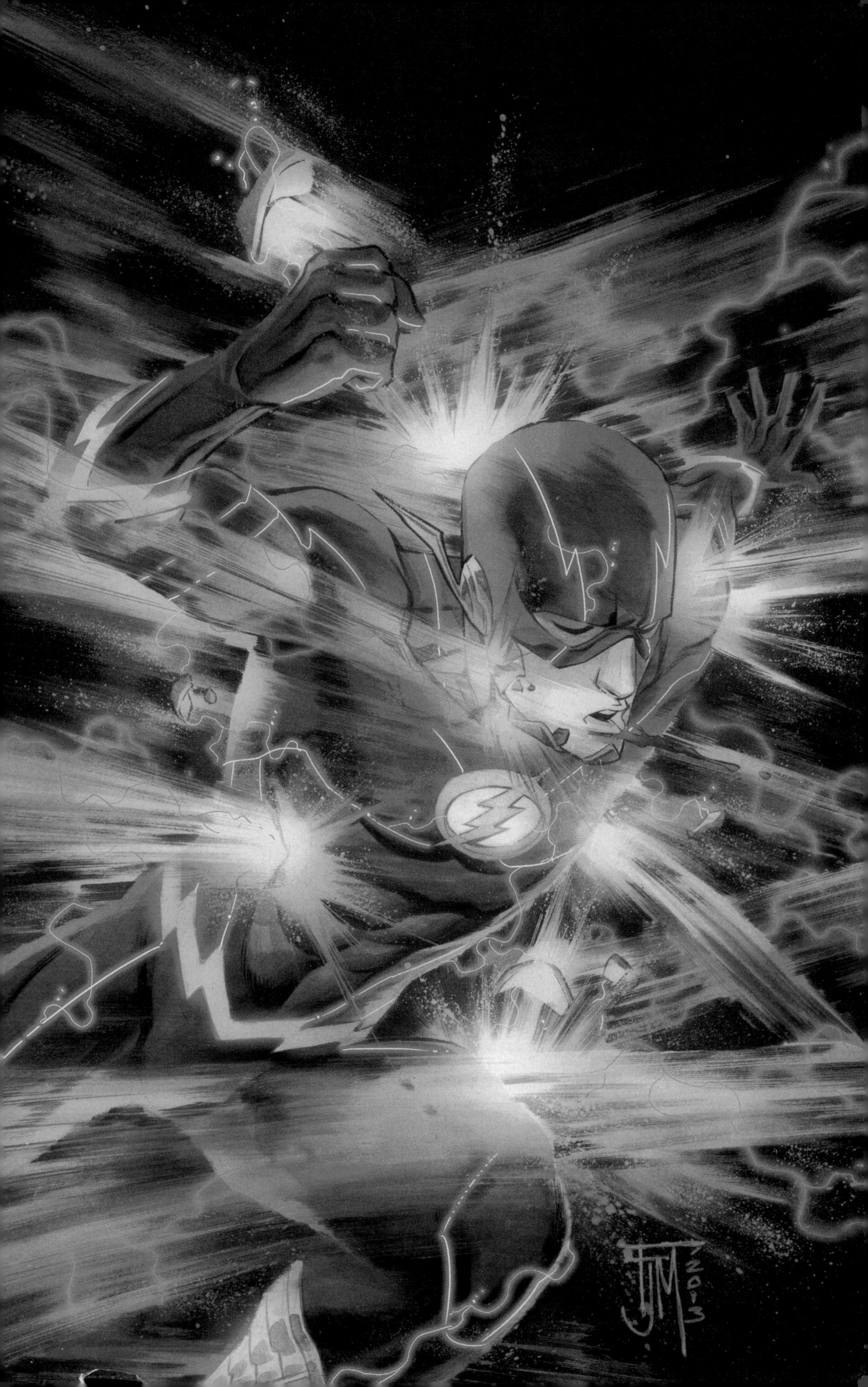

FRANCIS MANAPUL & BRIAN BUCCELLATO writers **FRANCIS MANAPUL** artist

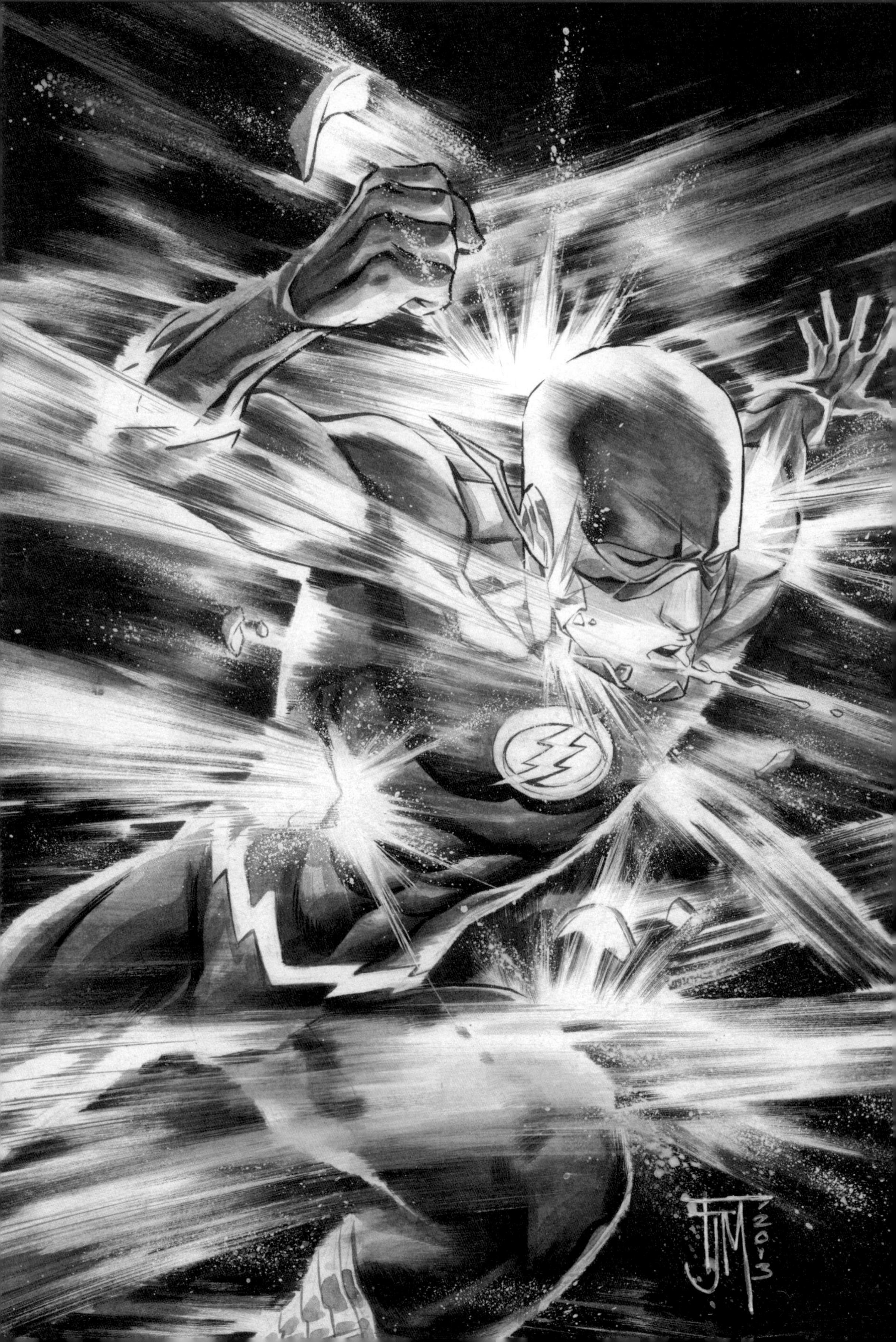

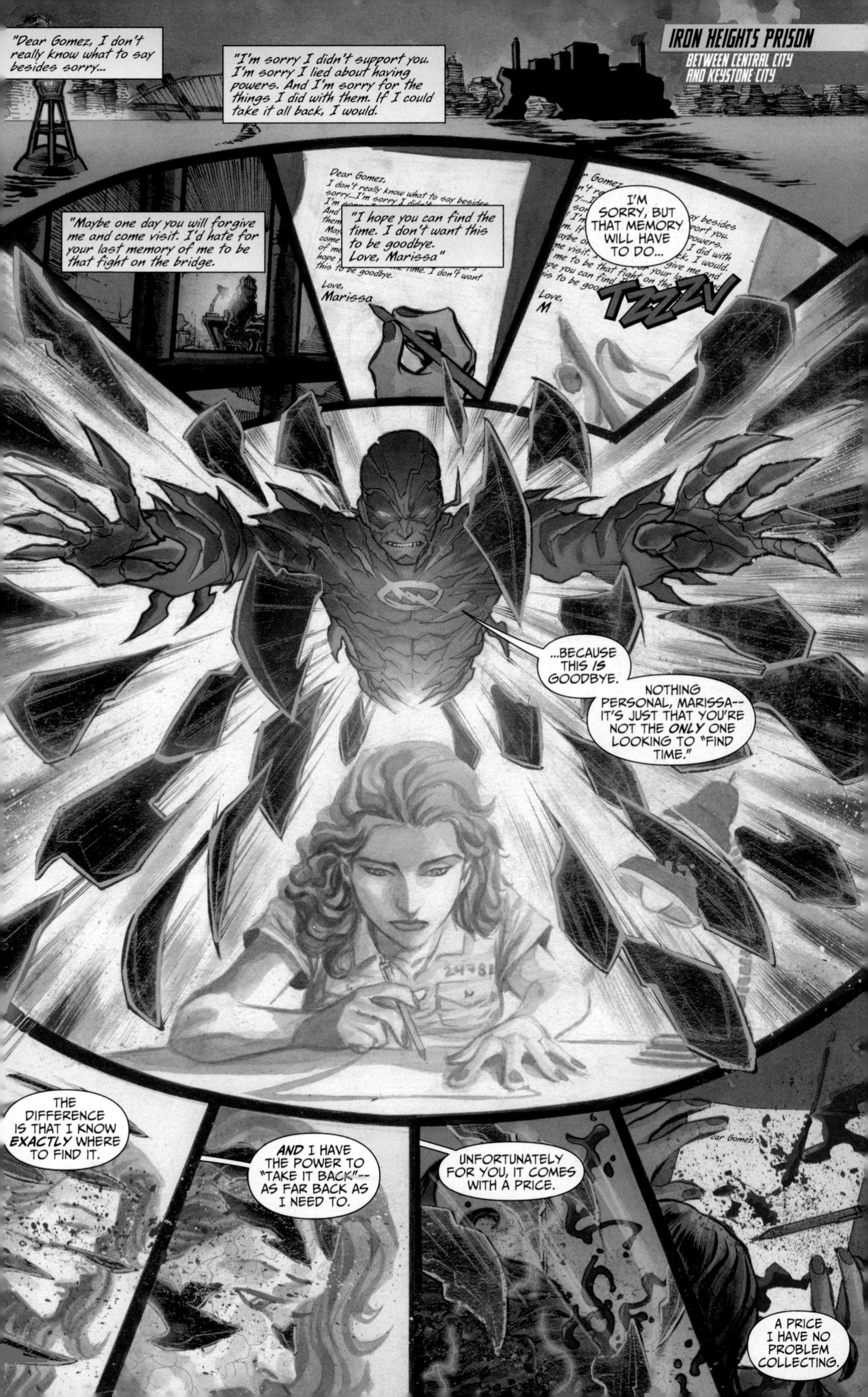

IRON HEIGHTS PRISON
BETWEEN CENTRAL CITY AND KEYSTONE CITY
"Dear Gomez, I don't really know what to say besides sorry...
"I'm sorry I didn't support you. I'm sorry I lied about having powers. And I'm sorry for the things I did with them. If I could take it all back, I would.
"Maybe one day you will forgive me and come visit. I'd hate for your last memory of me to be that fight on the bridge.
Dear Gomez,
"I hope you can find the time. I don't want this to be goodbye. Love, Marissa"
Love, Marissa
I'M SORRY, BUT THAT MEMORY WILL HAVE TO DO...
TZZZV
...BECAUSE THIS *IS* GOODBYE.
NOTHING PERSONAL, MARISSA-- IT'S JUST THAT YOU'RE NOT THE *ONLY* ONE LOOKING TO "FIND TIME."
THE DIFFERENCE IS THAT I KNOW *EXACTLY* WHERE TO FIND IT.
AND I HAVE THE POWER TO "TAKE IT BACK"-- AS FAR BACK AS I NEED TO.
UNFORTUNATELY FOR YOU, IT COMES WITH A PRICE.
A PRICE I HAVE NO PROBLEM COLLECTING.

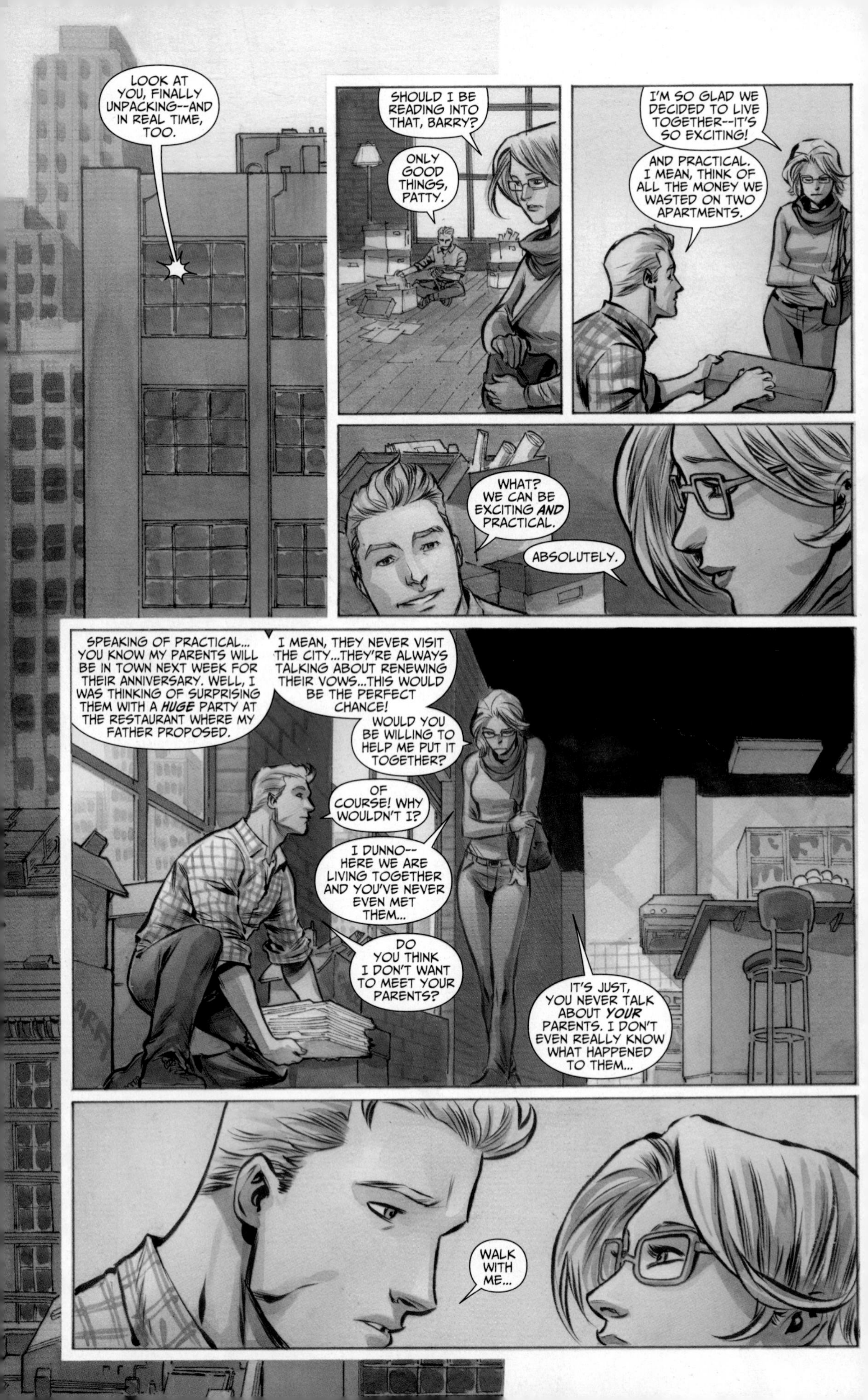
LOOK AT YOU, FINALLY UNPACKING--AND IN REAL TIME, TOO.
SHOULD I BE READING INTO THAT, BARRY?
ONLY GOOD THINGS, PATTY.
I'M SO GLAD WE DECIDED TO LIVE TOGETHER--IT'S SO EXCITING!
AND PRACTICAL. I MEAN, THINK OF ALL THE MONEY WE WASTED ON TWO APARTMENTS.
WHAT? WE CAN BE EXCITING AND PRACTICAL.
ABSOLUTELY.
SPEAKING OF PRACTICAL... YOU KNOW MY PARENTS WILL BE IN TOWN NEXT WEEK FOR THEIR ANNIVERSARY. WELL, I WAS THINKING OF SURPRISING THEM WITH A HUGE PARTY AT THE RESTAURANT WHERE MY FATHER PROPOSED.
I MEAN, THEY NEVER VISIT THE CITY...THEY'RE ALWAYS TALKING ABOUT RENEWING THEIR VOWS...THIS WOULD BE THE PERFECT CHANCE!
WOULD YOU BE WILLING TO HELP ME PUT IT TOGETHER?
OF COURSE! WHY WOULDN'T I?
I DUNNO-- HERE WE ARE LIVING TOGETHER AND YOU'VE NEVER EVEN MET THEM...
DO YOU THINK I DON'T WANT TO MEET YOUR PARENTS?
IT'S JUST, YOU NEVER TALK ABOUT YOUR PARENTS. I DON'T EVEN REALLY KNOW WHAT HAPPENED TO THEM...
WALK WITH ME...

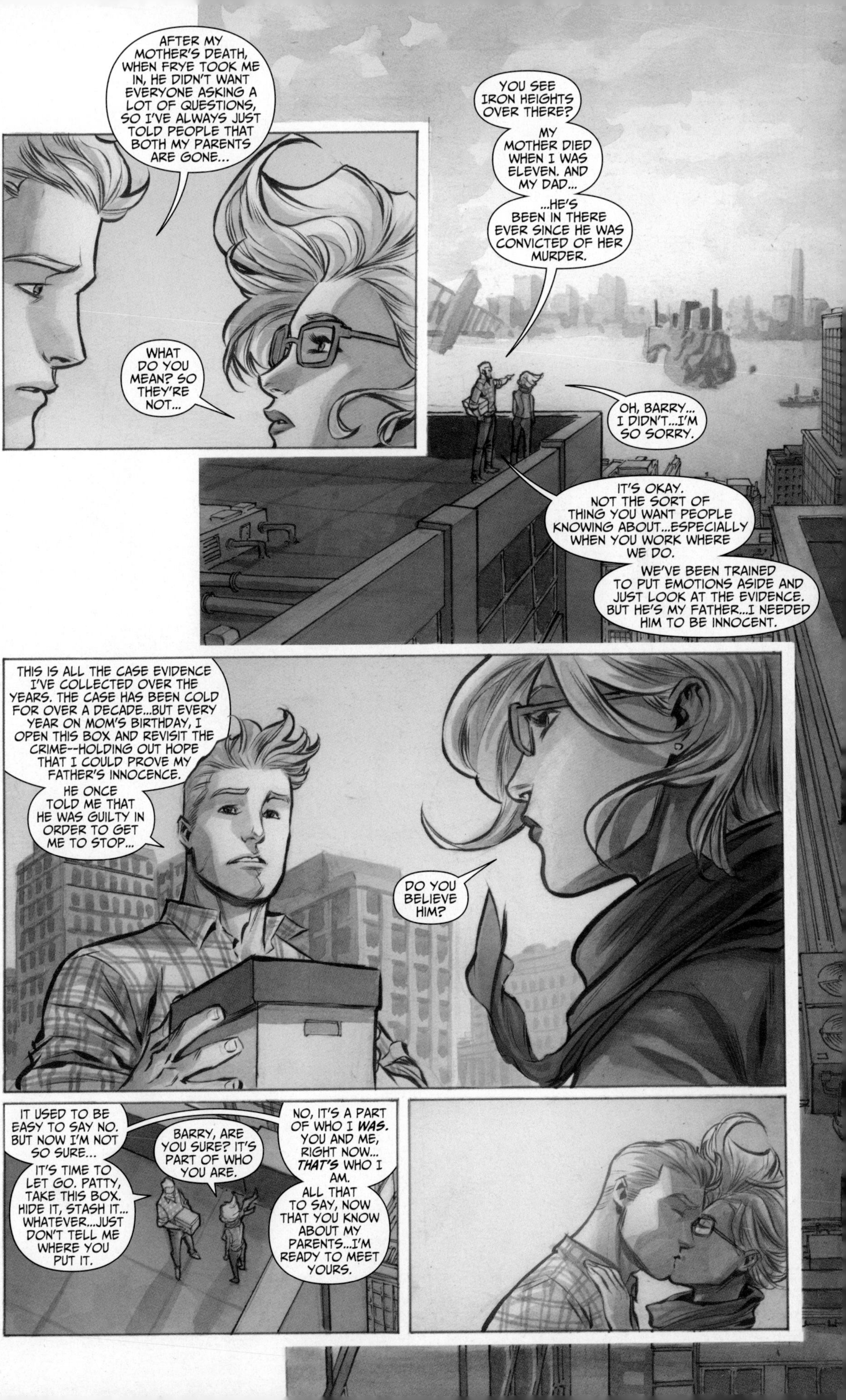
AFTER MY MOTHER'S DEATH, WHEN FRYE TOOK ME IN, HE DIDN'T WANT EVERYONE ASKING A LOT OF QUESTIONS, SO I'VE ALWAYS JUST TOLD PEOPLE THAT BOTH MY PARENTS ARE GONE...
WHAT DO YOU MEAN? SO THEY'RE NOT...
YOU SEE IRON HEIGHTS OVER THERE?
MY MOTHER DIED WHEN I WAS ELEVEN. AND MY DAD...
...HE'S BEEN IN THERE EVER SINCE HE WAS CONVICTED OF HER MURDER.
OH, BARRY... I DIDN'T...I'M SO SORRY.
IT'S OKAY. NOT THE SORT OF THING YOU WANT PEOPLE KNOWING ABOUT...ESPECIALLY WHEN YOU WORK WHERE WE DO.
WE'VE BEEN TRAINED TO PUT EMOTIONS ASIDE AND JUST LOOK AT THE EVIDENCE. BUT HE'S MY FATHER...I NEEDED HIM TO BE INNOCENT.
THIS IS ALL THE CASE EVIDENCE I'VE COLLECTED OVER THE YEARS. THE CASE HAS BEEN COLD FOR OVER A DECADE...BUT EVERY YEAR ON MOM'S BIRTHDAY, I OPEN THIS BOX AND REVISIT THE CRIME--HOLDING OUT HOPE THAT I COULD PROVE MY FATHER'S INNOCENCE.
HE ONCE TOLD ME THAT HE WAS GUILTY IN ORDER TO GET ME TO STOP...
DO YOU BELIEVE HIM?
IT USED TO BE EASY TO SAY NO. BUT NOW I'M NOT SO SURE...
IT'S TIME TO LET GO. PATTY, TAKE THIS BOX. HIDE IT, STASH IT... WHATEVER...JUST DON'T TELL ME WHERE YOU PUT IT.
BARRY, ARE YOU SURE? IT'S PART OF WHO YOU ARE.
NO, IT'S A PART OF WHO I *WAS.* YOU AND ME, RIGHT NOW... *THAT'S* WHO I AM.
ALL THAT TO SAY, NOW THAT YOU KNOW ABOUT MY PARENTS...I'M READY TO MEET YOURS.

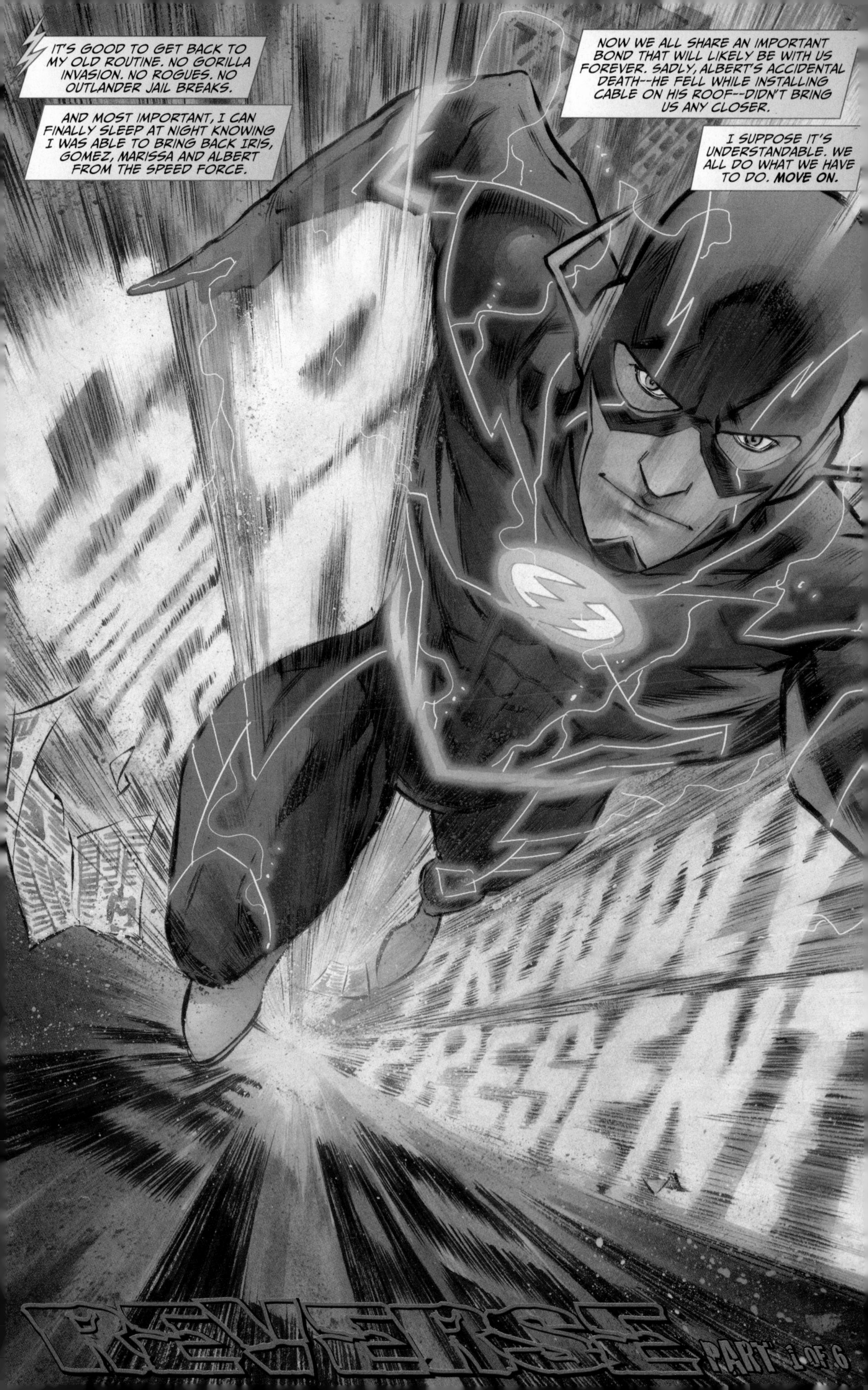
IT'S GOOD TO GET BACK TO MY OLD ROUTINE. NO GORILLA INVASION. NO ROGUES. NO OUTLANDER JAIL BREAKS.
AND MOST IMPORTANT, I CAN FINALLY SLEEP AT NIGHT KNOWING I WAS ABLE TO BRING BACK IRIS, GOMEZ, MARISSA AND ALBERT FROM THE SPEED FORCE.
NOW WE ALL SHARE AN IMPORTANT BOND THAT WILL LIKELY BE WITH US FOREVER. SADLY, ALBERT'S ACCIDENTAL DEATH--HE FELL WHILE INSTALLING CABLE ON HIS ROOF--DIDN'T BRING US ANY CLOSER.
I SUPPOSE IT'S UNDERSTANDABLE. WE ALL DO WHAT WE HAVE TO DO. **MOVE ON.**
REVERSE
PART 1 OF 6

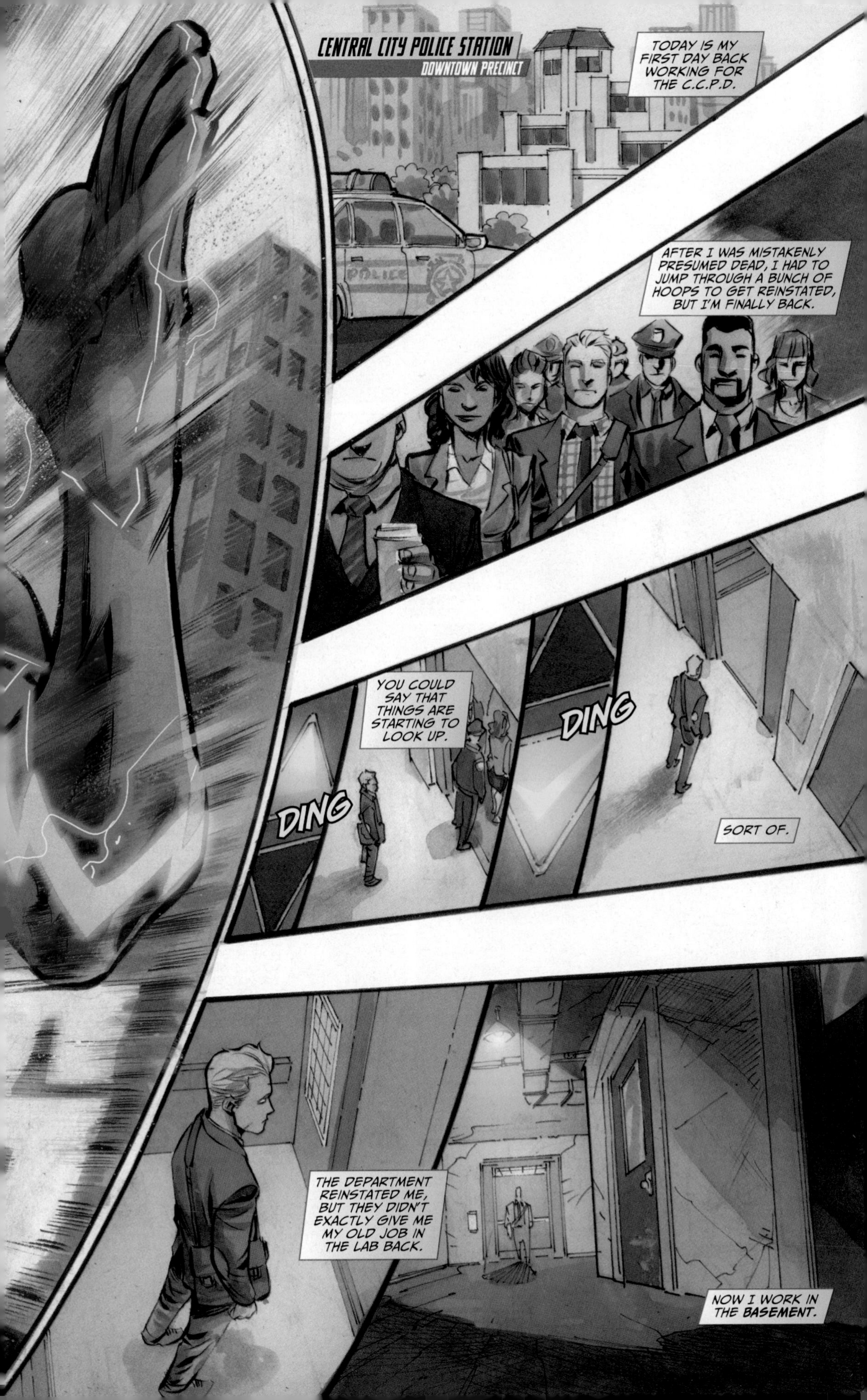
CENTRAL CITY POLICE STATION
DOWNTOWN PRECINCT
TODAY IS MY FIRST DAY BACK WORKING FOR THE C.C.P.D.
AFTER I WAS MISTAKENLY PRESUMED DEAD, I HAD TO JUMP THROUGH A BUNCH OF HOOPS TO GET REINSTATED, BUT I'M FINALLY BACK.
YOU COULD SAY THAT THINGS ARE STARTING TO LOOK UP.
DING
DING
SORT OF.
THE DEPARTMENT REINSTATED ME, BUT THEY DIDN'T EXACTLY GIVE ME MY OLD JOB IN THE LAB BACK.
NOW I WORK IN THE BASEMENT.

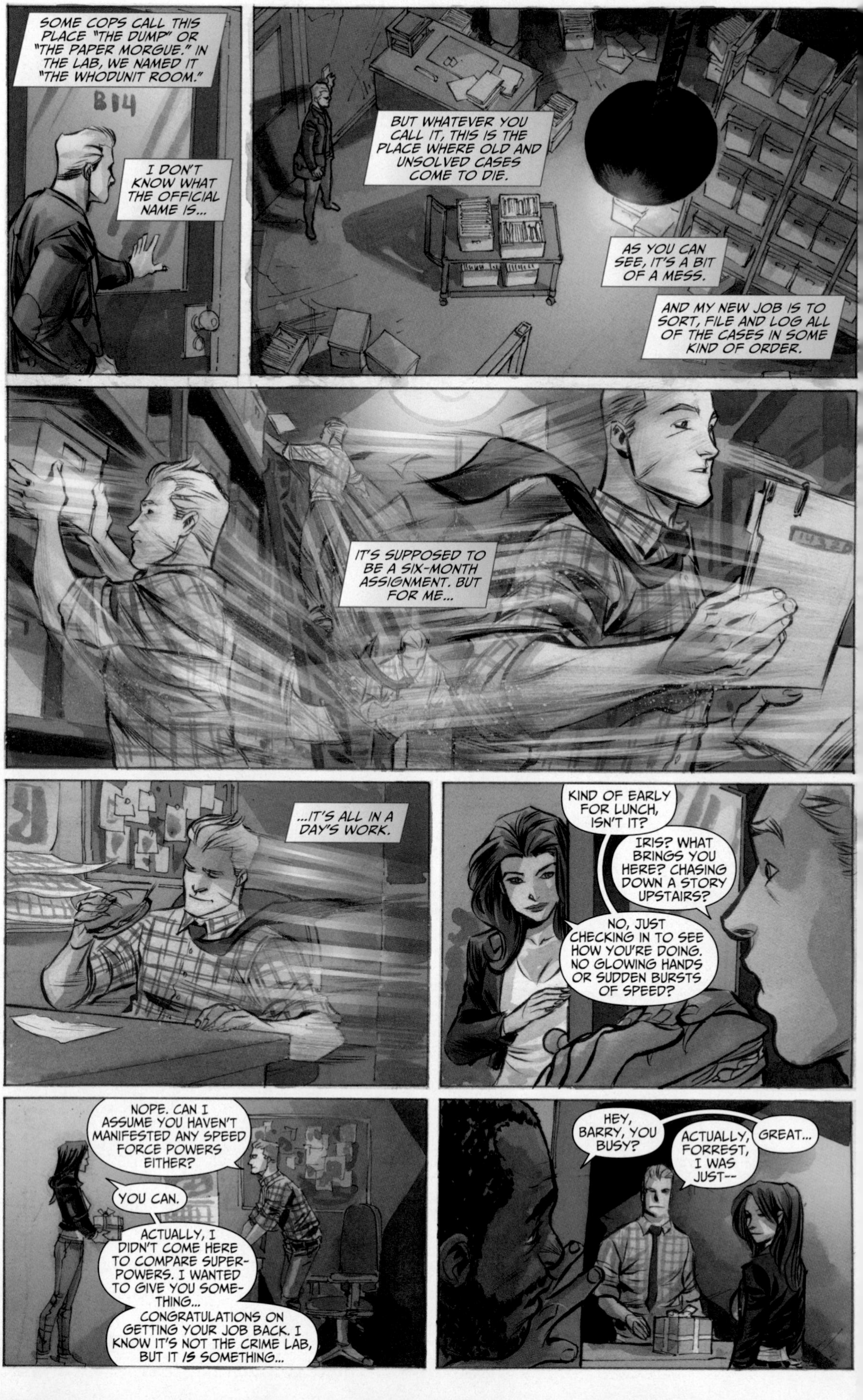
SOME COPS CALL THIS PLACE "THE DUMP" OR "THE PAPER MORGUE." IN THE LAB, WE NAMED IT "THE WHODUNIT ROOM."
B14
I DON'T KNOW WHAT THE OFFICIAL NAME IS...
BUT WHATEVER YOU CALL IT, THIS IS THE PLACE WHERE OLD AND UNSOLVED CASES COME TO DIE.
AS YOU CAN SEE, IT'S A BIT OF A MESS.
AND MY NEW JOB IS TO SORT, FILE AND LOG ALL OF THE CASES IN SOME KIND OF ORDER.
IT'S SUPPOSED TO BE A SIX-MONTH ASSIGNMENT. BUT FOR ME...
...IT'S ALL IN A DAY'S WORK.
KIND OF EARLY FOR LUNCH, ISN'T IT?
IRIS? WHAT BRINGS YOU HERE? CHASING DOWN A STORY UPSTAIRS?
NO, JUST CHECKING IN TO SEE HOW YOU'RE DOING. NO GLOWING HANDS OR SUDDEN BURSTS OF SPEED?
NOPE. CAN I ASSUME YOU HAVEN'T MANIFESTED ANY SPEED FORCE POWERS EITHER?
YOU CAN.
ACTUALLY, I DIDN'T COME HERE TO COMPARE SUPER-POWERS. I WANTED TO GIVE YOU SOME-THING...
CONGRATULATIONS ON GETTING YOUR JOB BACK. I KNOW IT'S NOT THE CRIME LAB, BUT IT IS SOMETHING...
HEY, BARRY, YOU BUSY?
ACTUALLY, FORREST, I WAS JUST--
GREAT...

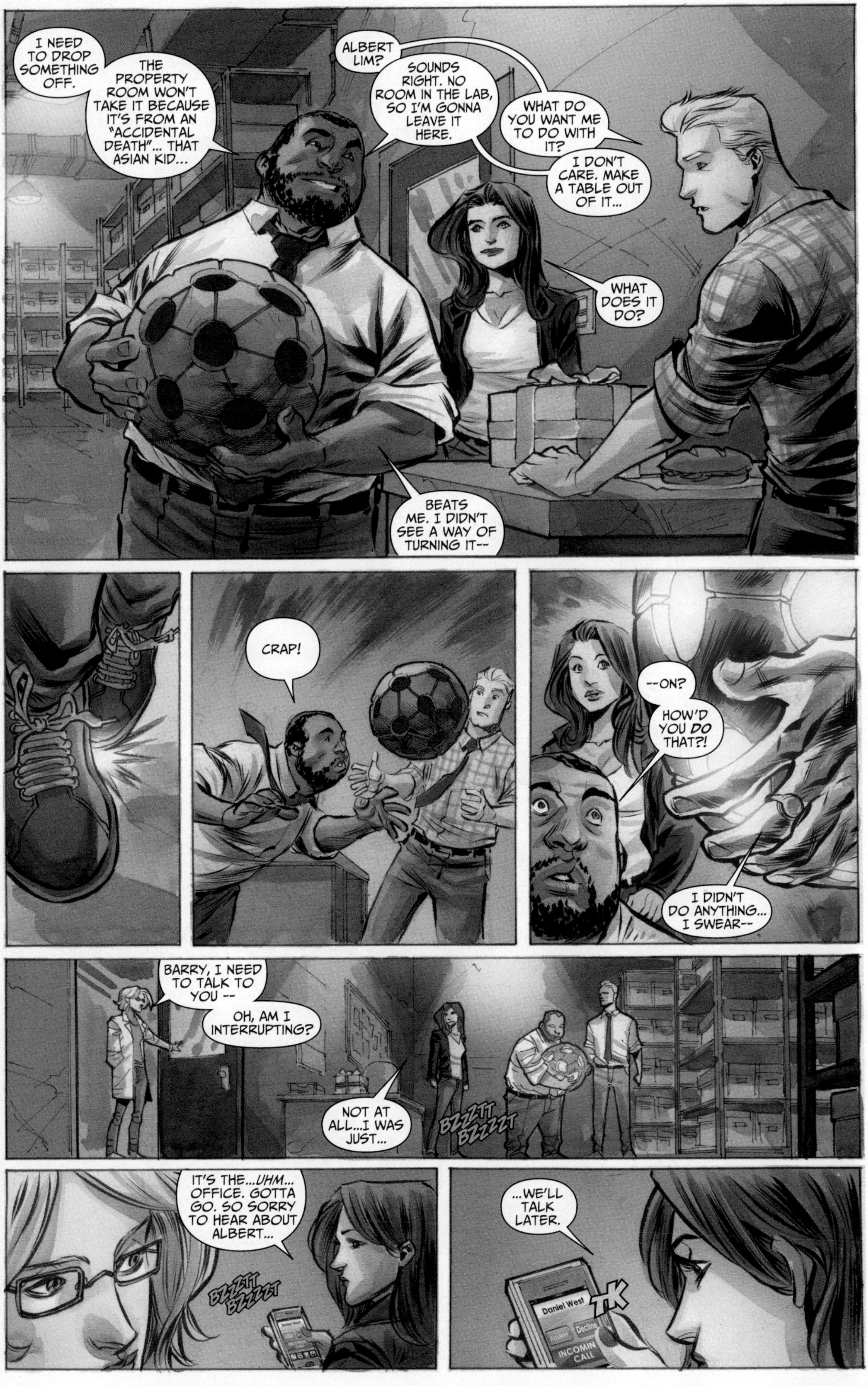
I NEED TO DROP SOMETHING OFF.
THE PROPERTY ROOM WON'T TAKE IT BECAUSE IT'S FROM AN "ACCIDENTAL DEATH"... THAT ASIAN KID...
ALBERT LIM?
SOUNDS RIGHT. NO ROOM IN THE LAB, SO I'M GONNA LEAVE IT HERE.
WHAT DO YOU WANT ME TO DO WITH IT?
I DON'T CARE. MAKE A TABLE OUT OF IT...
WHAT DOES IT DO?
BEATS ME. I DIDN'T SEE A WAY OF TURNING IT--
CRAP!
--ON?
HOW'D YOU *DO* THAT?!
I DIDN'T DO ANYTHING... I SWEAR--
BARRY, I NEED TO TALK TO YOU --
OH, AM I INTERRUPTING?
NOT AT ALL...I WAS JUST...
BZZZTT BZZZZT
IT'S THE...*UHM*... OFFICE. GOTTA GO. SO SORRY TO HEAR ABOUT ALBERT...
BZZZTT BZZZZT
...WE'LL TALK LATER.
Daniel West
Answer
Decline
INCOMIN CALL
TK

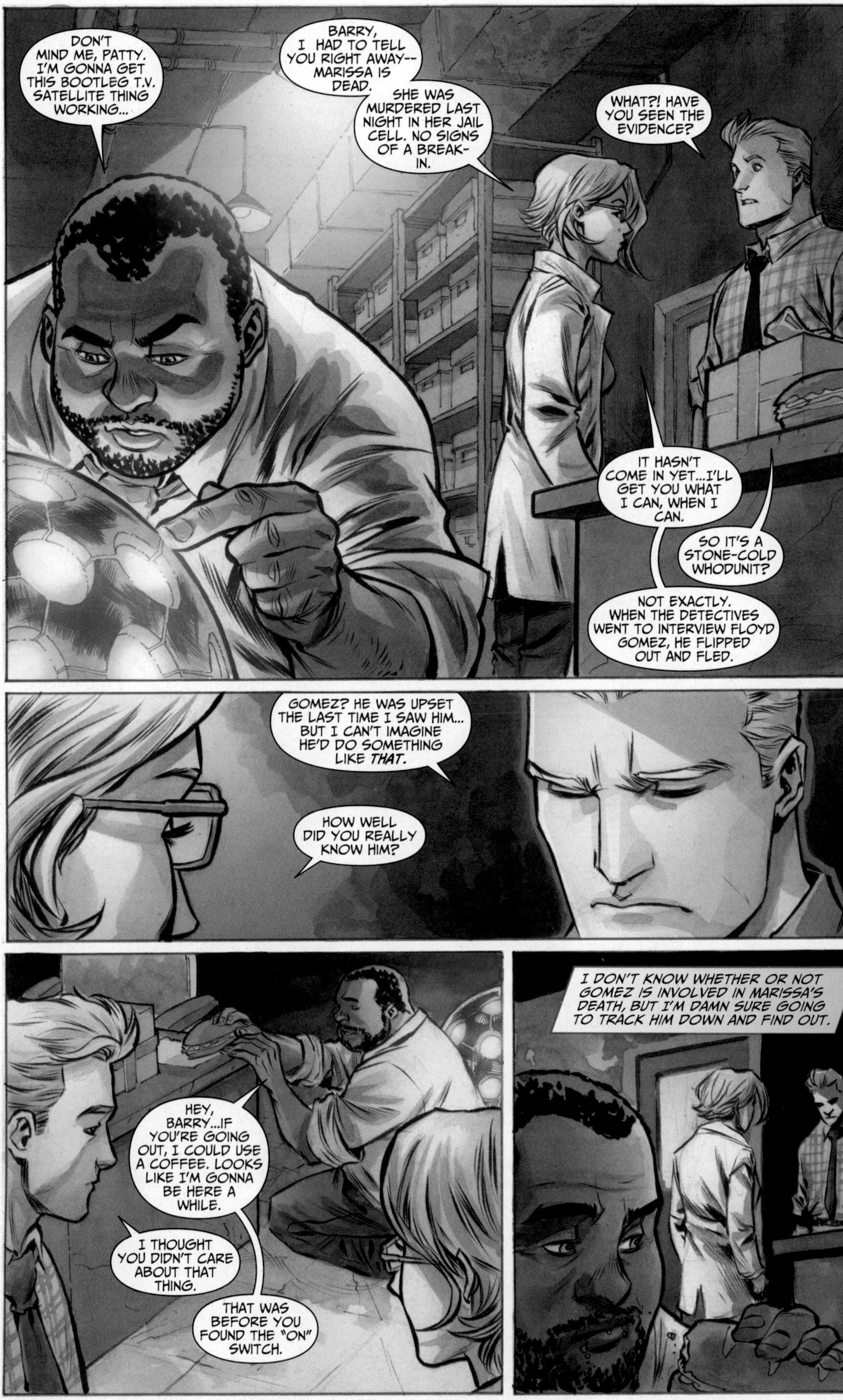
DON'T MIND ME, PATTY. I'M GONNA GET THIS BOOTLEG T.V. SATELLITE THING WORKING...
BARRY, I HAD TO TELL YOU RIGHT AWAY-- MARISSA IS DEAD.
SHE WAS MURDERED LAST NIGHT IN HER JAIL CELL. NO SIGNS OF A BREAK-IN.
WHAT?! HAVE YOU SEEN THE EVIDENCE?
IT HASN'T COME IN YET...I'LL GET YOU WHAT I CAN, WHEN I CAN.
SO IT'S A STONE-COLD WHODUNIT?
NOT EXACTLY. WHEN THE DETECTIVES WENT TO INTERVIEW FLOYD GOMEZ, HE FLIPPED OUT AND FLED.
GOMEZ? HE WAS UPSET THE LAST TIME I SAW HIM... BUT I CAN'T IMAGINE HE'D DO SOMETHING LIKE *THAT.*
HOW WELL DID YOU REALLY KNOW HIM?
HEY, BARRY...IF YOU'RE GOING OUT, I COULD USE A COFFEE. LOOKS LIKE I'M GONNA BE HERE A WHILE.
I THOUGHT YOU DIDN'T CARE ABOUT THAT THING.
THAT WAS BEFORE YOU FOUND THE "ON" SWITCH.
I DON'T KNOW WHETHER OR NOT GOMEZ IS INVOLVED IN MARISSA'S DEATH, BUT I'M DAMN SURE GOING TO TRACK HIM DOWN AND FIND OUT.

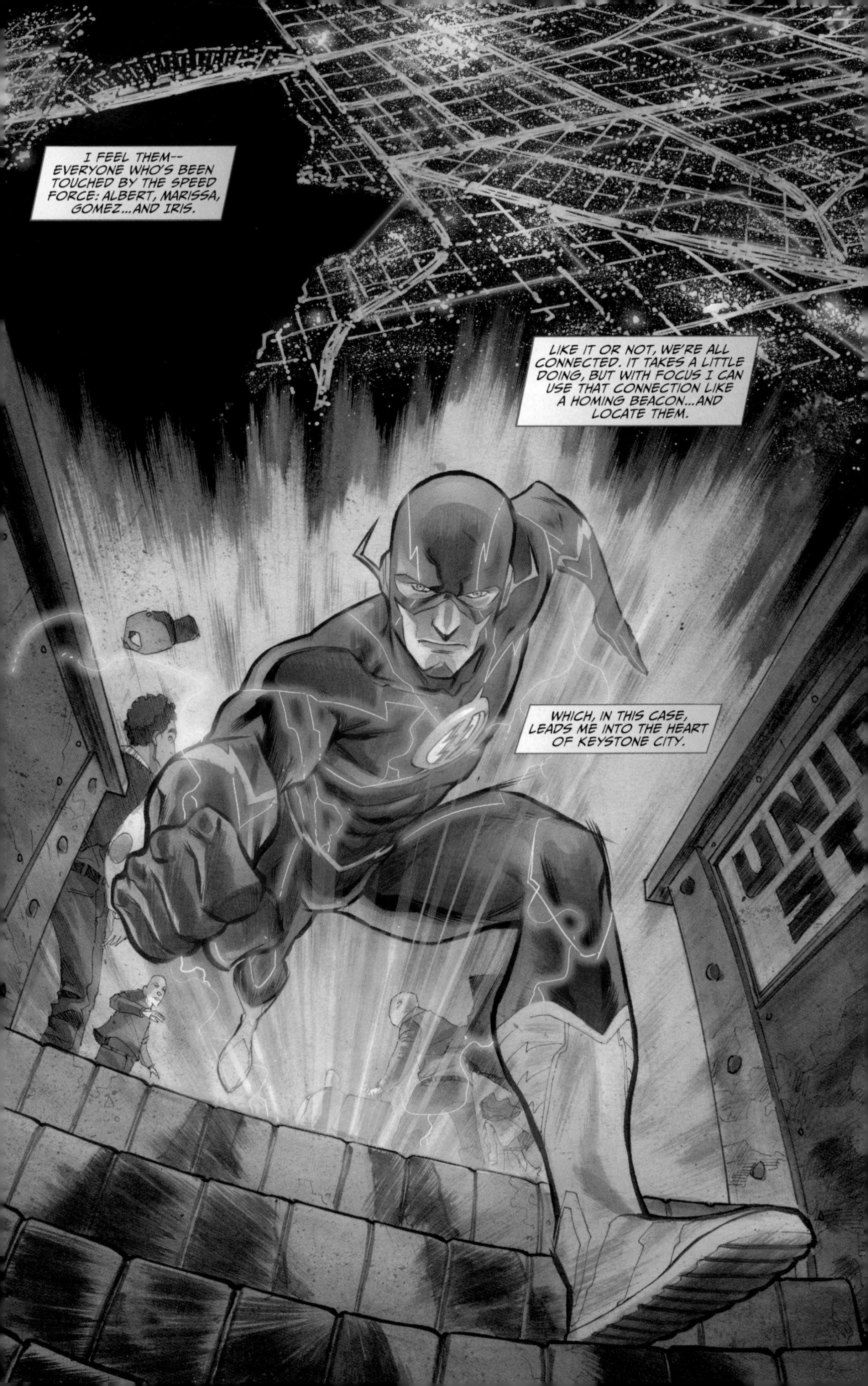
I FEEL THEM--EVERYONE WHO'S BEEN TOUCHED BY THE SPEED FORCE: ALBERT, MARISSA, GOMEZ...AND IRIS.
LIKE IT OR NOT, WE'RE ALL CONNECTED. IT TAKES A LITTLE DOING, BUT WITH FOCUS I CAN USE THAT CONNECTION LIKE A HOMING BEACON...AND LOCATE THEM.
WHICH, IN THIS CASE, LEADS ME INTO THE HEART OF KEYSTONE CITY.

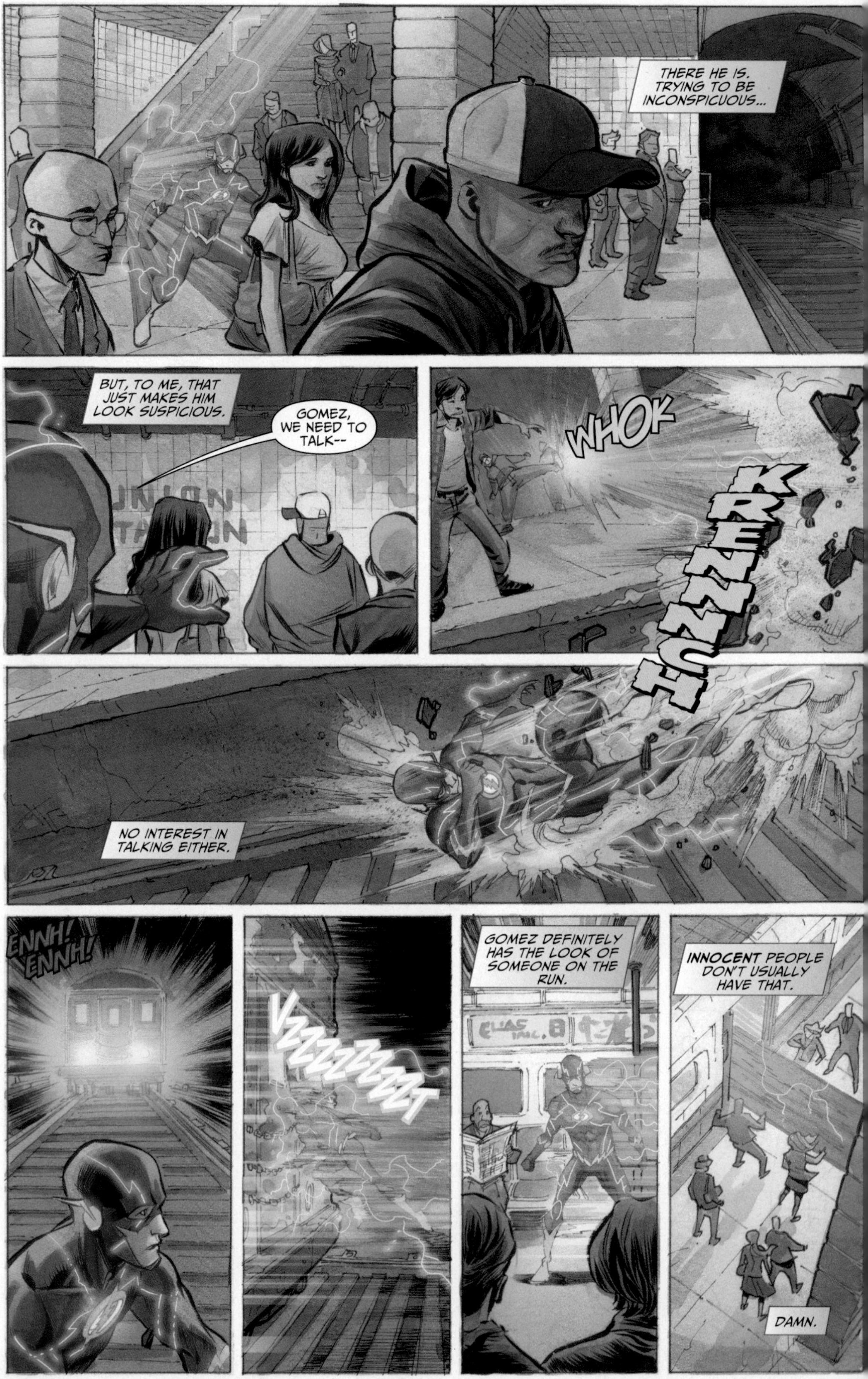
THERE HE IS. TRYING TO BE INCONSPICUOUS...
BUT, TO ME, THAT JUST MAKES HIM LOOK SUSPICIOUS.
GOMEZ, WE NEED TO TALK--
UNION STATION
WHOK
KRENNCH
NO INTEREST IN TALKING EITHER.
ENNH! ENNH!
VZZZZZZZZZT
GOMEZ DEFINITELY HAS THE LOOK OF SOMEONE ON THE RUN.
INNOCENT PEOPLE DON'T USUALLY HAVE THAT.
DAMN.

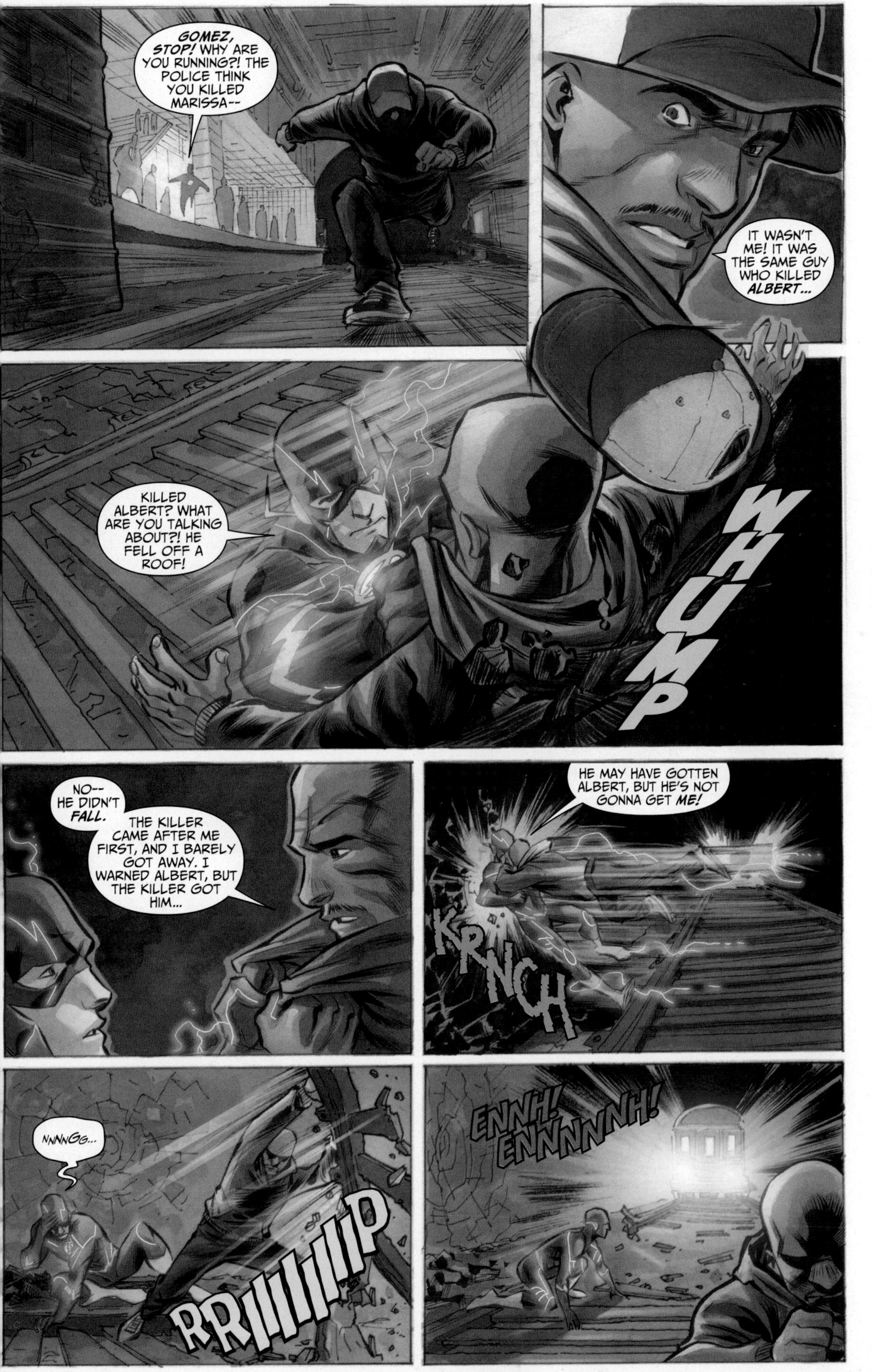
GOMEZ, STOP! WHY ARE YOU RUNNING?! THE POLICE THINK YOU KILLED MARISSA--
IT WASN'T ME! IT WAS THE SAME GUY WHO KILLED ALBERT...
KILLED ALBERT? WHAT ARE YOU TALKING ABOUT?! HE FELL OFF A ROOF!
WHUMP
NO-- HE DIDN'T FALL.
THE KILLER CAME AFTER ME FIRST, AND I BARELY GOT AWAY. I WARNED ALBERT, BUT THE KILLER GOT HIM...
HE MAY HAVE GOTTEN ALBERT, BUT HE'S NOT GONNA GET ME!
KRNCH
NNNNGG...
RRIIIIIIIP
ENNH! ENNNNNH!

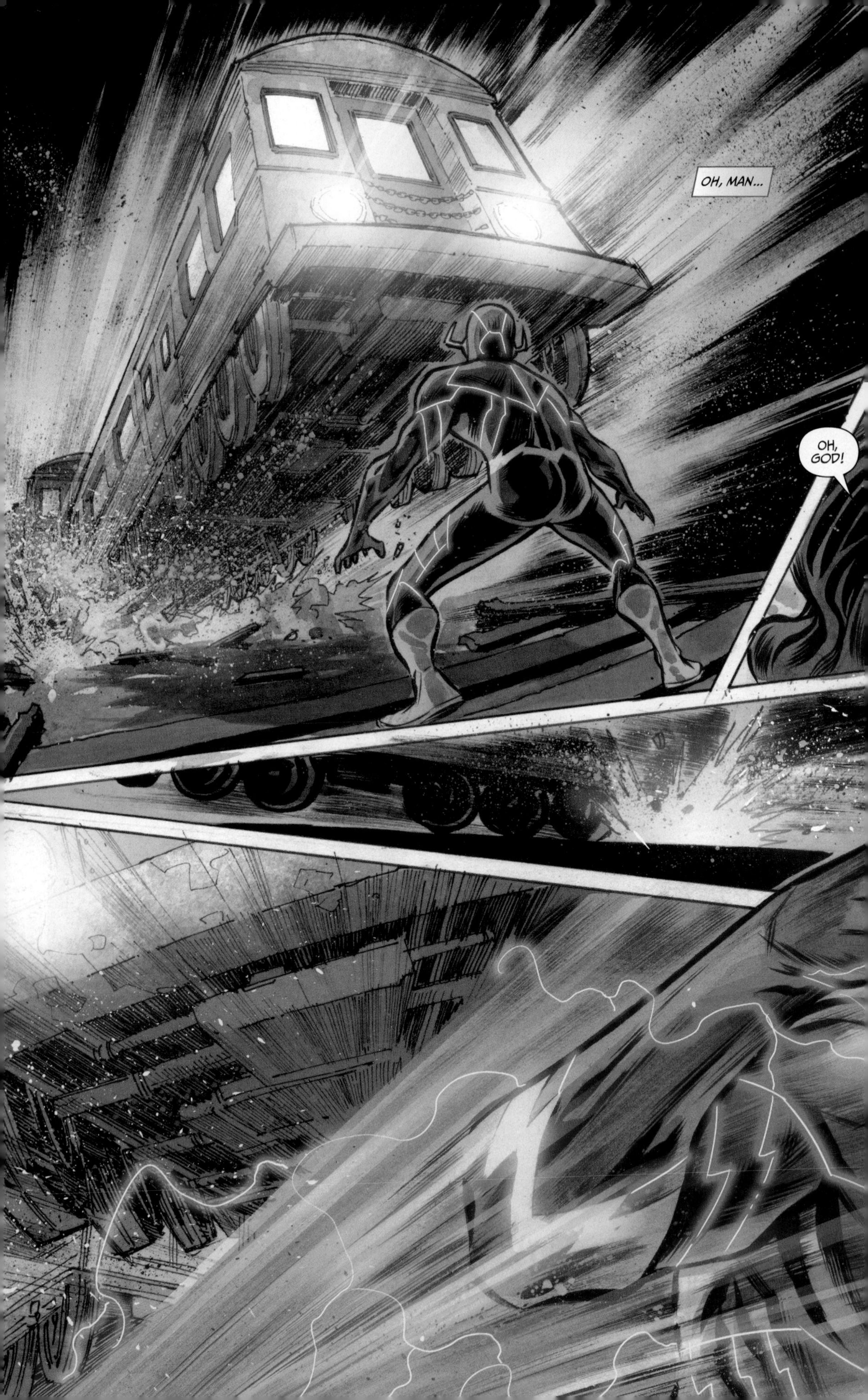
OH, MAN...
OH, GOD!

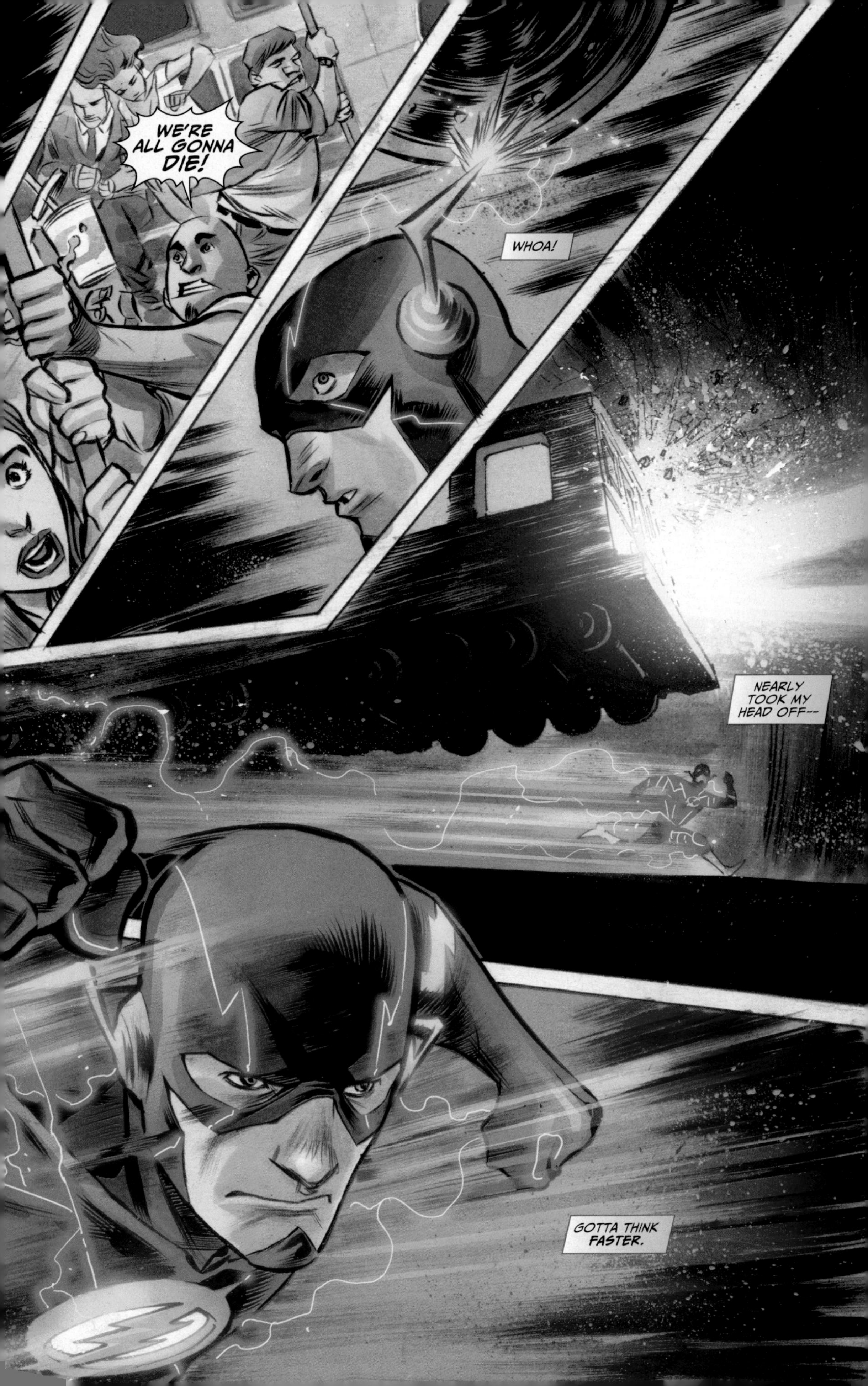
WE'RE ALL GONNA DIE!
WHOA!
NEARLY TOOK MY HEAD OFF--
GOTTA THINK FASTER.

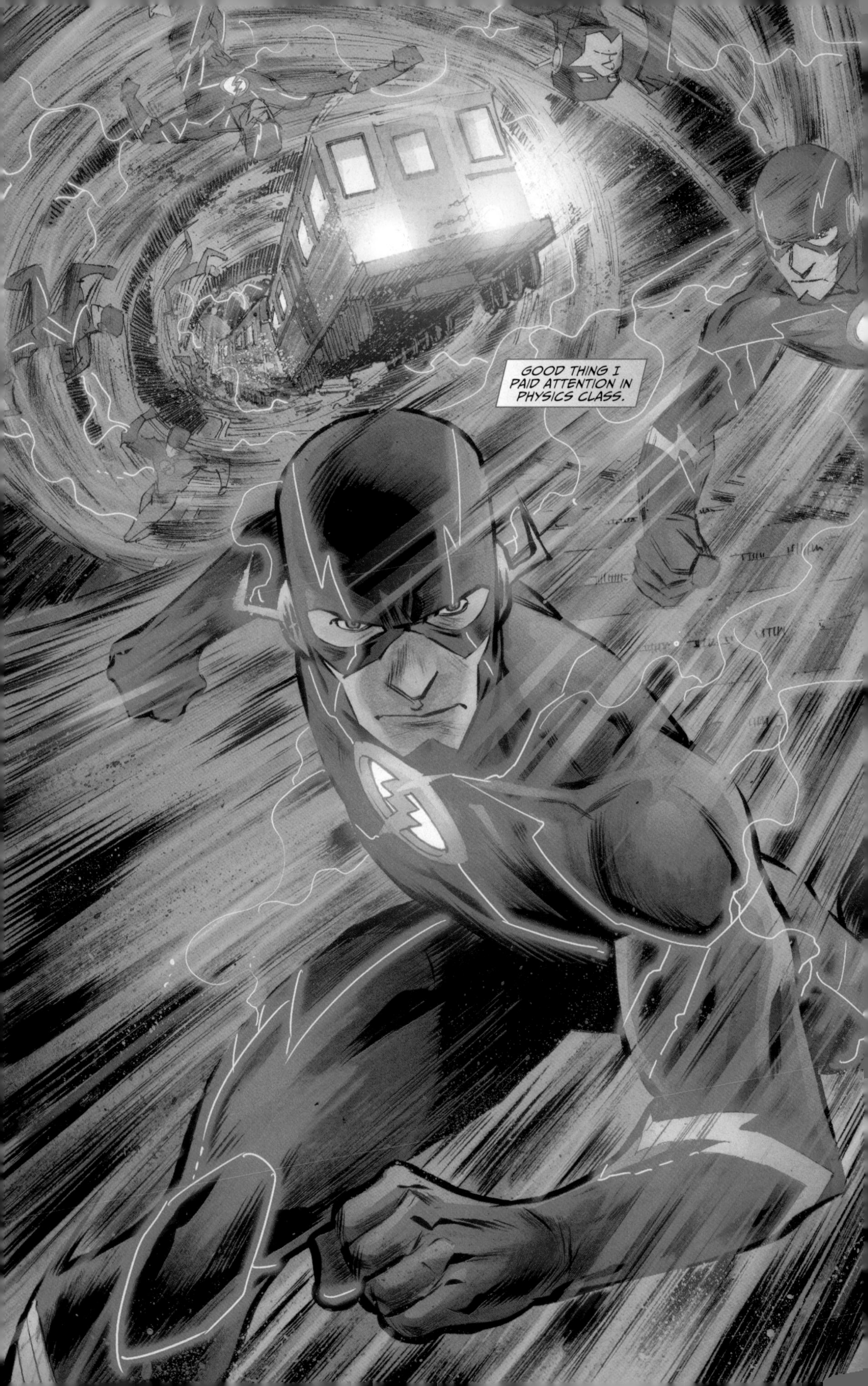
GOOD THING I PAID ATTENTION IN PHYSICS CLASS.

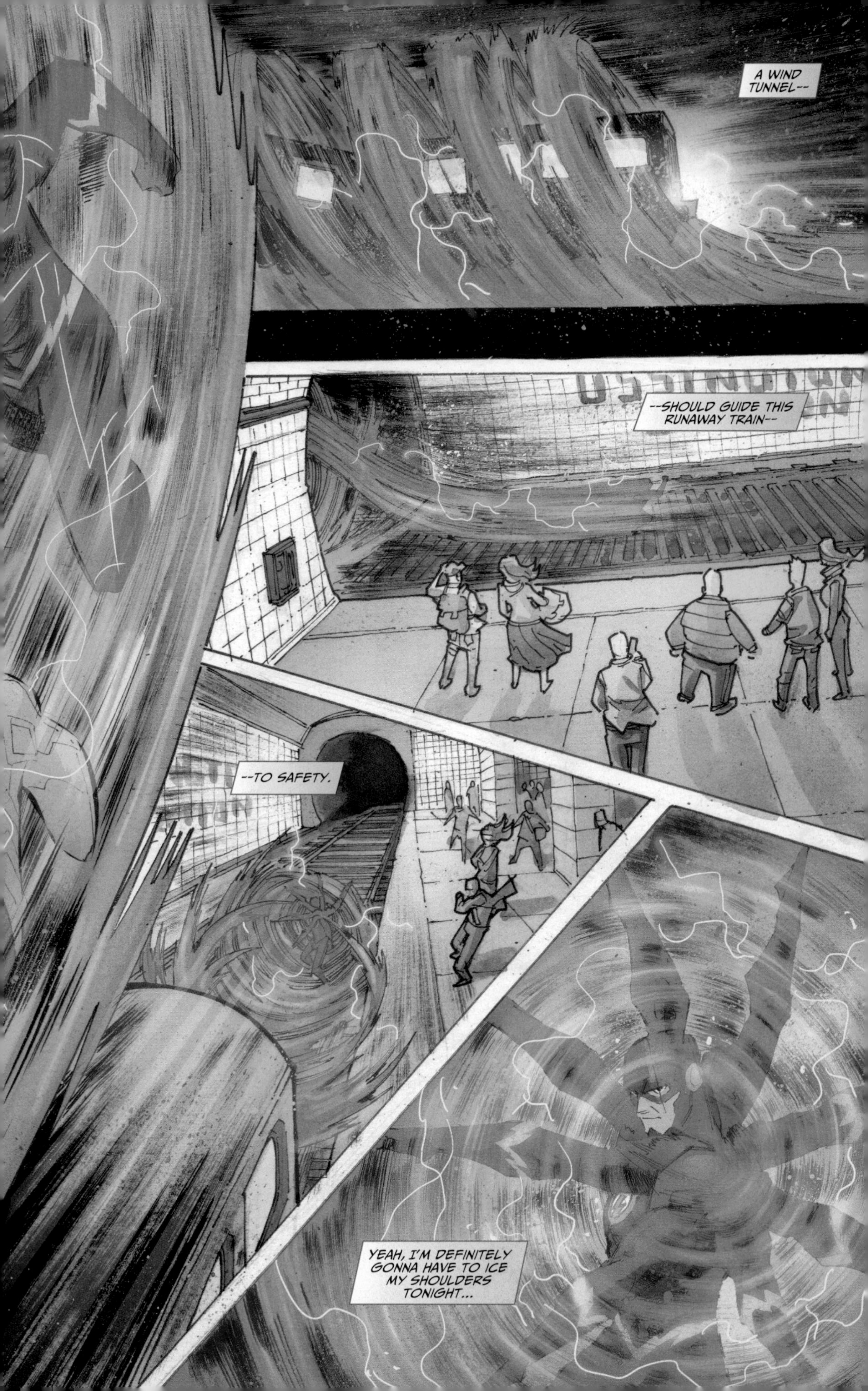
A WIND TUNNEL--
--SHOULD GUIDE THIS RUNAWAY TRAIN--
--TO SAFETY.
YEAH, I'M DEFINITELY GONNA HAVE TO ICE MY SHOULDERS TONIGHT...

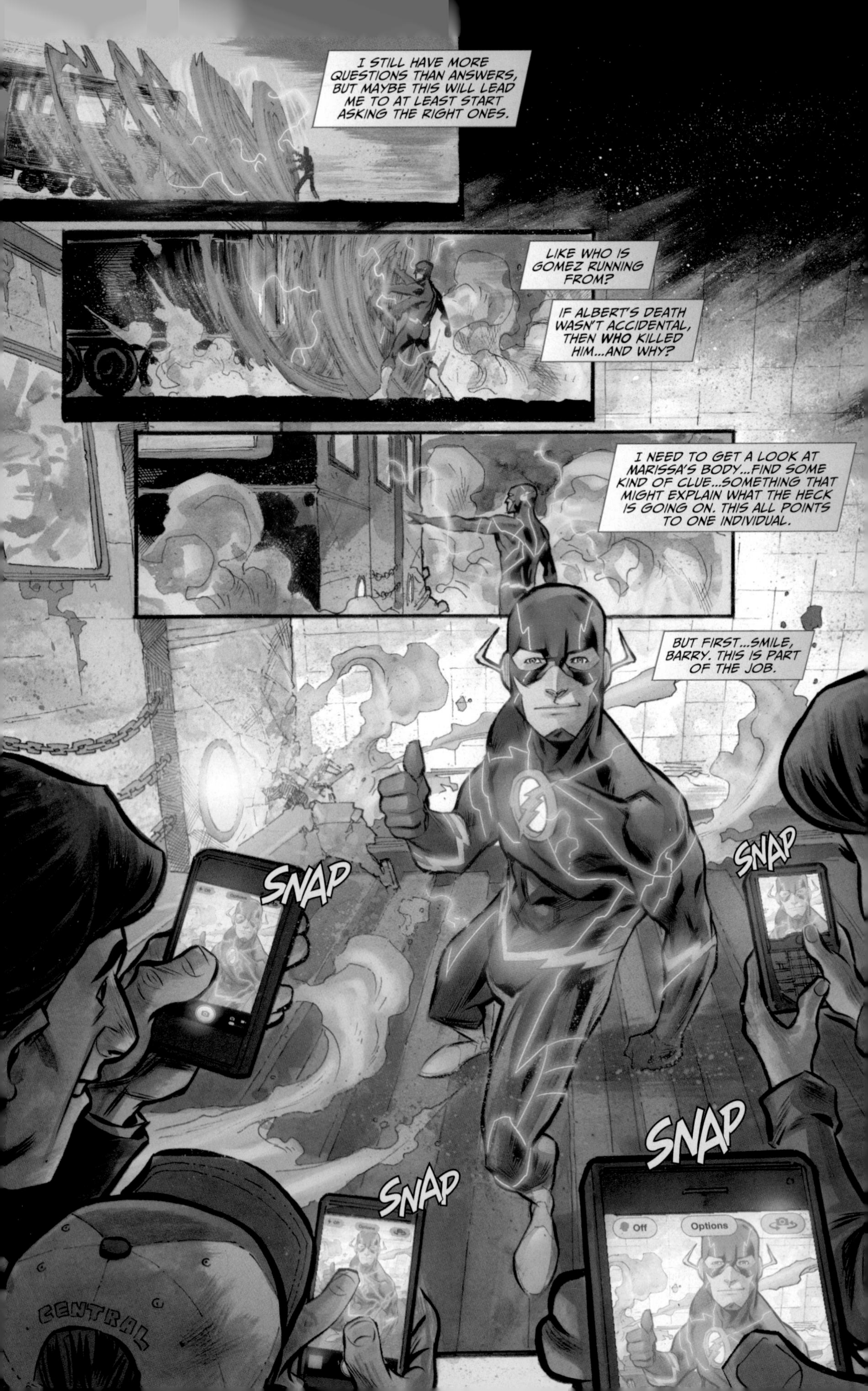

I STILL HAVE MORE QUESTIONS THAN ANSWERS, BUT MAYBE THIS WILL LEAD ME TO AT LEAST START ASKING THE RIGHT ONES.
LIKE WHO IS GOMEZ RUNNING FROM?
IF ALBERT'S DEATH WASN'T ACCIDENTAL, THEN WHO KILLED HIM...AND WHY?
I NEED TO GET A LOOK AT MARISSA'S BODY...FIND SOME KIND OF CLUE...SOMETHING THAT MIGHT EXPLAIN WHAT THE HECK IS GOING ON. THIS ALL POINTS TO ONE INDIVIDUAL.
BUT FIRST...SMILE, BARRY. THIS IS PART OF THE JOB.
SNAP
SNAP
SNAP
SNAP
Off
Options
CENTRAL

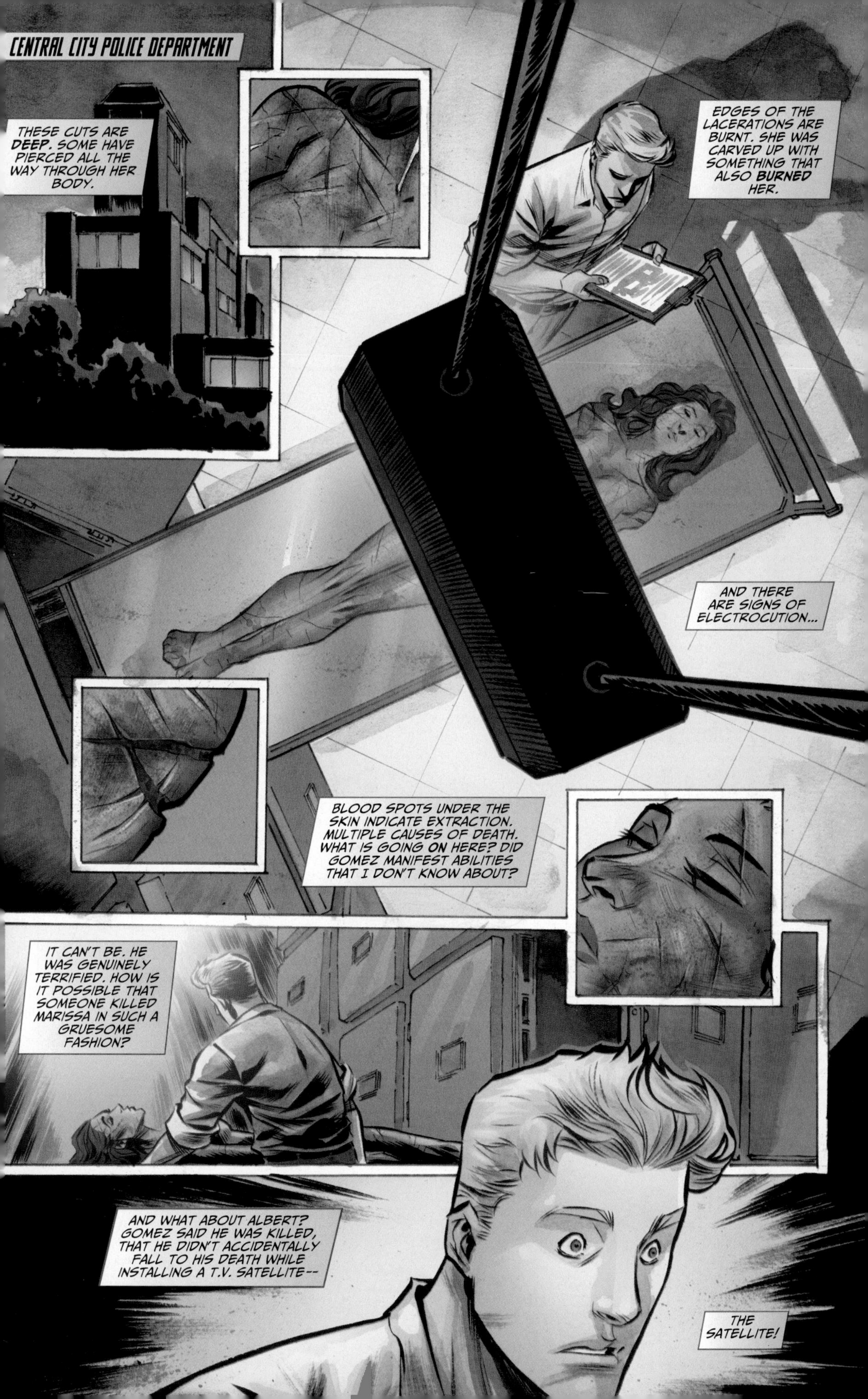
CENTRAL CITY POLICE DEPARTMENT
THESE CUTS ARE DEEP. SOME HAVE PIERCED ALL THE WAY THROUGH HER BODY.
EDGES OF THE LACERATIONS ARE BURNT. SHE WAS CARVED UP WITH SOMETHING THAT ALSO BURNED HER.
AND THERE ARE SIGNS OF ELECTROCUTION...
BLOOD SPOTS UNDER THE SKIN INDICATE EXTRACTION. MULTIPLE CAUSES OF DEATH. WHAT IS GOING ON HERE? DID GOMEZ MANIFEST ABILITIES THAT I DON'T KNOW ABOUT?
IT CAN'T BE. HE WAS GENUINELY TERRIFIED. HOW IS IT POSSIBLE THAT SOMEONE KILLED MARISSA IN SUCH A GRUESOME FASHION?
AND WHAT ABOUT ALBERT? GOMEZ SAID HE WAS KILLED, THAT HE DIDN'T ACCIDENTALLY FALL TO HIS DEATH WHILE INSTALLING A T.V. SATELLITE--
THE SATELLITE!

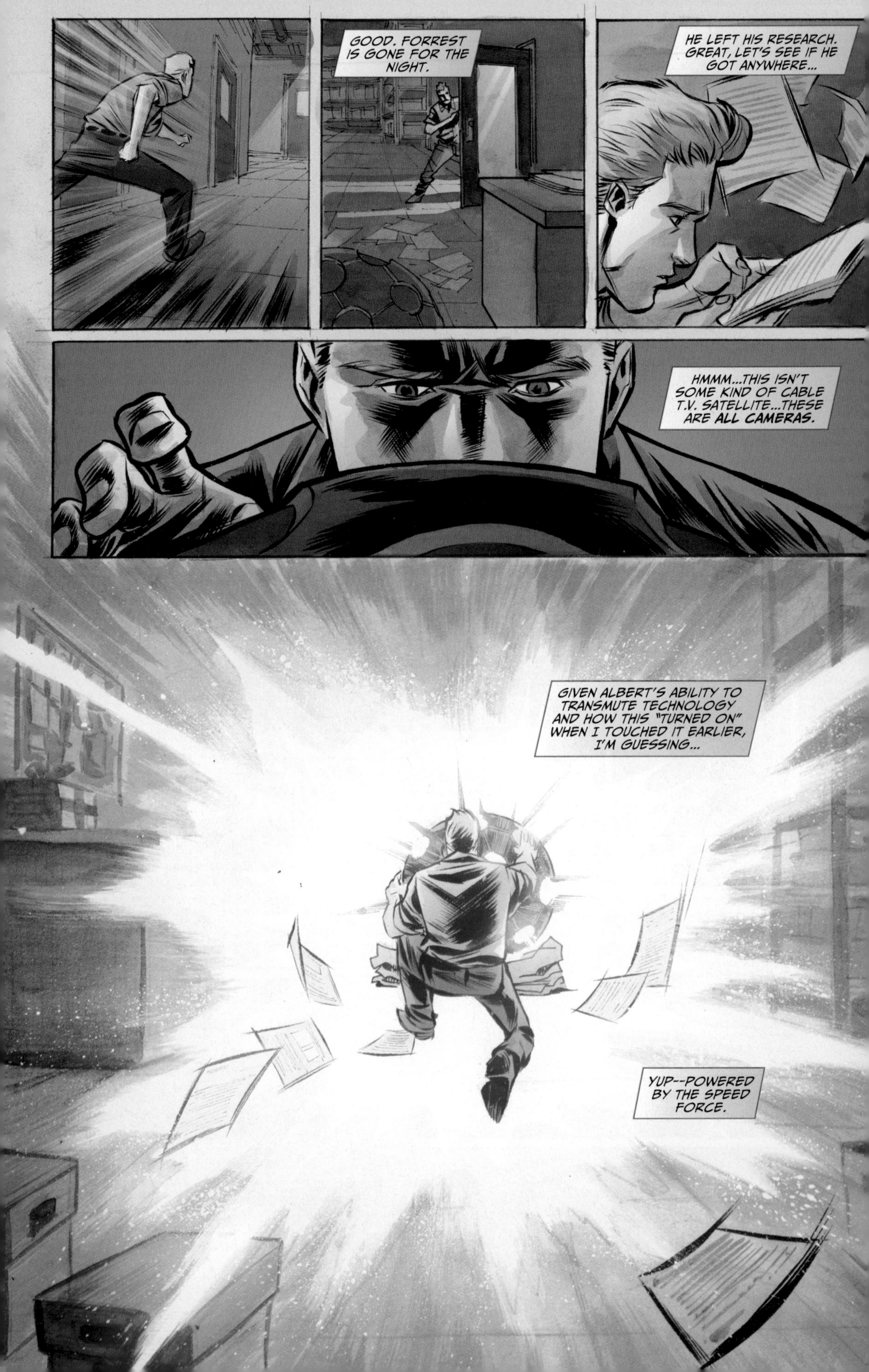
GOOD. FORREST IS GONE FOR THE NIGHT.
HE LEFT HIS RESEARCH. GREAT, LET'S SEE IF HE GOT ANYWHERE...
HMMM...THIS ISN'T SOME KIND OF CABLE T.V. SATELLITE...THESE ARE ALL CAMERAS.
GIVEN ALBERT'S ABILITY TO TRANSMUTE TECHNOLOGY AND HOW THIS "TURNED ON" WHEN I TOUCHED IT EARLIER, I'M GUESSING...
YUP--POWERED BY THE SPEED FORCE.

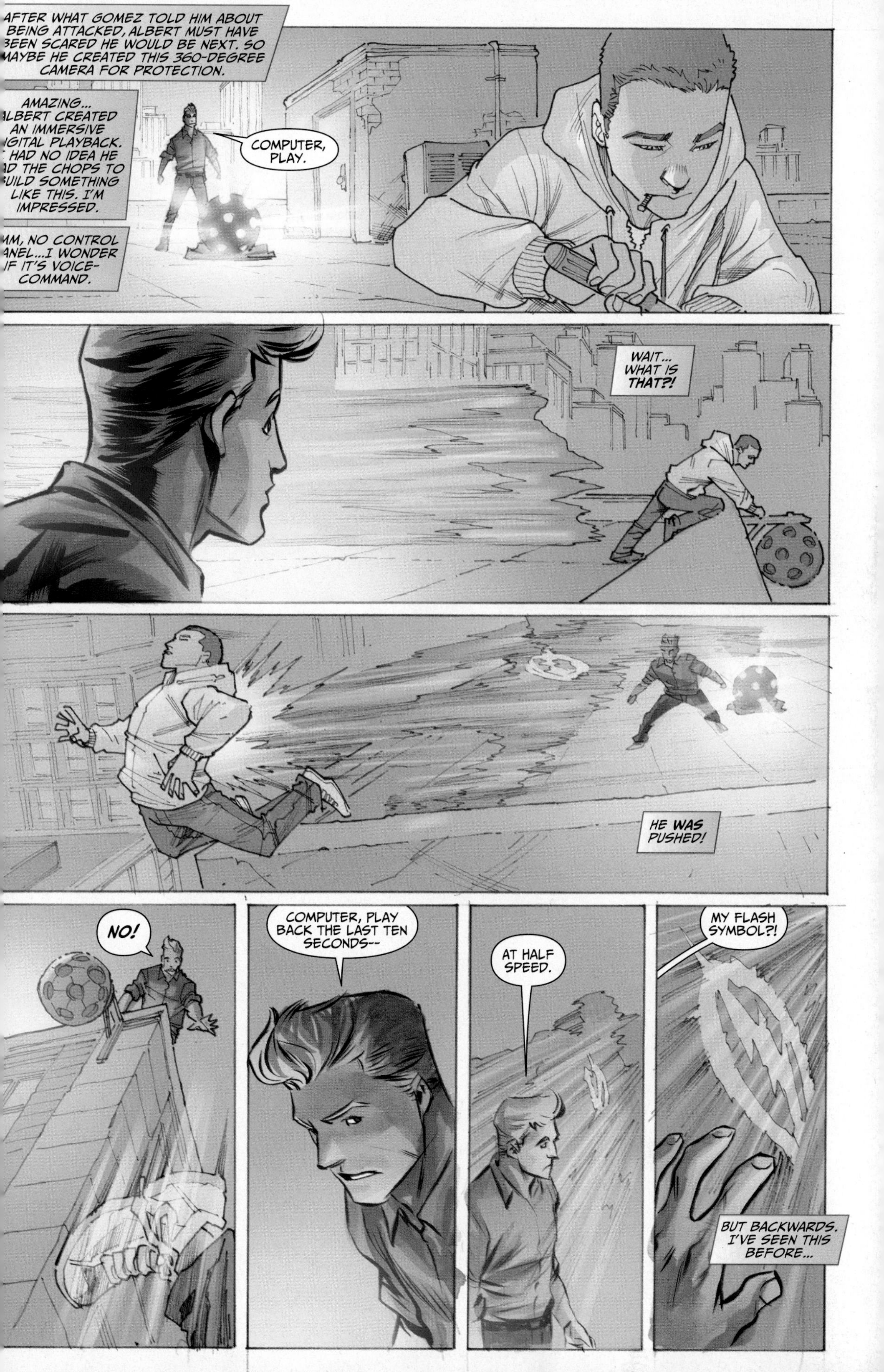
AFTER WHAT GOMEZ TOLD HIM ABOUT BEING ATTACKED, ALBERT MUST HAVE BEEN SCARED HE WOULD BE NEXT. SO MAYBE HE CREATED THIS 360-DEGREE CAMERA FOR PROTECTION.
AMAZING... ALBERT CREATED AN IMMERSIVE DIGITAL PLAYBACK. I HAD NO IDEA HE HAD THE CHOPS TO BUILD SOMETHING LIKE THIS. I'M IMPRESSED.
MM, NO CONTROL ANEL...I WONDER IF IT'S VOICE-COMMAND.
COMPUTER, PLAY.
WAIT... WHAT IS THAT?!
HE WAS PUSHED!
NO!
COMPUTER, PLAY BACK THE LAST TEN SECONDS--
AT HALF SPEED.
MY FLASH SYMBOL?!
BUT BACKWARDS. I'VE SEEN THIS BEFORE...

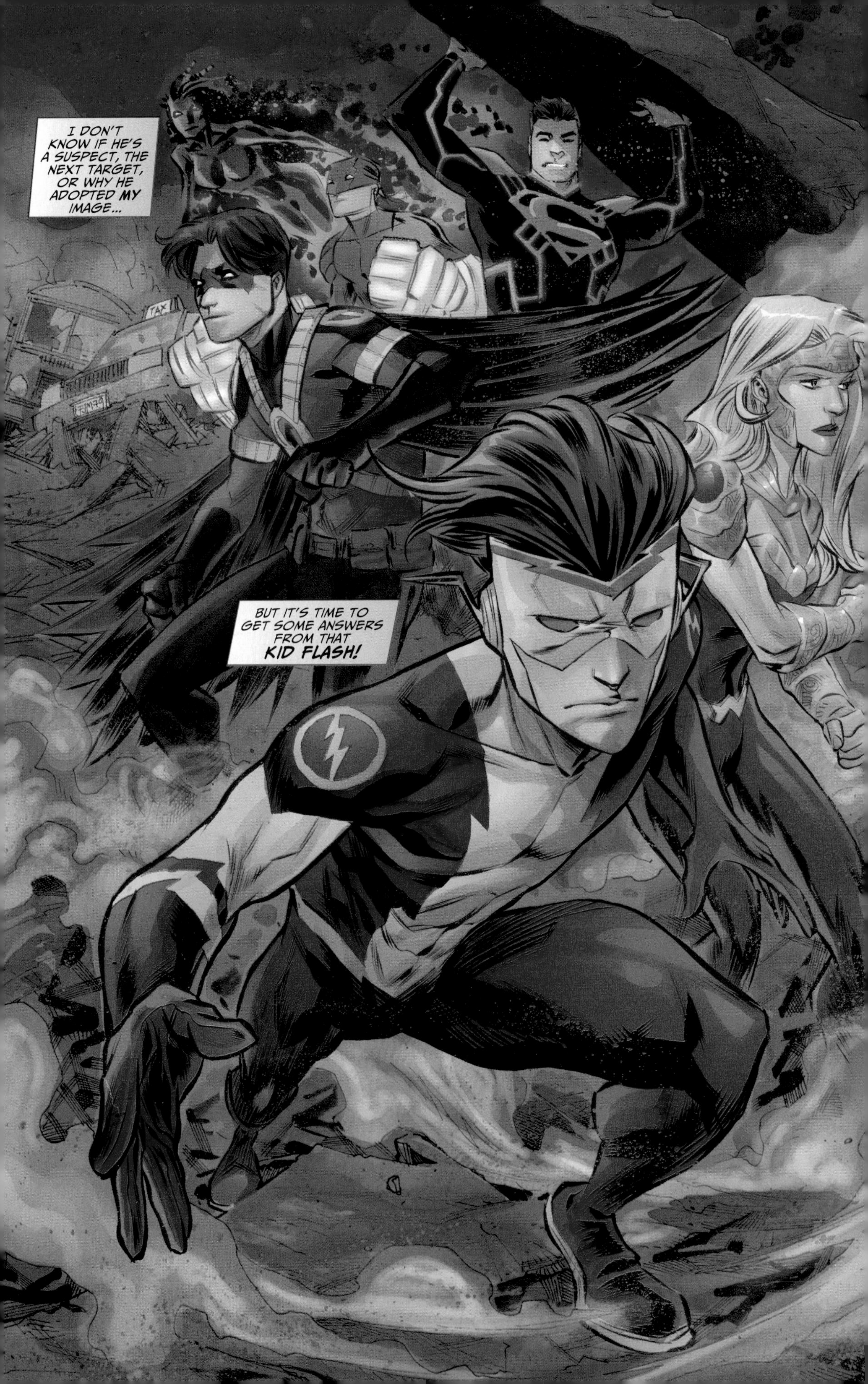
I DON'T KNOW IF HE'S A SUSPECT, THE NEXT TARGET, OR WHY HE ADOPTED MY IMAGE...
BUT IT'S TIME TO GET SOME ANSWERS FROM THAT KID FLASH!

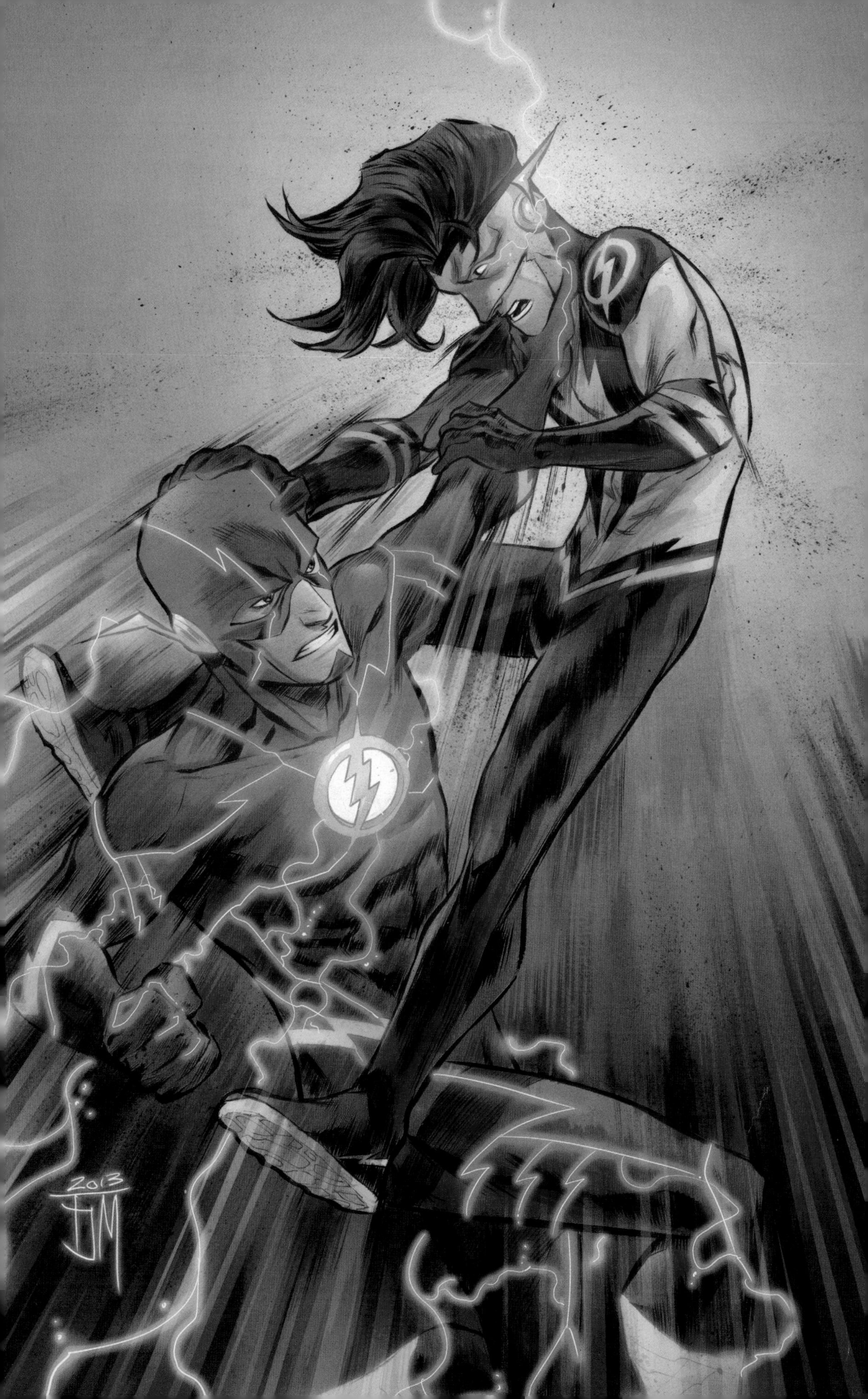

FRANCIS MANAPUL & BRIAN BUCCELLATO writers FRANCIS MANAPUL artist

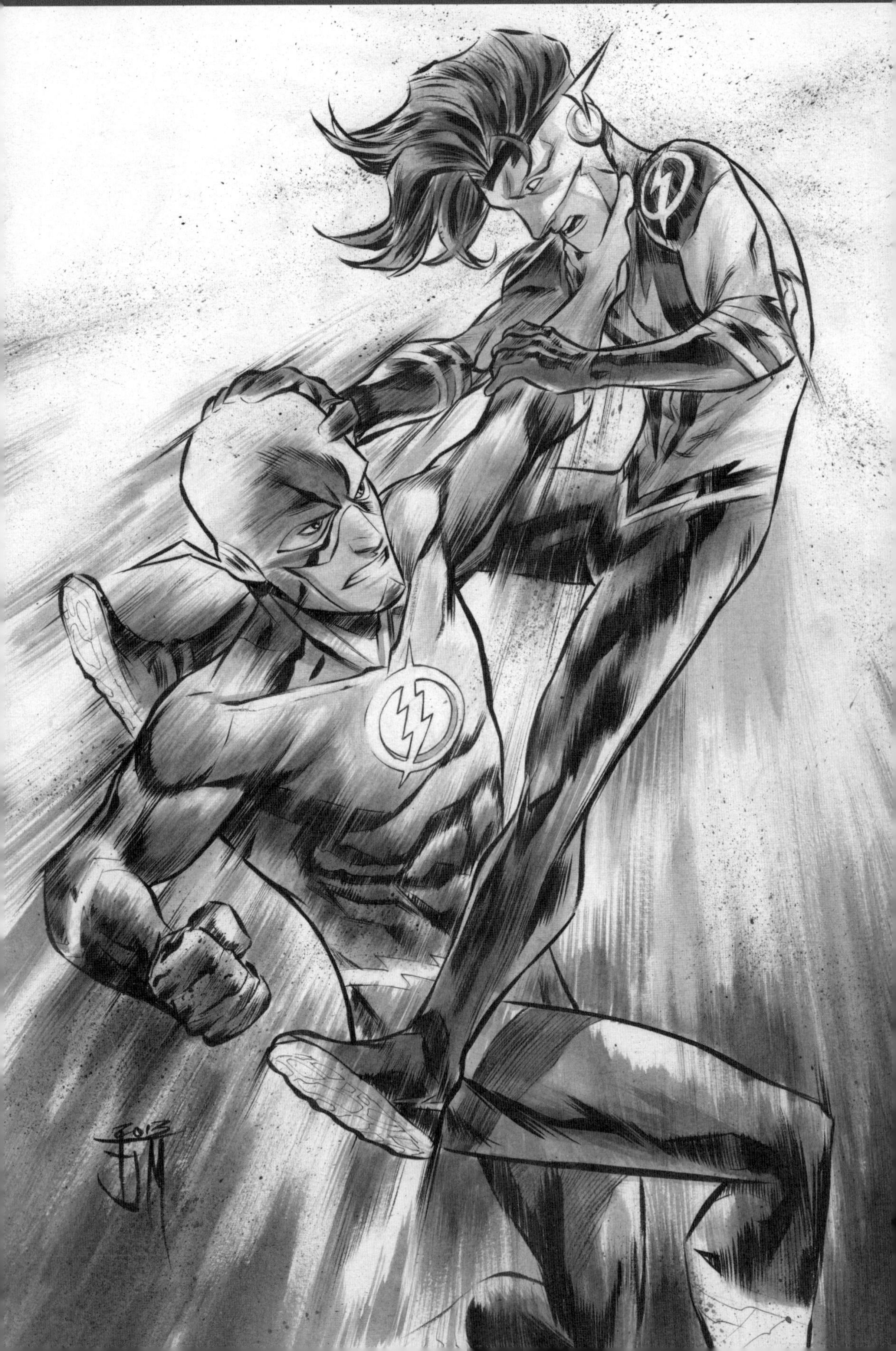

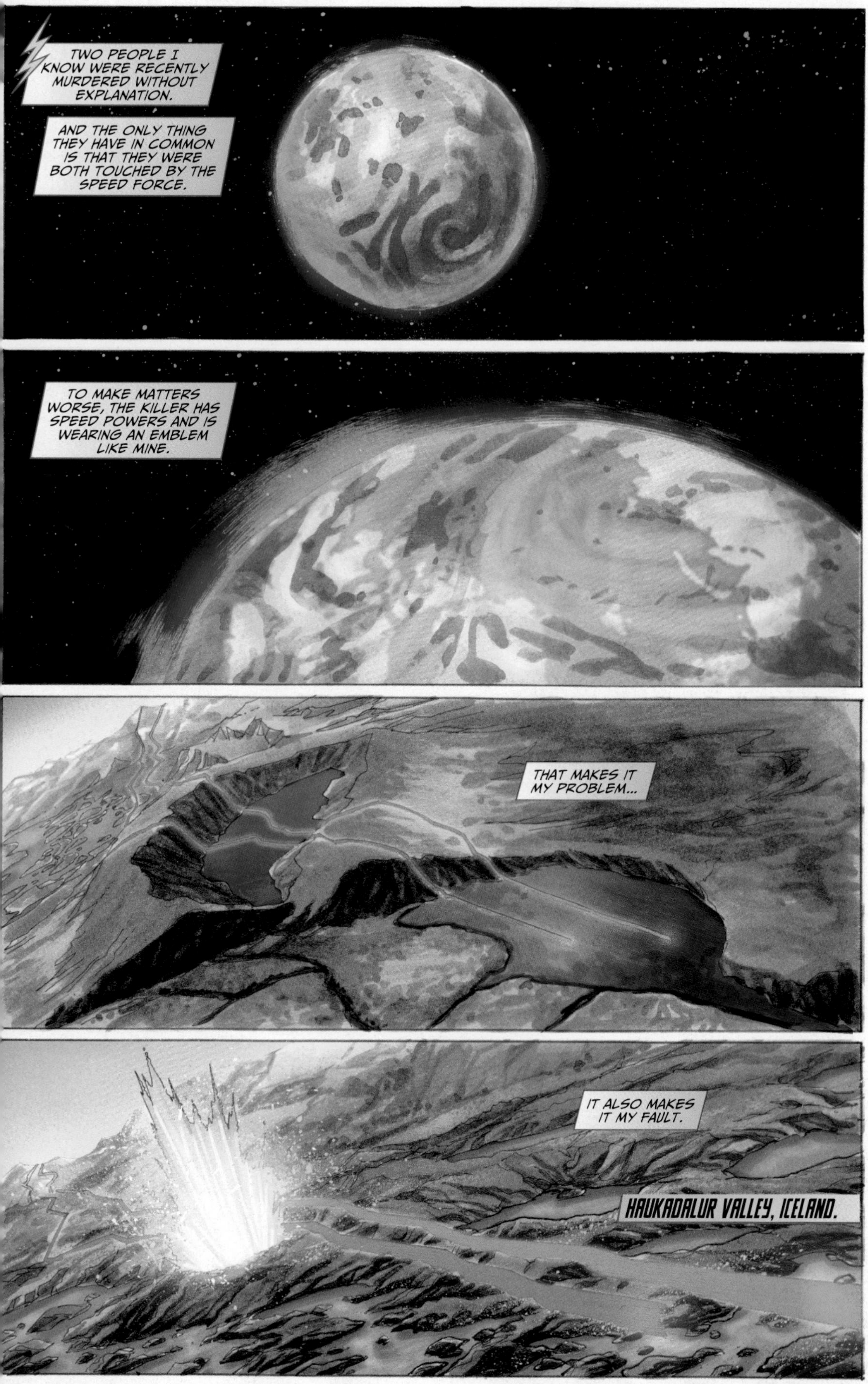
TWO PEOPLE I KNOW WERE RECENTLY MURDERED WITHOUT EXPLANATION.
AND THE ONLY THING THEY HAVE IN COMMON IS THAT THEY WERE BOTH TOUCHED BY THE SPEED FORCE.
TO MAKE MATTERS WORSE, THE KILLER HAS SPEED POWERS AND IS WEARING AN EMBLEM LIKE MINE.
THAT MAKES IT MY PROBLEM...
IT ALSO MAKES IT MY FAULT.
HAUKADALUR VALLEY, ICELAND.

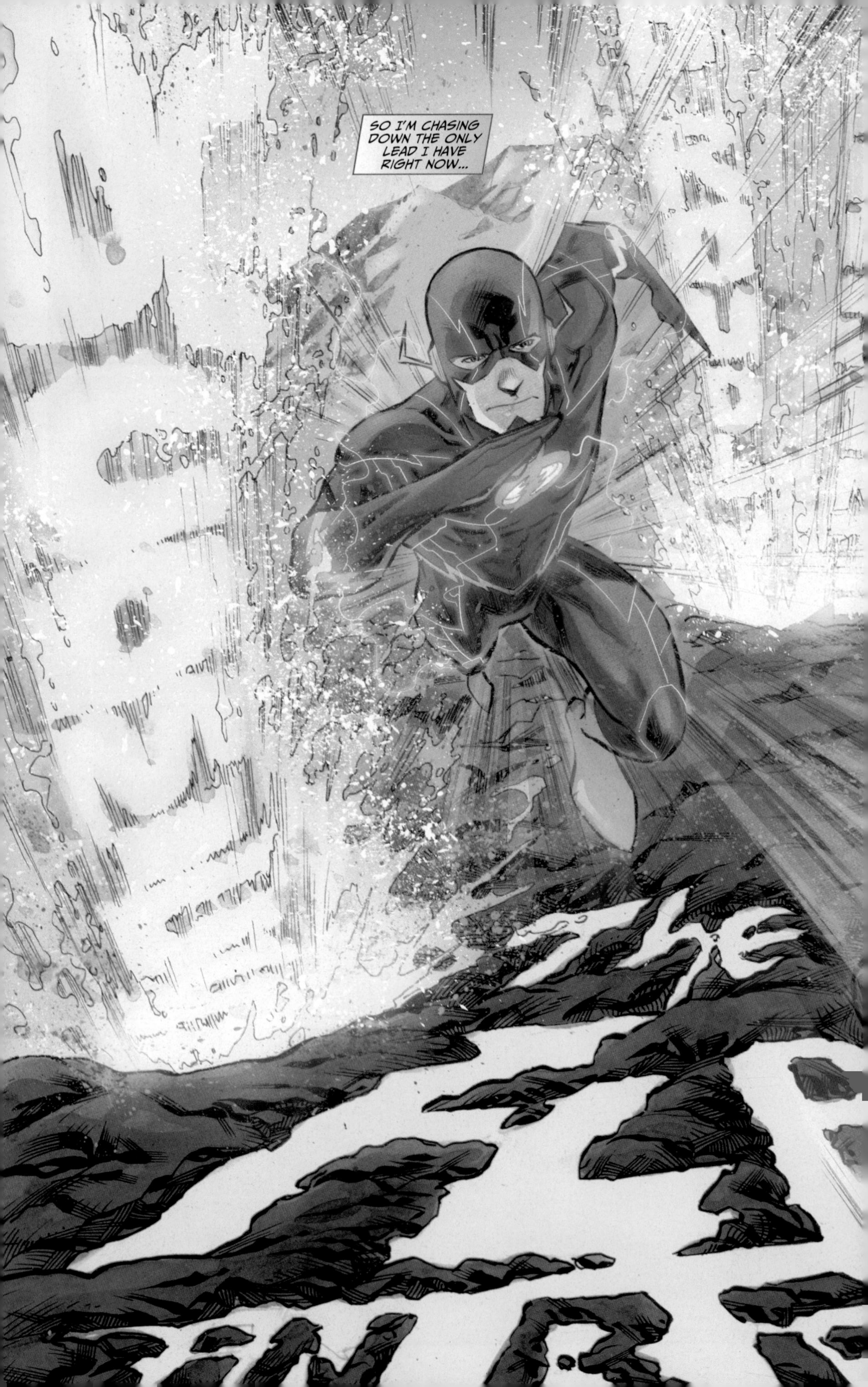
SO I'M CHASING DOWN THE ONLY LEAD I HAVE RIGHT NOW...

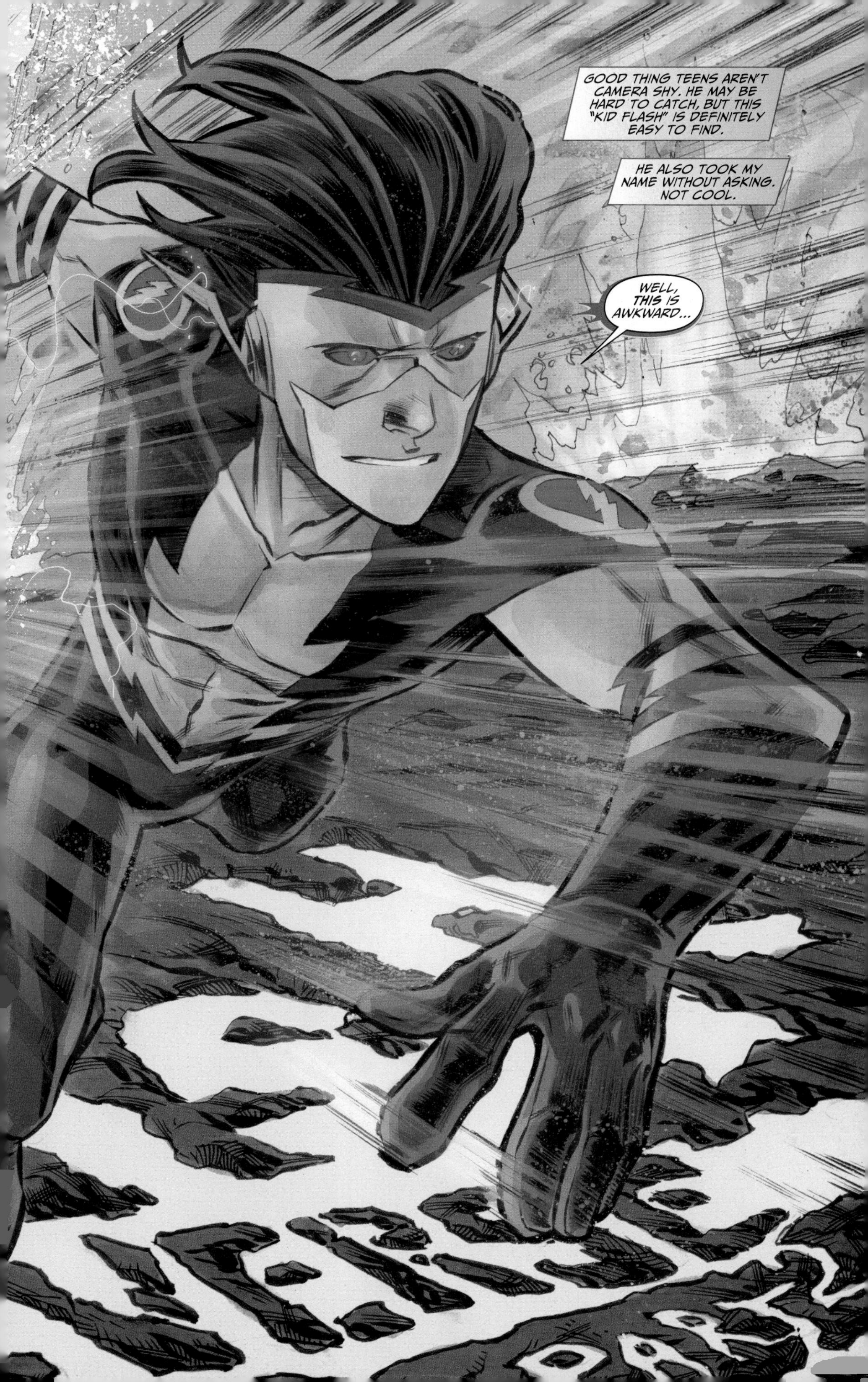
GOOD THING TEENS AREN'T CAMERA SHY. HE MAY BE HARD TO CATCH, BUT THIS "KID FLASH" IS DEFINITELY EASY TO FIND.
HE ALSO TOOK MY NAME WITHOUT ASKING. NOT COOL.
WELL, THIS IS AWKWARD...

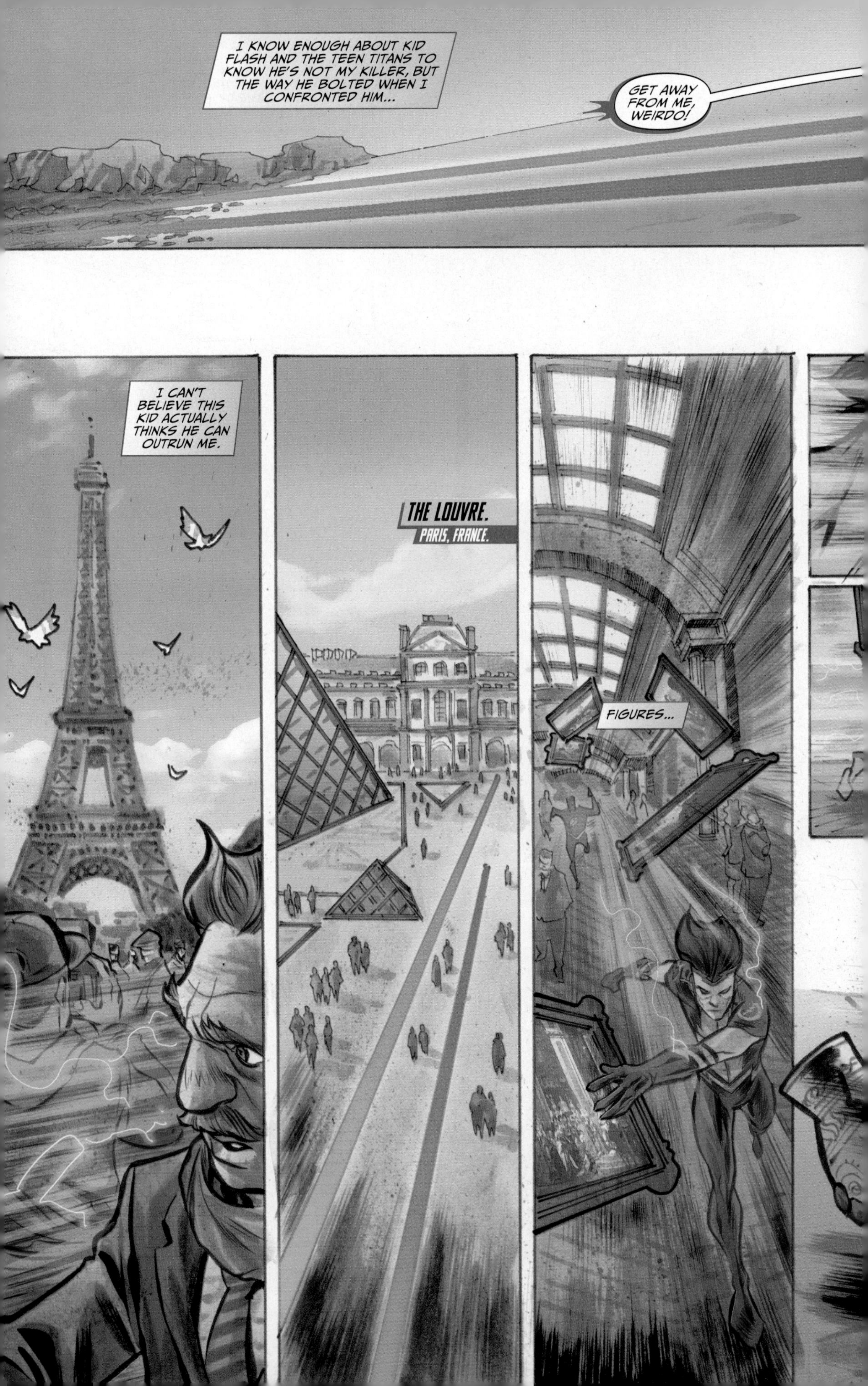

I KNOW ENOUGH ABOUT KID FLASH AND THE TEEN TITANS TO KNOW HE'S NOT MY KILLER, BUT THE WAY HE BOLTED WHEN I CONFRONTED HIM...
GET AWAY FROM ME, WEIRDO!
I CAN'T BELIEVE THIS KID ACTUALLY THINKS HE CAN OUTRUN ME.
THE LOUVRE.
PARIS, FRANCE.
FIGURES...

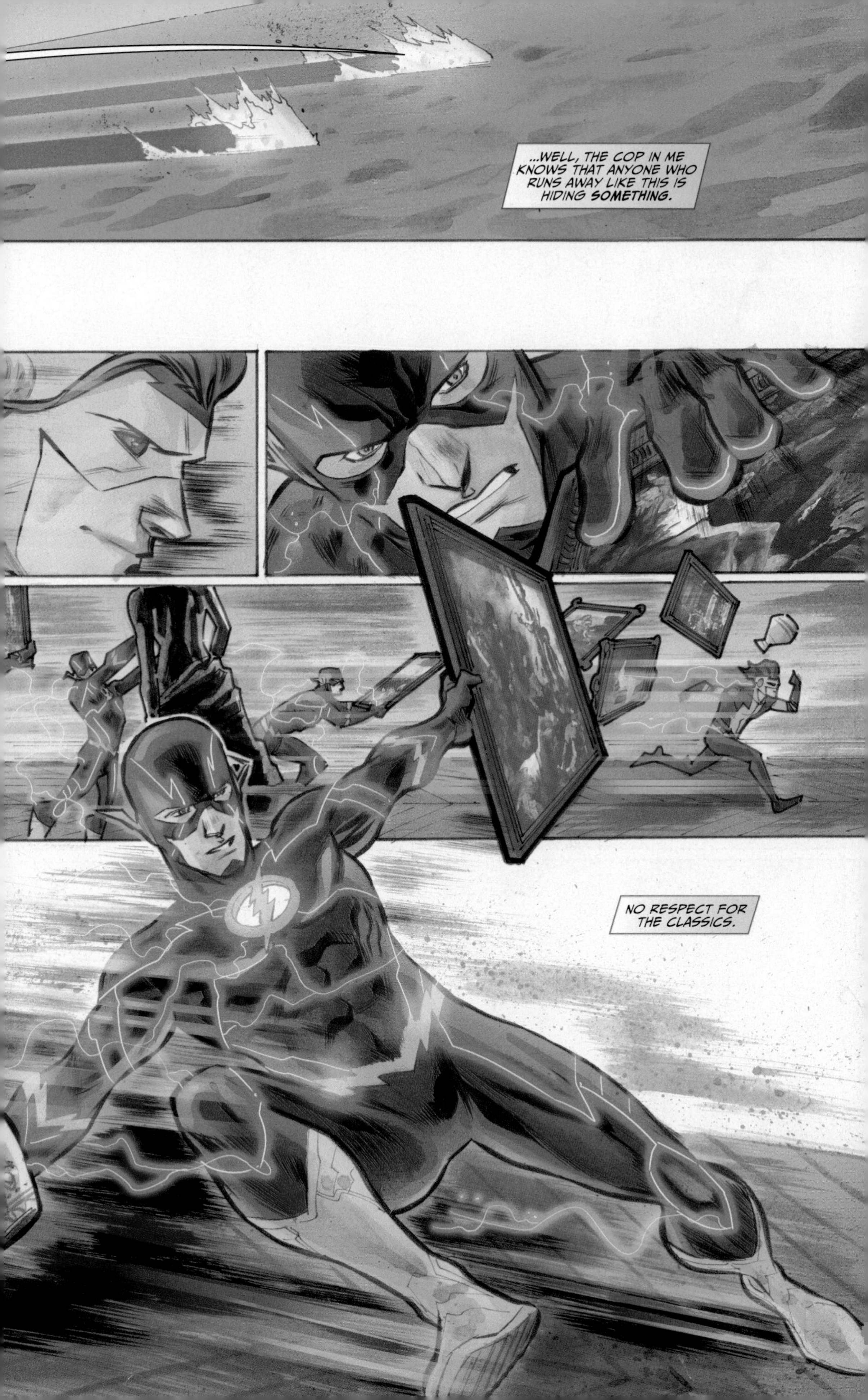
...WELL, THE COP IN ME KNOWS THAT ANYONE WHO RUNS AWAY LIKE THIS IS HIDING SOMETHING.
NO RESPECT FOR THE CLASSICS.

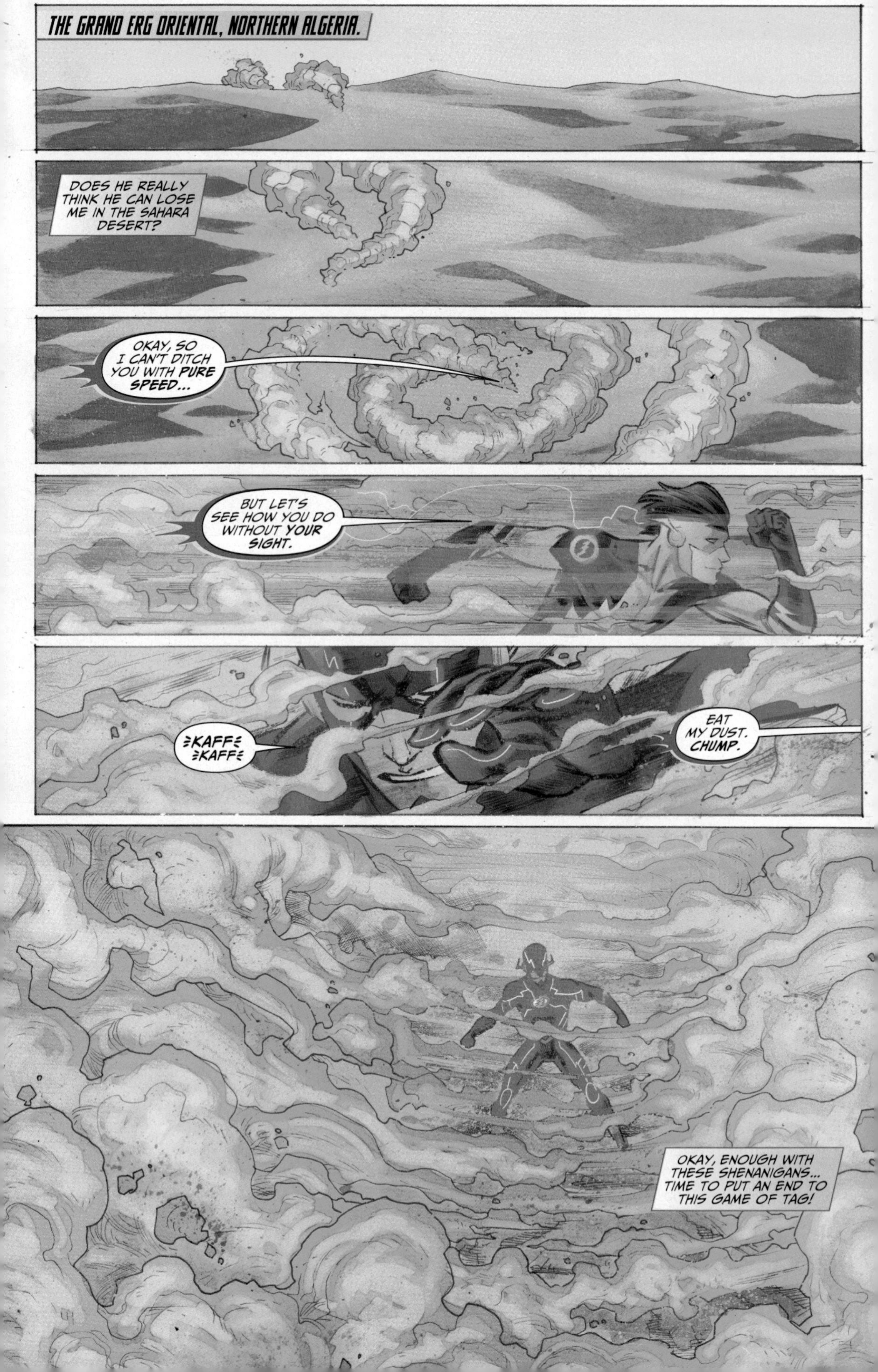
THE GRAND ERG ORIENTAL, NORTHERN ALGERIA.
DOES HE REALLY THINK HE CAN LOSE ME IN THE SAHARA DESERT?
OKAY, SO I CAN'T DITCH YOU WITH PURE SPEED...
BUT LET'S SEE HOW YOU DO WITHOUT YOUR SIGHT.
KAFF KAFF
EAT MY DUST. CHUMP.
OKAY, ENOUGH WITH THESE SHENANIGANS... TIME TO PUT AN END TO THIS GAME OF TAG!

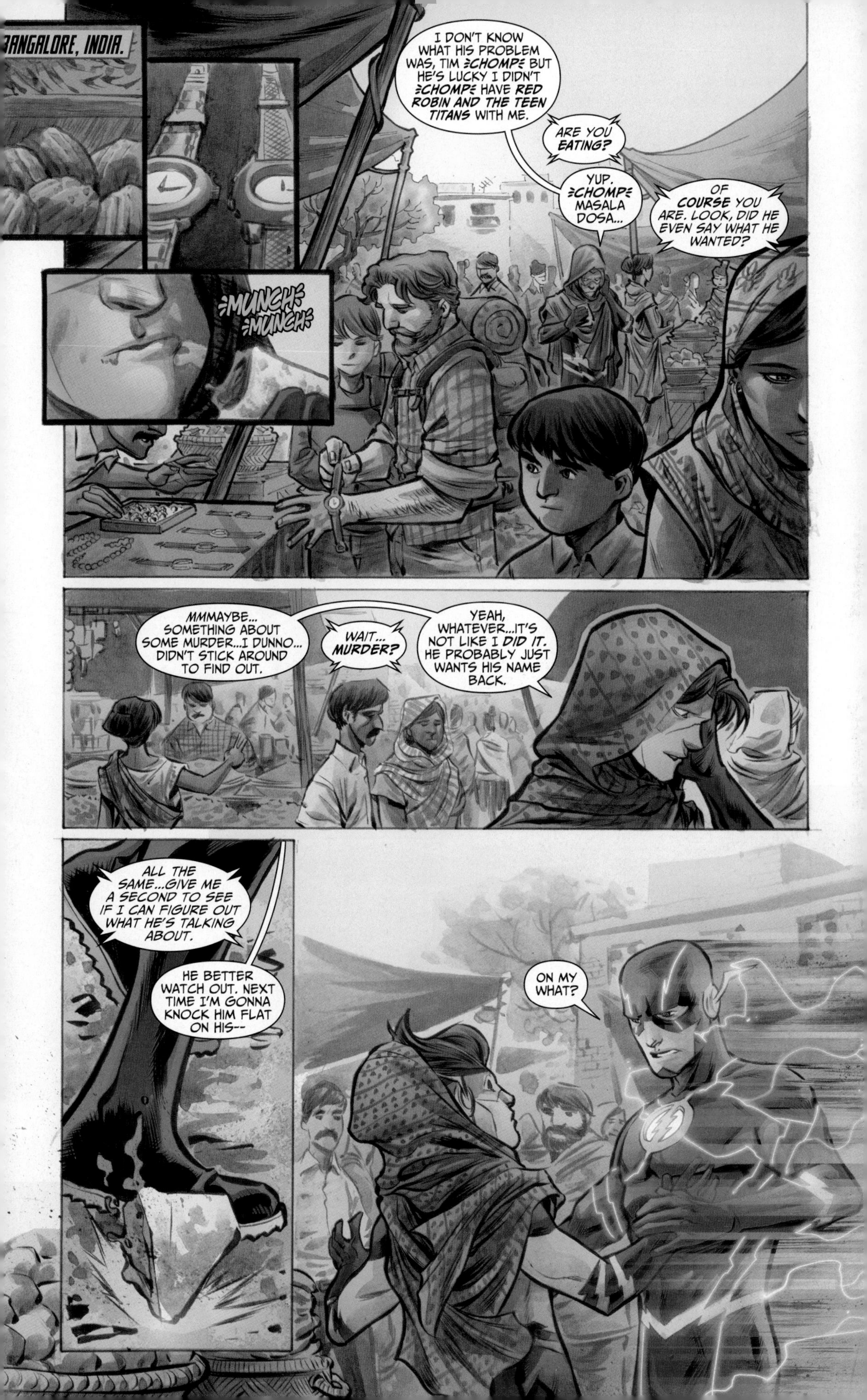
BANGALORE, INDIA.
I DON'T KNOW WHAT HIS PROBLEM WAS, TIM CHOMP BUT HE'S LUCKY I DIDN'T CHOMP HAVE RED ROBIN AND THE TEEN TITANS WITH ME.
ARE YOU EATING?
YUP. CHOMP MASALA DOSA...
OF COURSE YOU ARE. LOOK, DID HE EVEN SAY WHAT HE WANTED?
MUNCH MUNCH
MMMAYBE... SOMETHING ABOUT SOME MURDER...I DUNNO... DIDN'T STICK AROUND TO FIND OUT.
WAIT... MURDER?
YEAH, WHATEVER...IT'S NOT LIKE I DID IT. HE PROBABLY JUST WANTS HIS NAME BACK.
ALL THE SAME...GIVE ME A SECOND TO SEE IF I CAN FIGURE OUT WHAT HE'S TALKING ABOUT.
HE BETTER WATCH OUT. NEXT TIME I'M GONNA KNOCK HIM FLAT ON HIS--
ON MY WHAT?

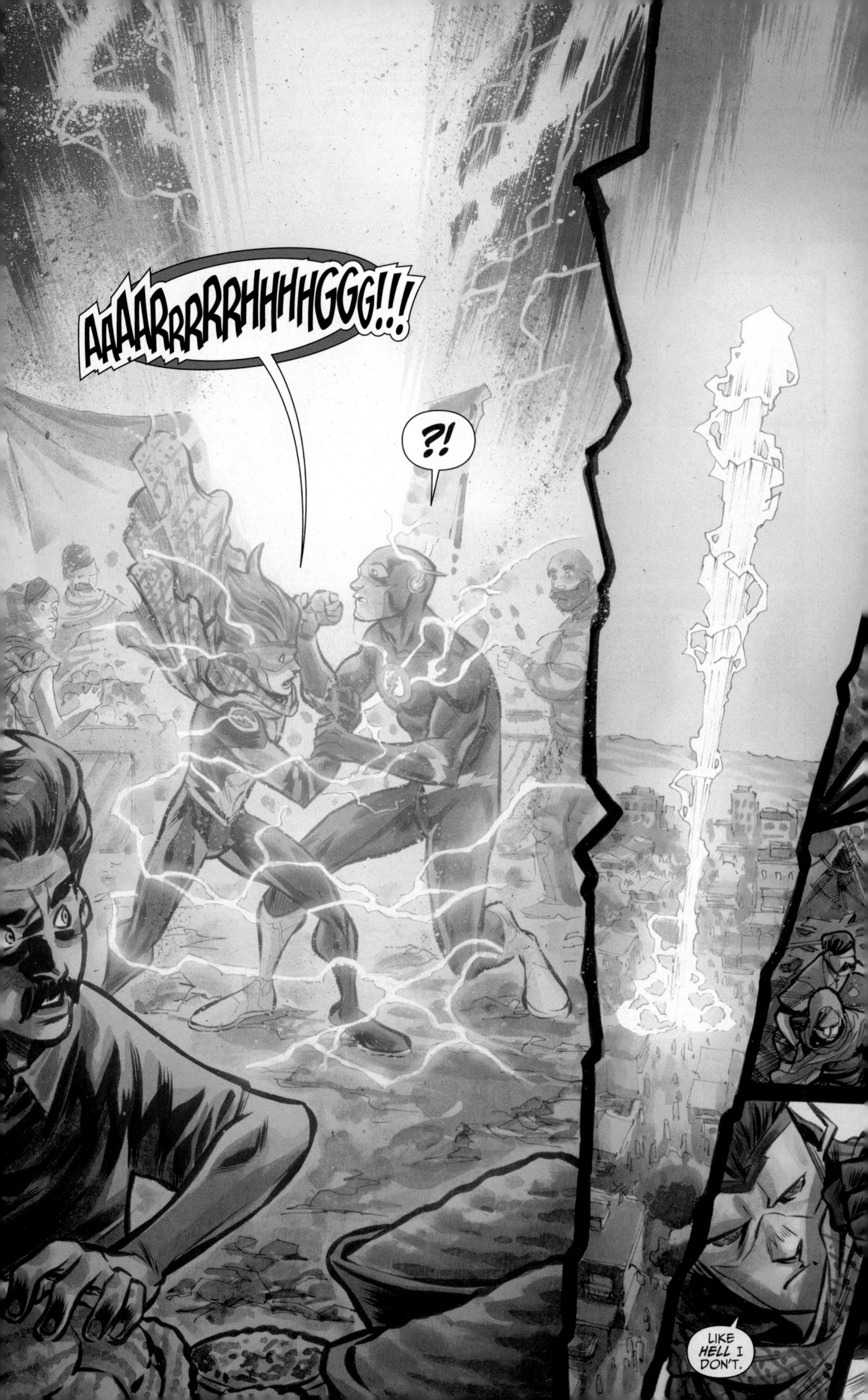
AAAARRRRRHHHHGGG!!!
?!
LIKE HELL I DON'T.

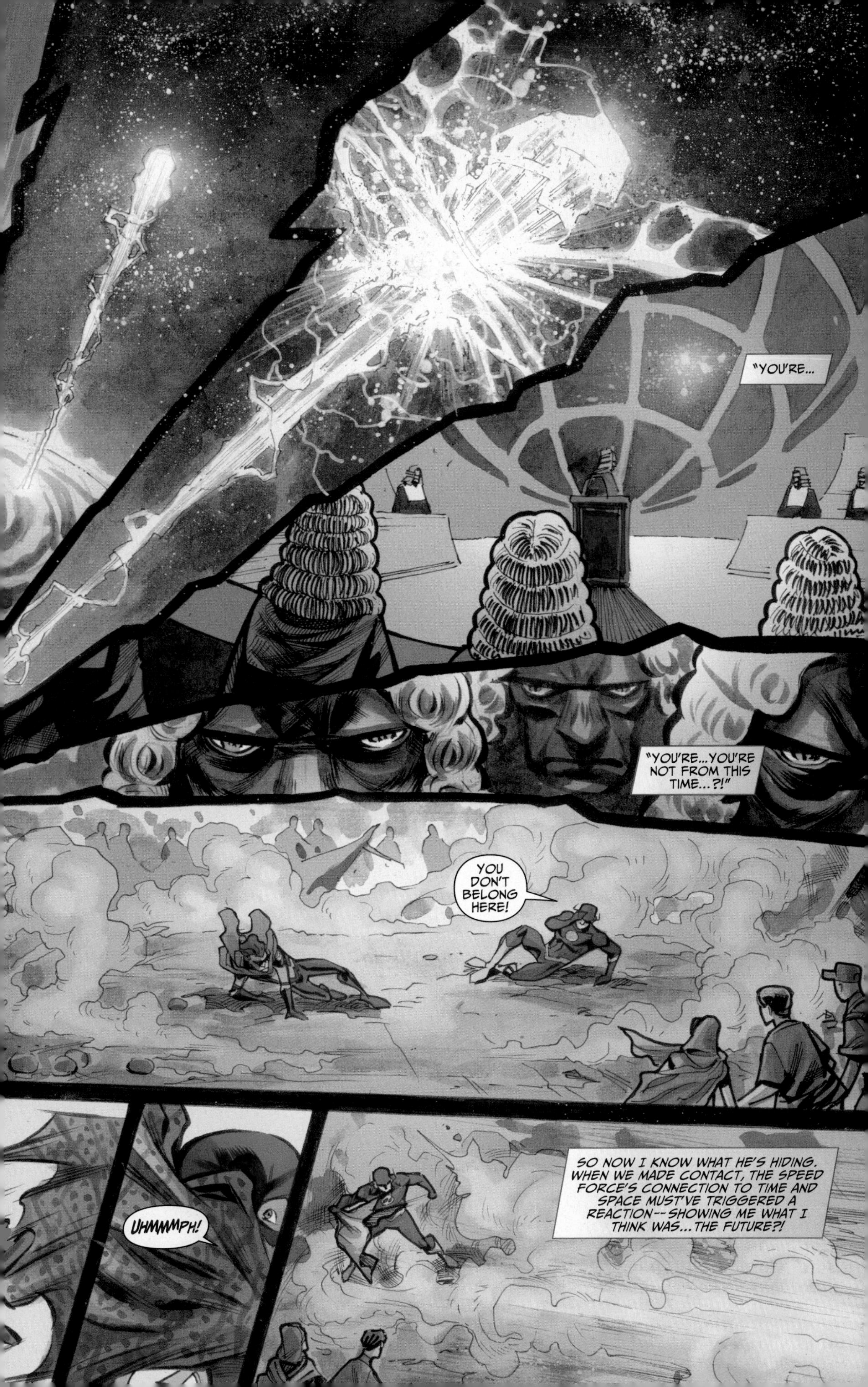
"YOU'RE...
"YOU'RE...YOU'RE NOT FROM THIS TIME...?!"
YOU DON'T BELONG HERE!
UHMMMPH!
SO NOW I KNOW WHAT HE'S HIDING. WHEN WE MADE CONTACT, THE SPEED FORCE'S CONNECTION TO TIME AND SPACE MUST'VE TRIGGERED A REACTION--SHOWING ME WHAT I THINK WAS...THE FUTURE?!

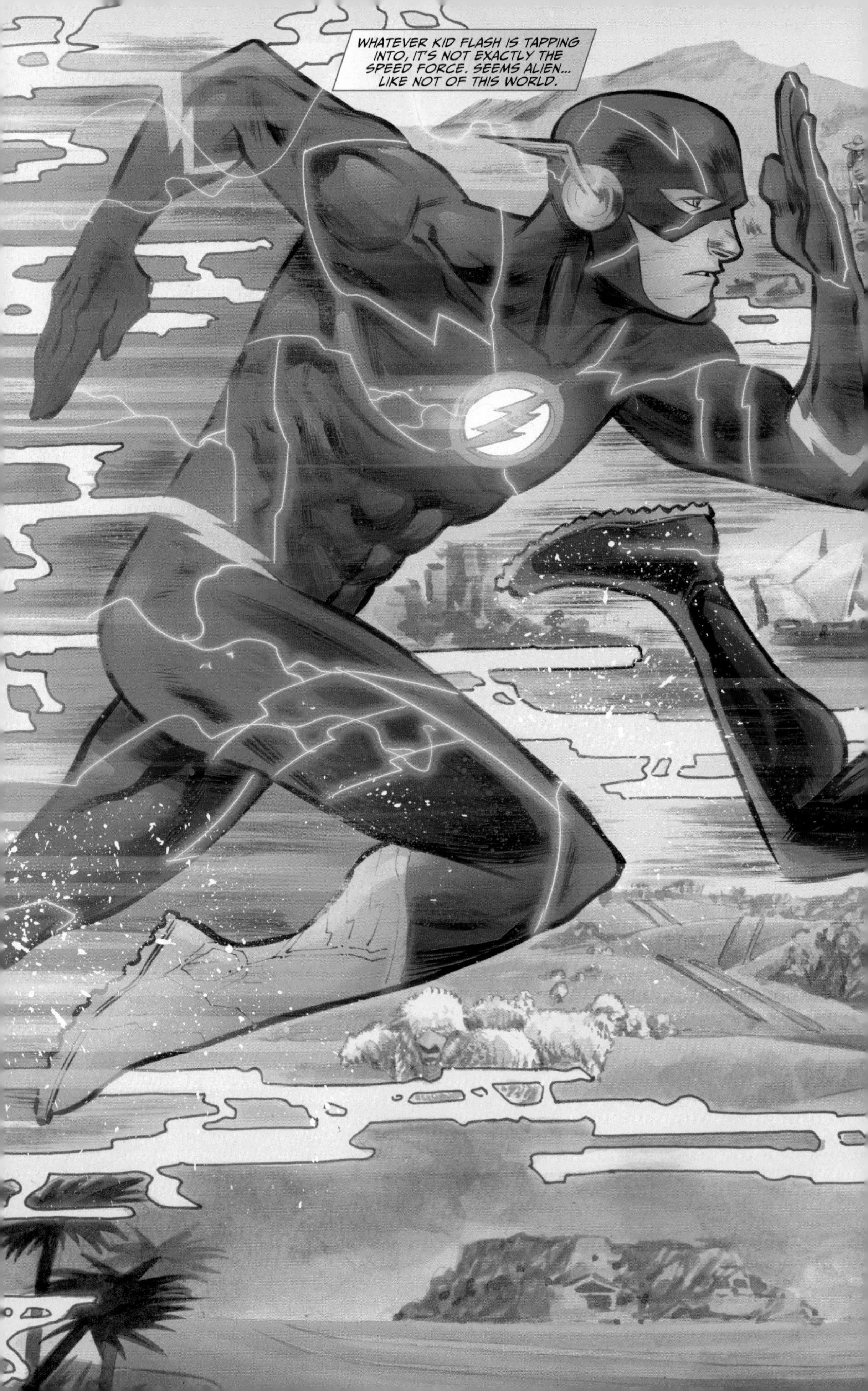
WHATEVER KID FLASH IS TAPPING INTO, IT'S NOT EXACTLY THE SPEED FORCE. SEEMS ALIEN... LIKE NOT OF THIS WORLD.

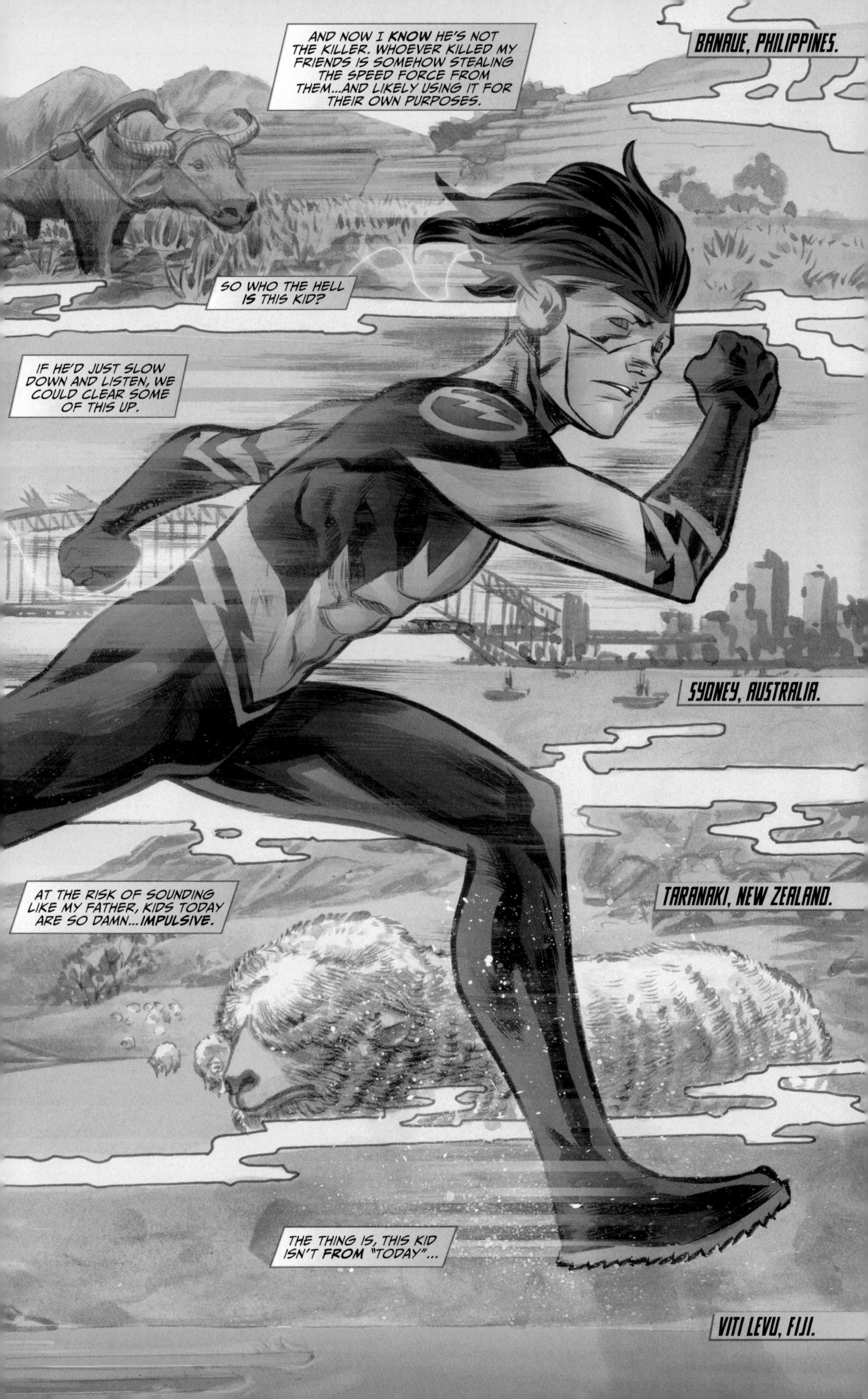
AND NOW I KNOW HE'S NOT THE KILLER. WHOEVER KILLED MY FRIENDS IS SOMEHOW STEALING THE SPEED FORCE FROM THEM...AND LIKELY USING IT FOR THEIR OWN PURPOSES.
BANAUE, PHILIPPINES.
SO WHO THE HELL IS THIS KID?
IF HE'D JUST SLOW DOWN AND LISTEN, WE COULD CLEAR SOME OF THIS UP.
SYDNEY, AUSTRALIA.
AT THE RISK OF SOUNDING LIKE MY FATHER, KIDS TODAY ARE SO DAMN...IMPULSIVE.
TARANAKI, NEW ZEALAND.
THE THING IS, THIS KID ISN'T FROM "TODAY"...
VITI LEVU, FIJI.

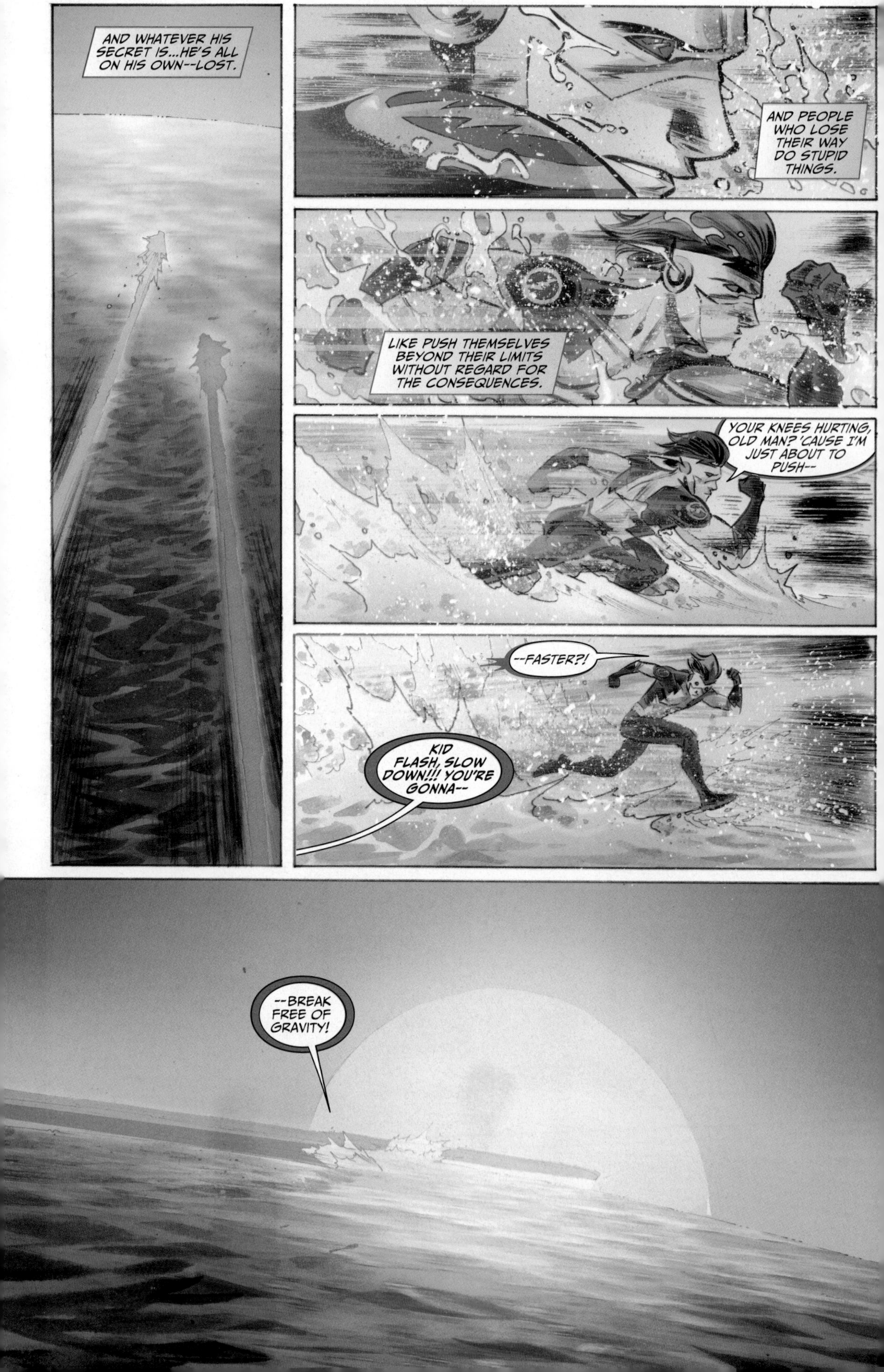
AND WHATEVER HIS SECRET IS...HE'S ALL ON HIS OWN--LOST.
AND PEOPLE WHO LOSE THEIR WAY DO STUPID THINGS.
LIKE PUSH THEMSELVES BEYOND THEIR LIMITS WITHOUT REGARD FOR THE CONSEQUENCES.
YOUR KNEES HURTING, OLD MAN? 'CAUSE I'M JUST ABOUT TO PUSH--
--FASTER?!
KID FLASH, SLOW DOWN!!! YOU'RE GONNA--
--BREAK FREE OF GRAVITY!

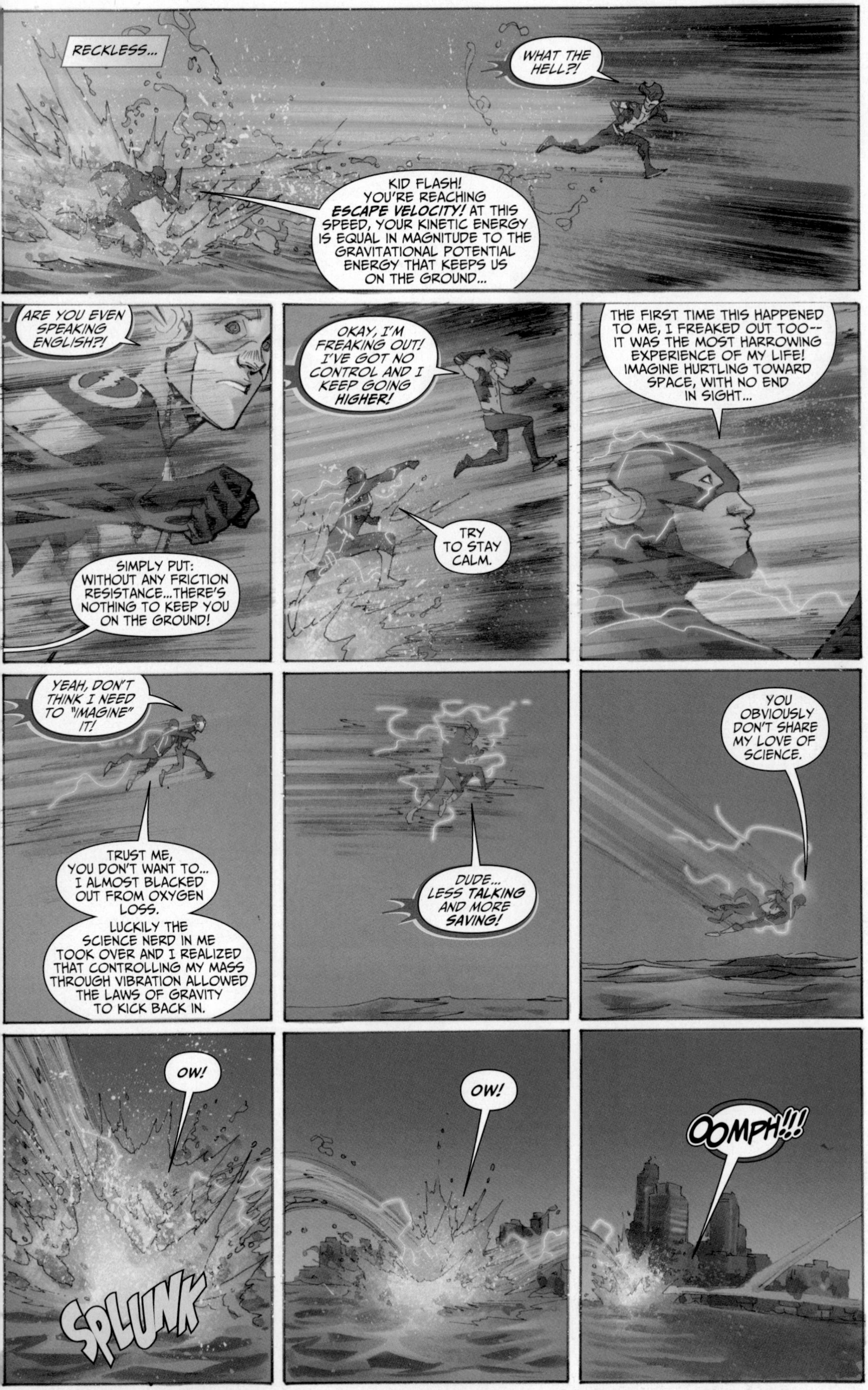
RECKLESS...
WHAT THE HELL?!
KID FLASH! YOU'RE REACHING ESCAPE VELOCITY! AT THIS SPEED, YOUR KINETIC ENERGY IS EQUAL IN MAGNITUDE TO THE GRAVITATIONAL POTENTIAL ENERGY THAT KEEPS US ON THE GROUND...
ARE YOU EVEN SPEAKING ENGLISH?!
SIMPLY PUT: WITHOUT ANY FRICTION RESISTANCE...THERE'S NOTHING TO KEEP YOU ON THE GROUND!
OKAY, I'M FREAKING OUT! I'VE GOT NO CONTROL AND I KEEP GOING HIGHER!
TRY TO STAY CALM.
THE FIRST TIME THIS HAPPENED TO ME, I FREAKED OUT TOO-- IT WAS THE MOST HARROWING EXPERIENCE OF MY LIFE! IMAGINE HURTLING TOWARD SPACE, WITH NO END IN SIGHT...
YEAH, DON'T THINK I NEED TO "IMAGINE" IT!
TRUST ME, YOU DON'T WANT TO... I ALMOST BLACKED OUT FROM OXYGEN LOSS.
LUCKILY THE SCIENCE NERD IN ME TOOK OVER AND I REALIZED THAT CONTROLLING MY MASS THROUGH VIBRATION ALLOWED THE LAWS OF GRAVITY TO KICK BACK IN.
DUDE... LESS TALKING AND MORE SAVING!
YOU OBVIOUSLY DON'T SHARE MY LOVE OF SCIENCE.
OW!
SPLUNK
OW!
OOMPH!!!

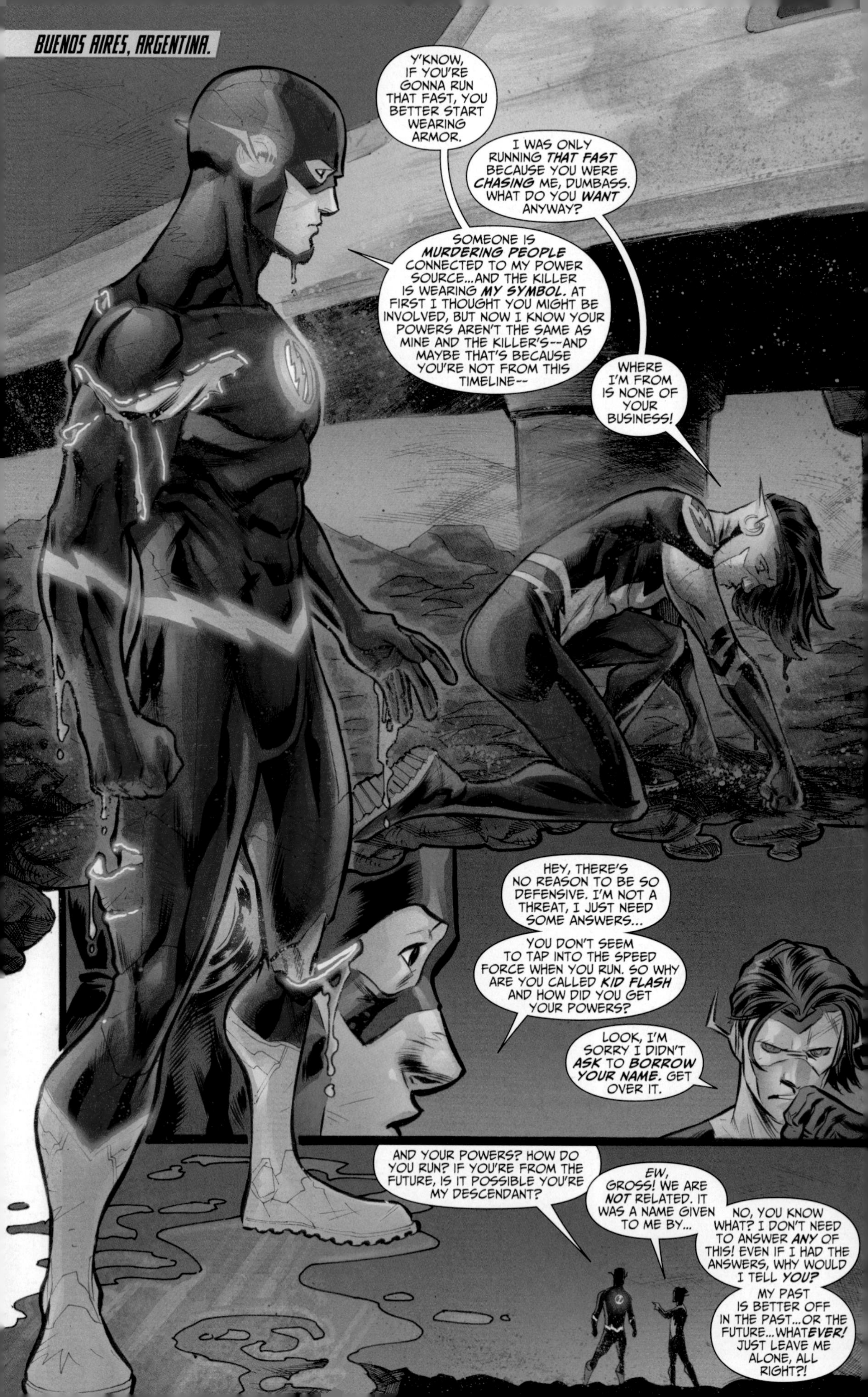
BUENOS AIRES, ARGENTINA.
Y'KNOW, IF YOU'RE GONNA RUN THAT FAST, YOU BETTER START WEARING ARMOR.
I WAS ONLY RUNNING THAT FAST BECAUSE YOU WERE CHASING ME, DUMBASS. WHAT DO YOU WANT ANYWAY?
SOMEONE IS MURDERING PEOPLE CONNECTED TO MY POWER SOURCE...AND THE KILLER IS WEARING MY SYMBOL. AT FIRST I THOUGHT YOU MIGHT BE INVOLVED, BUT NOW I KNOW YOUR POWERS AREN'T THE SAME AS MINE AND THE KILLER'S--AND MAYBE THAT'S BECAUSE YOU'RE NOT FROM THIS TIMELINE--
WHERE I'M FROM IS NONE OF YOUR BUSINESS!
HEY, THERE'S NO REASON TO BE SO DEFENSIVE. I'M NOT A THREAT, I JUST NEED SOME ANSWERS...
YOU DON'T SEEM TO TAP INTO THE SPEED FORCE WHEN YOU RUN. SO WHY ARE YOU CALLED KID FLASH AND HOW DID YOU GET YOUR POWERS?
LOOK, I'M SORRY I DIDN'T ASK TO BORROW YOUR NAME. GET OVER IT.
AND YOUR POWERS? HOW DO YOU RUN? IF YOU'RE FROM THE FUTURE, IS IT POSSIBLE YOU'RE MY DESCENDANT?
EW, GROSS! WE ARE NOT RELATED. IT WAS A NAME GIVEN TO ME BY...
NO, YOU KNOW WHAT? I DON'T NEED TO ANSWER ANY OF THIS! EVEN IF I HAD THE ANSWERS, WHY WOULD I TELL YOU?
MY PAST IS BETTER OFF IN THE PAST...OR THE FUTURE...WHATEVER! JUST LEAVE ME ALONE, ALL RIGHT?!

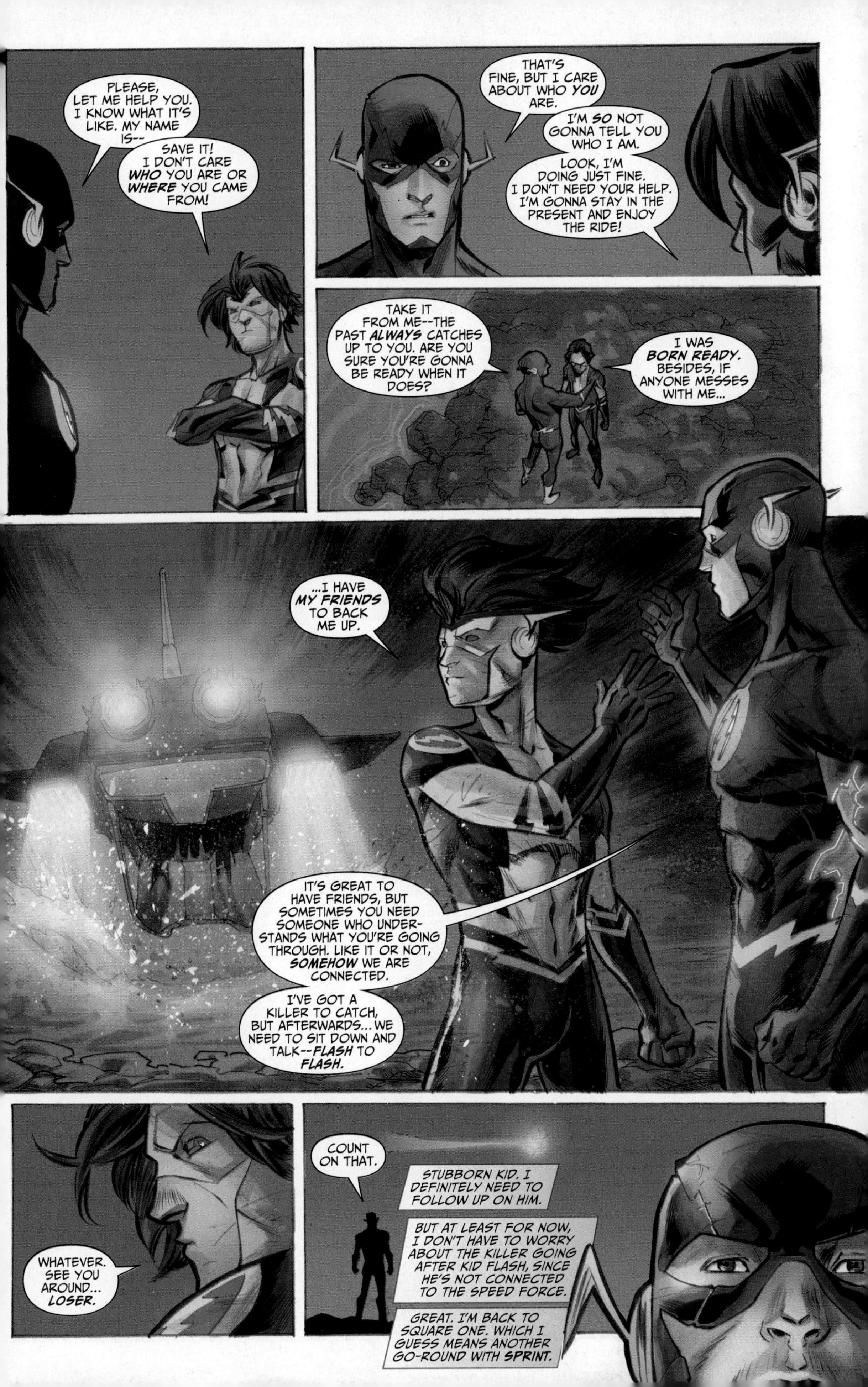
PLEASE, LET ME HELP YOU. I KNOW WHAT IT'S LIKE. MY NAME IS--
SAVE IT! I DON'T CARE WHO YOU ARE OR WHERE YOU CAME FROM!
THAT'S FINE, BUT I CARE ABOUT WHO YOU ARE.
I'M SO NOT GONNA TELL YOU WHO I AM.
LOOK, I'M DOING JUST FINE. I DON'T NEED YOUR HELP. I'M GONNA STAY IN THE PRESENT AND ENJOY THE RIDE!
TAKE IT FROM ME--THE PAST ALWAYS CATCHES UP TO YOU. ARE YOU SURE YOU'RE GONNA BE READY WHEN IT DOES?
I WAS BORN READY. BESIDES, IF ANYONE MESSES WITH ME...
...I HAVE MY FRIENDS TO BACK ME UP.
IT'S GREAT TO HAVE FRIENDS, BUT SOMETIMES YOU NEED SOMEONE WHO UNDERSTANDS WHAT YOU'RE GOING THROUGH. LIKE IT OR NOT, SOMEHOW WE ARE CONNECTED.
I'VE GOT A KILLER TO CATCH, BUT AFTERWARDS... WE NEED TO SIT DOWN AND TALK--FLASH TO FLASH.
WHATEVER. SEE YOU AROUND... LOSER.
COUNT ON THAT.
STUBBORN KID. I DEFINITELY NEED TO FOLLOW UP ON HIM.
BUT AT LEAST FOR NOW, I DON'T HAVE TO WORRY ABOUT THE KILLER GOING AFTER KID FLASH, SINCE HE'S NOT CONNECTED TO THE SPEED FORCE.
GREAT. I'M BACK TO SQUARE ONE. WHICH I GUESS MEANS ANOTHER GO-ROUND WITH SPRINT.

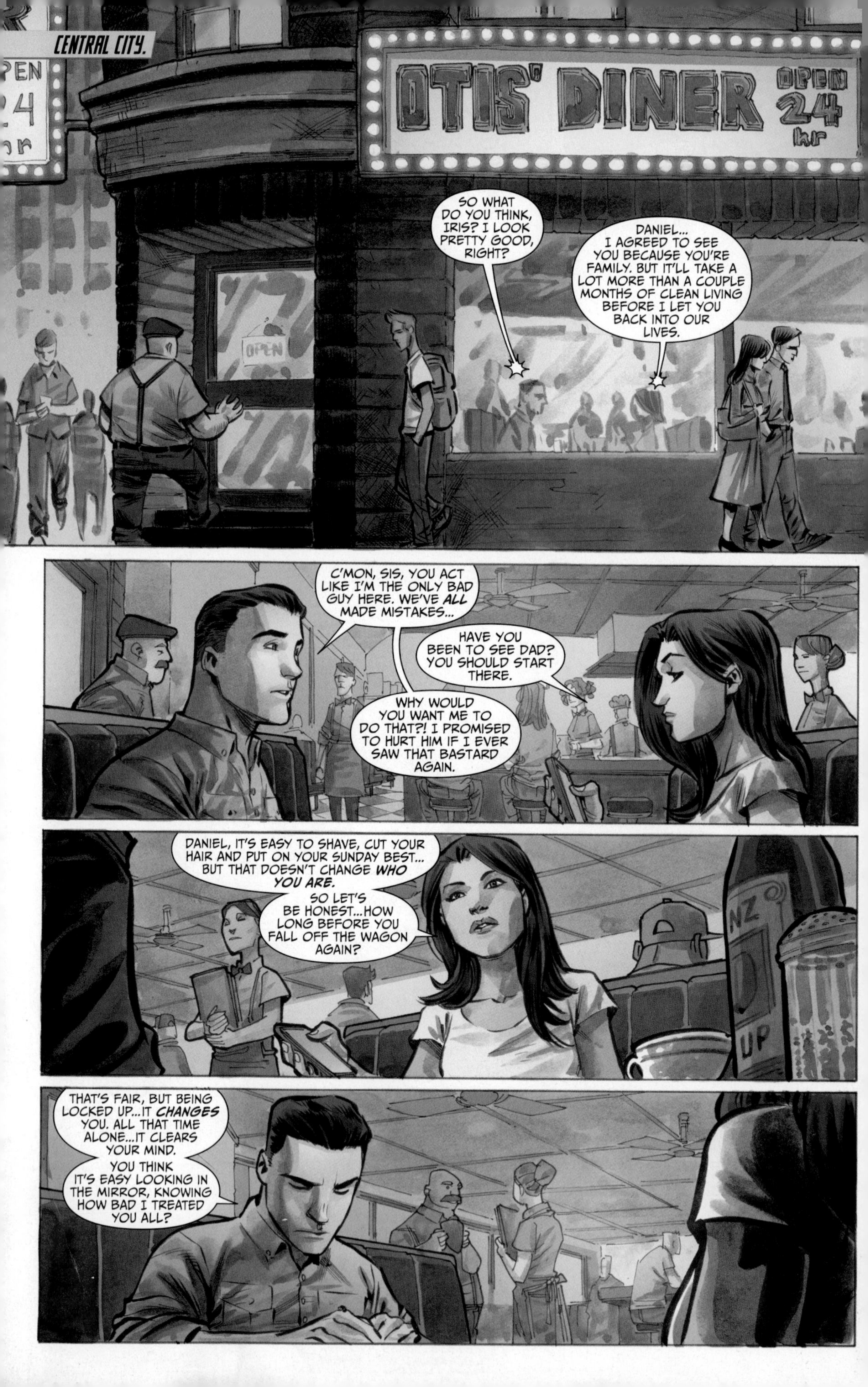
CENTRAL CITY.
OTIS' DINER OPEN 24 hr
OPEN
SO WHAT DO YOU THINK, IRIS? I LOOK PRETTY GOOD, RIGHT?
DANIEL... I AGREED TO SEE YOU BECAUSE YOU'RE FAMILY. BUT IT'LL TAKE A LOT MORE THAN A COUPLE MONTHS OF CLEAN LIVING BEFORE I LET YOU BACK INTO OUR LIVES.
C'MON, SIS, YOU ACT LIKE I'M THE ONLY BAD GUY HERE. WE'VE ALL MADE MISTAKES...
HAVE YOU BEEN TO SEE DAD? YOU SHOULD START THERE.
WHY WOULD YOU WANT ME TO DO THAT?! I PROMISED TO HURT HIM IF I EVER SAW THAT BASTARD AGAIN.
DANIEL, IT'S EASY TO SHAVE, CUT YOUR HAIR AND PUT ON YOUR SUNDAY BEST... BUT THAT DOESN'T CHANGE WHO YOU ARE.
SO LET'S BE HONEST...HOW LONG BEFORE YOU FALL OFF THE WAGON AGAIN?
THAT'S FAIR, BUT BEING LOCKED UP...IT CHANGES YOU. ALL THAT TIME ALONE...IT CLEARS YOUR MIND.
YOU THINK IT'S EASY LOOKING IN THE MIRROR, KNOWING HOW BAD I TREATED YOU ALL?

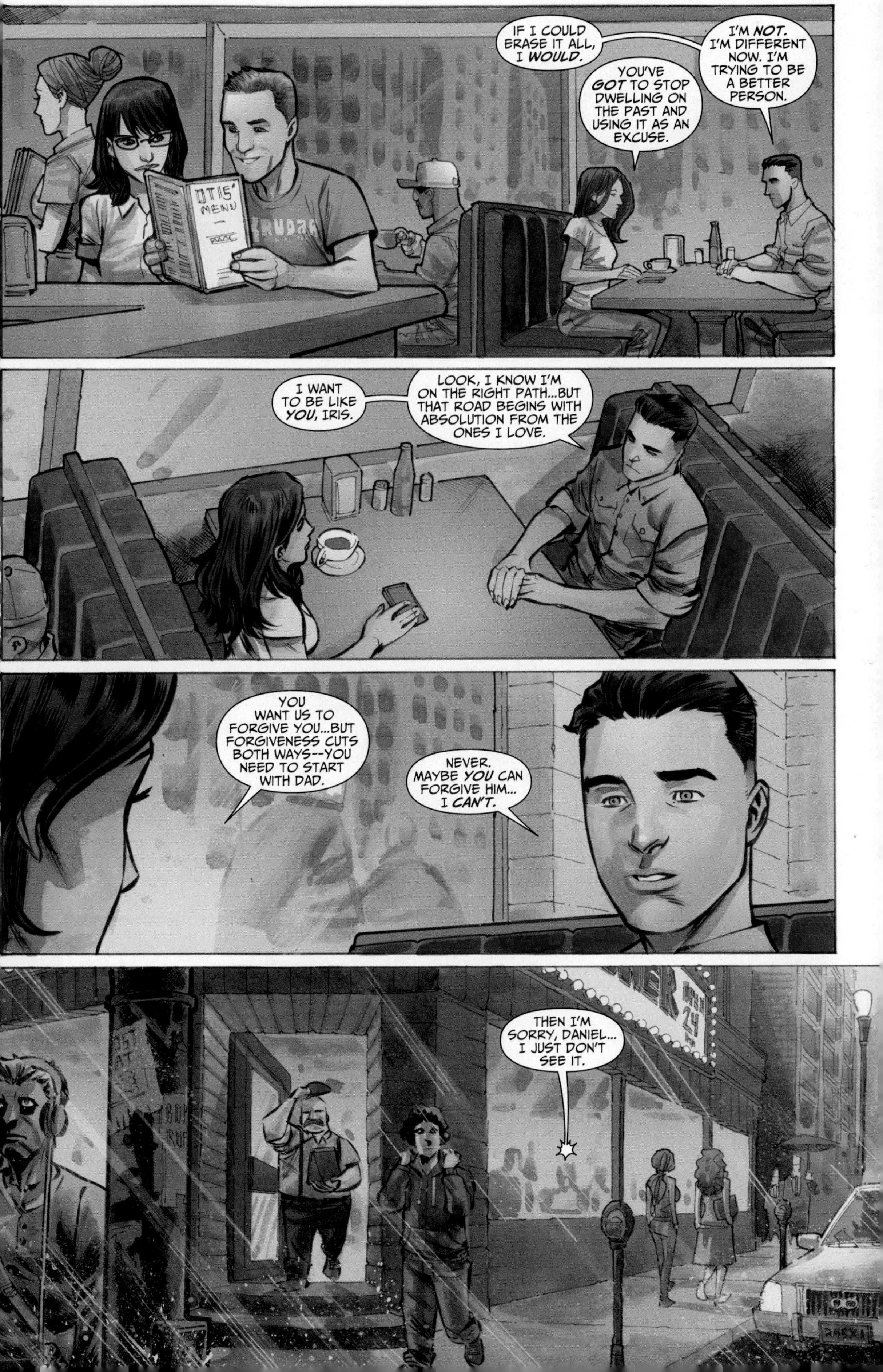

YOU'VE GOT TO STOP DWELLING ON THE PAST AND USING IT AS AN EXCUSE.
IF I COULD ERASE IT ALL, I WOULD.
I'M NOT. I'M DIFFERENT NOW. I'M TRYING TO BE A BETTER PERSON.
I WANT TO BE LIKE YOU, IRIS.
LOOK, I KNOW I'M ON THE RIGHT PATH...BUT THAT ROAD BEGINS WITH ABSOLUTION FROM THE ONES I LOVE.
YOU WANT US TO FORGIVE YOU...BUT FORGIVENESS CUTS BOTH WAYS--YOU NEED TO START WITH DAD.
NEVER. MAYBE YOU CAN FORGIVE HIM... I CAN'T.
THEN I'M SORRY, DANIEL... I JUST DON'T SEE IT.

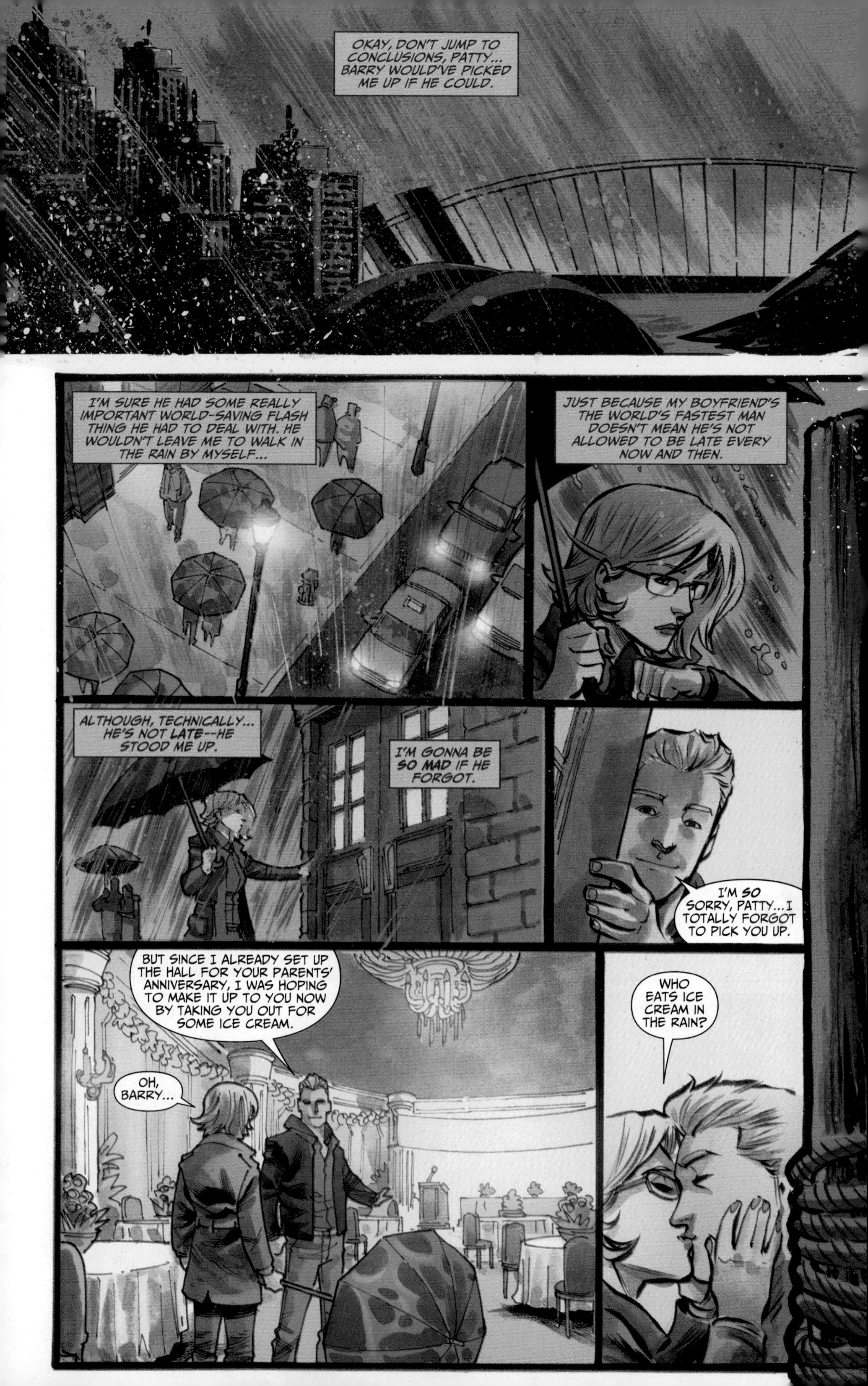
OKAY, DON'T JUMP TO CONCLUSIONS, PATTY... BARRY WOULD'VE PICKED ME UP IF HE COULD.
I'M SURE HE HAD SOME REALLY IMPORTANT WORLD-SAVING FLASH THING HE HAD TO DEAL WITH. HE WOULDN'T LEAVE ME TO WALK IN THE RAIN BY MYSELF...
JUST BECAUSE MY BOYFRIEND'S THE WORLD'S FASTEST MAN DOESN'T MEAN HE'S NOT ALLOWED TO BE LATE EVERY NOW AND THEN.
ALTHOUGH, TECHNICALLY... HE'S NOT LATE--HE STOOD ME UP.
I'M GONNA BE SO MAD IF HE FORGOT.
I'M SO SORRY, PATTY...I TOTALLY FORGOT TO PICK YOU UP.
BUT SINCE I ALREADY SET UP THE HALL FOR YOUR PARENTS' ANNIVERSARY, I WAS HOPING TO MAKE IT UP TO YOU NOW BY TAKING YOU OUT FOR SOME ICE CREAM.
OH, BARRY...
WHO EATS ICE CREAM IN THE RAIN?

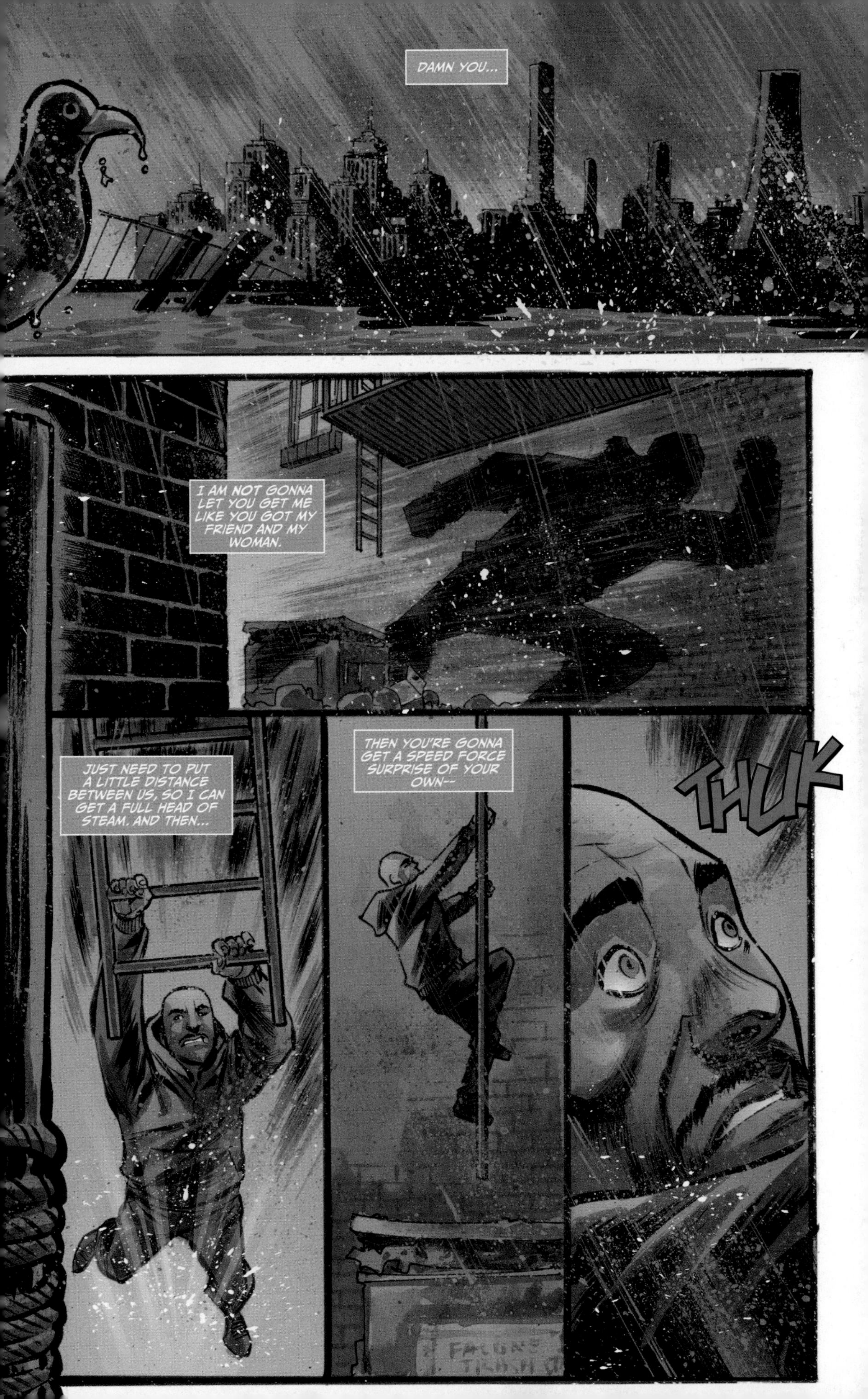
DAMN YOU...
I AM NOT GONNA LET YOU GET ME LIKE YOU GOT MY FRIEND AND MY WOMAN.
JUST NEED TO PUT A LITTLE DISTANCE BETWEEN US, SO I CAN GET A FULL HEAD OF STEAM. AND THEN...
THEN YOU'RE GONNA GET A SPEED FORCE SURPRISE OF YOUR OWN--
THUK

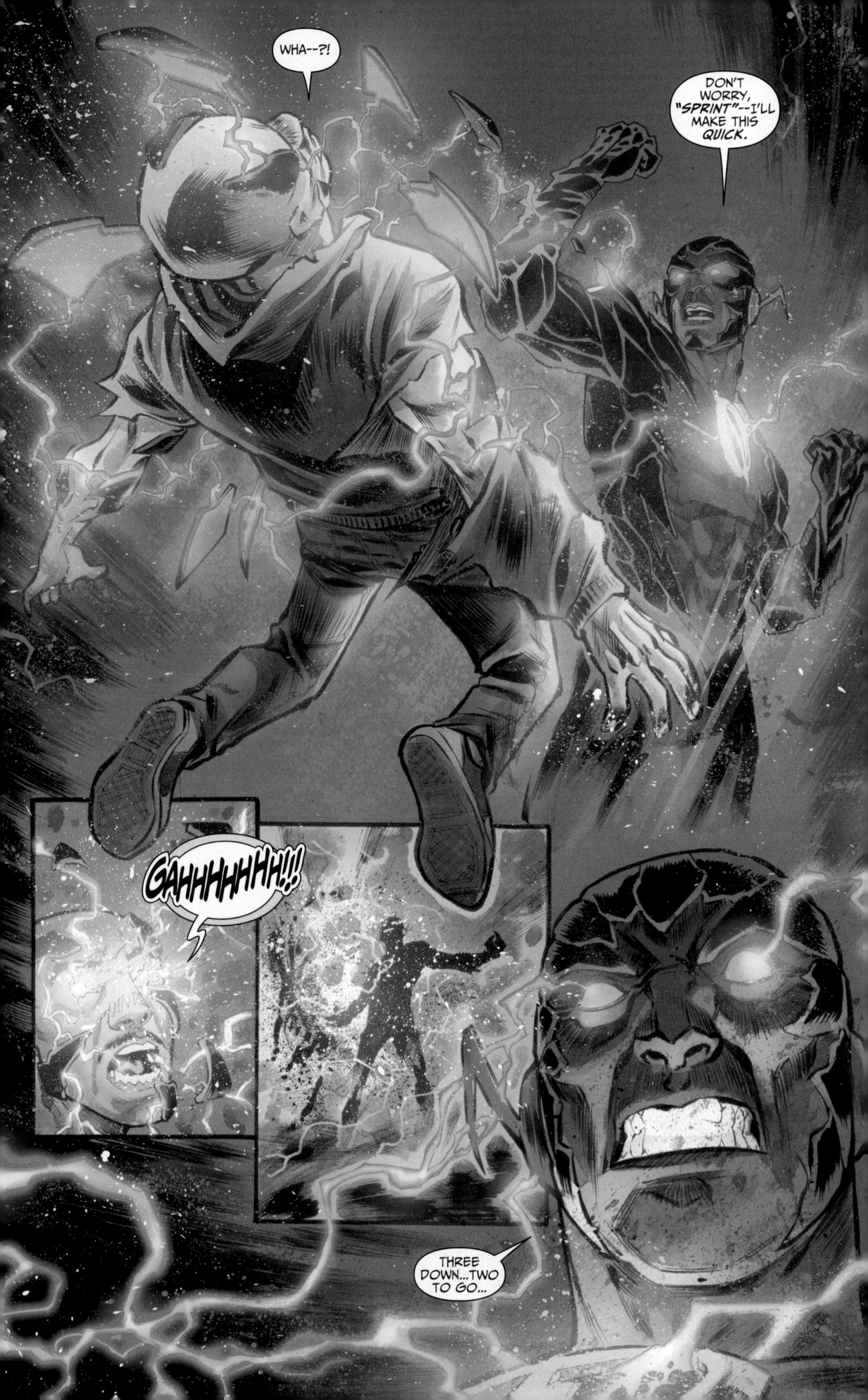
WHA--?!
DON'T WORRY, "SPRINT"--I'LL MAKE THIS QUICK.
GAHHHHHHH!!!
THREE DOWN...TWO TO GO...

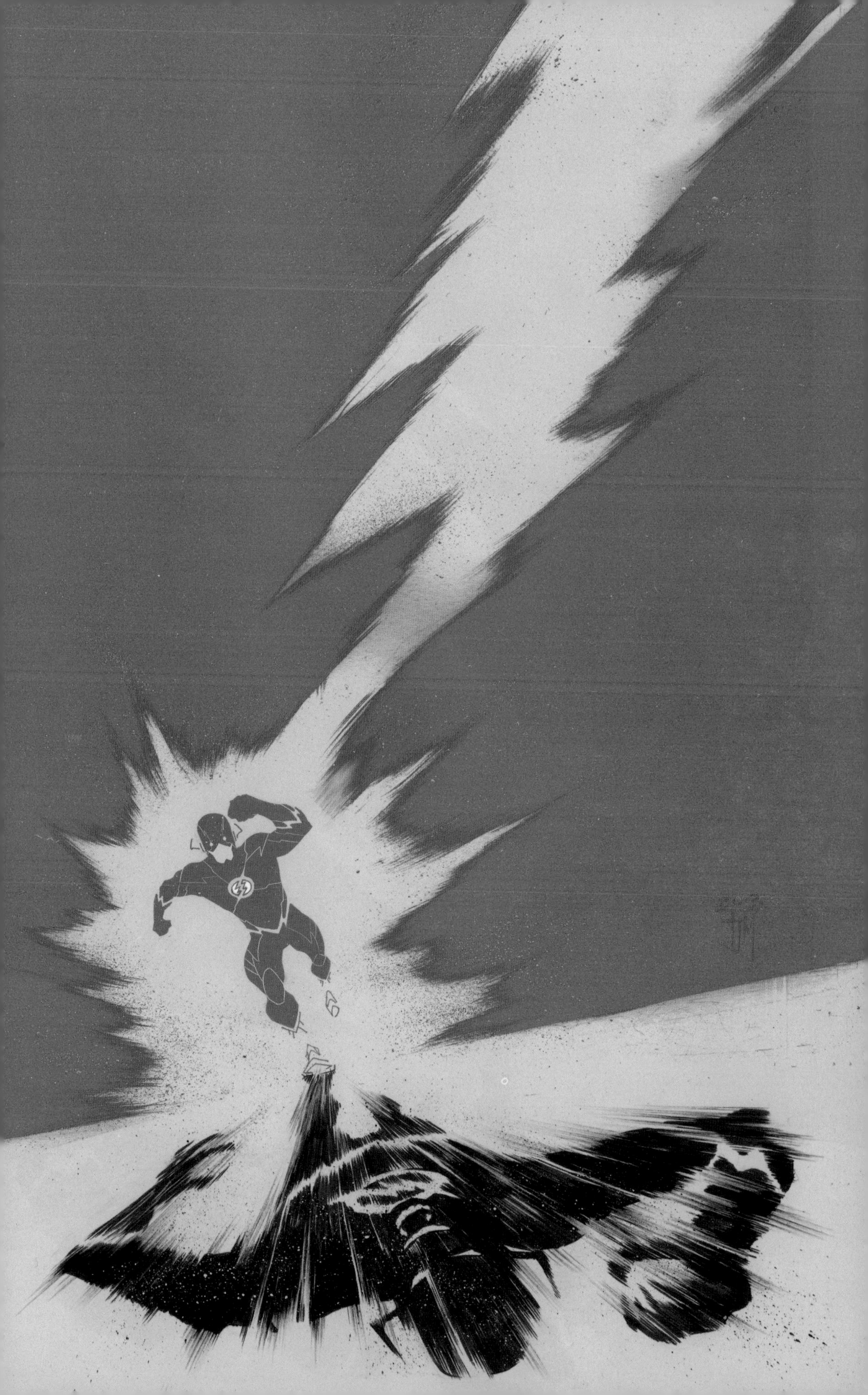

FRANCIS MANAPUL & BRIAN BUCCELLATO writers FRANCIS MANAPUL artist

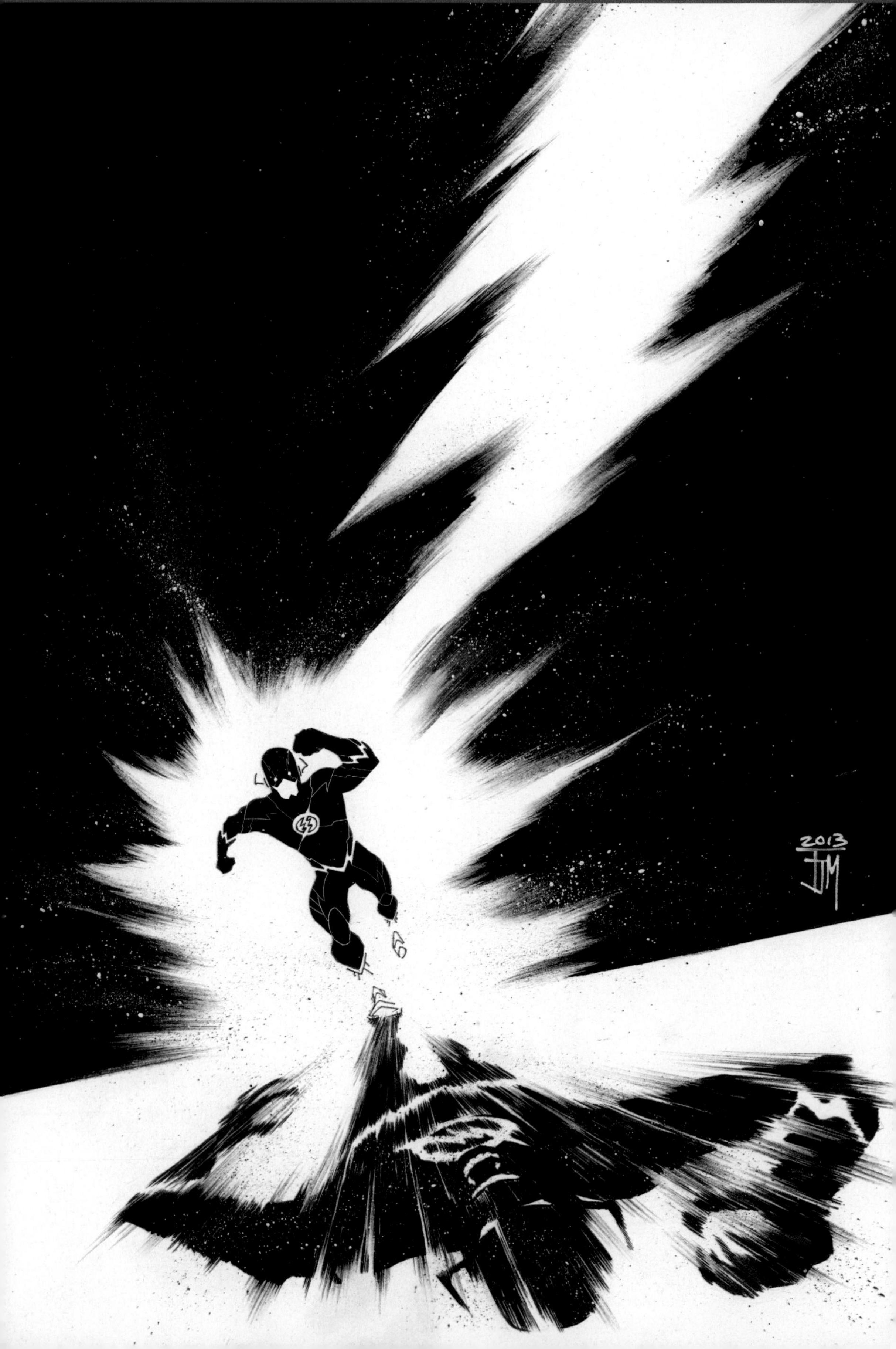
2013

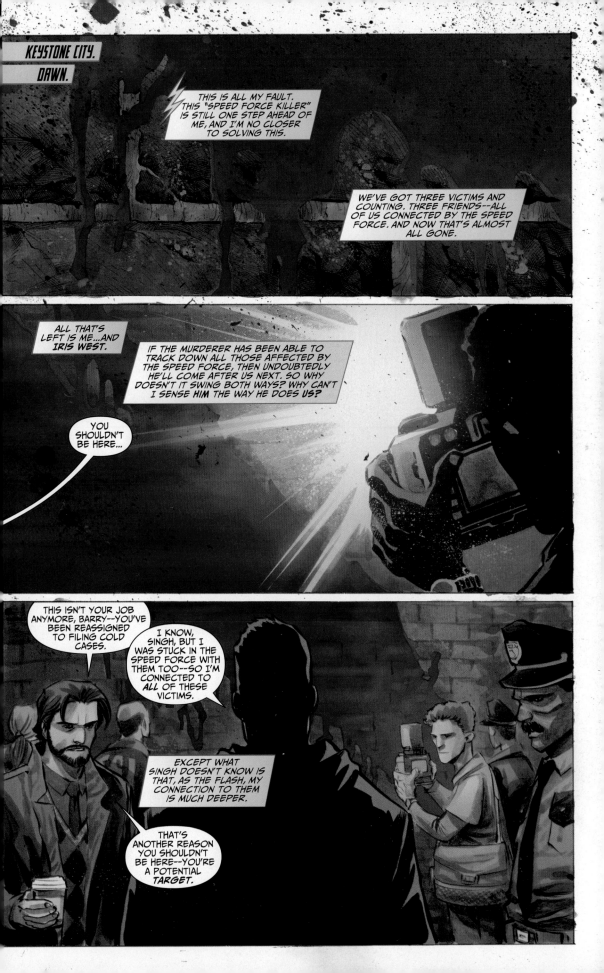

KEYSTONE CITY.
DAWN.

THIS IS ALL MY FAULT. THIS "SPEED FORCE KILLER" IS STILL ONE STEP AHEAD OF ME, AND I'M NO CLOSER TO SOLVING THIS.

WE'VE GOT THREE VICTIMS AND COUNTING. THREE FRIENDS--ALL OF US CONNECTED BY THE SPEED FORCE. AND NOW THAT'S ALMOST ALL GONE.

ALL THAT'S LEFT IS ME...AND IRIS WEST.

IF THE MURDERER HAS BEEN ABLE TO TRACK DOWN ALL THOSE AFFECTED BY THE SPEED FORCE, THEN UNDOUBTEDLY HE'LL COME AFTER US NEXT. SO WHY DOESN'T IT SWING BOTH WAYS? WHY CAN'T I SENSE HIM THE WAY HE DOES US?

YOU SHOULDN'T BE HERE...

THIS ISN'T YOUR JOB ANYMORE, BARRY--YOU'VE BEEN REASSIGNED TO FILING COLD CASES.

I KNOW, SINGH, BUT I WAS STUCK IN THE SPEED FORCE WITH THEM TOO--SO I'M CONNECTED TO ALL OF THESE VICTIMS.

EXCEPT WHAT SINGH DOESN'T KNOW IS THAT, AS THE FLASH, MY CONNECTION TO THEM IS MUCH DEEPER.

THAT'S ANOTHER REASON YOU SHOULDN'T BE HERE--YOU'RE A POTENTIAL TARGET.

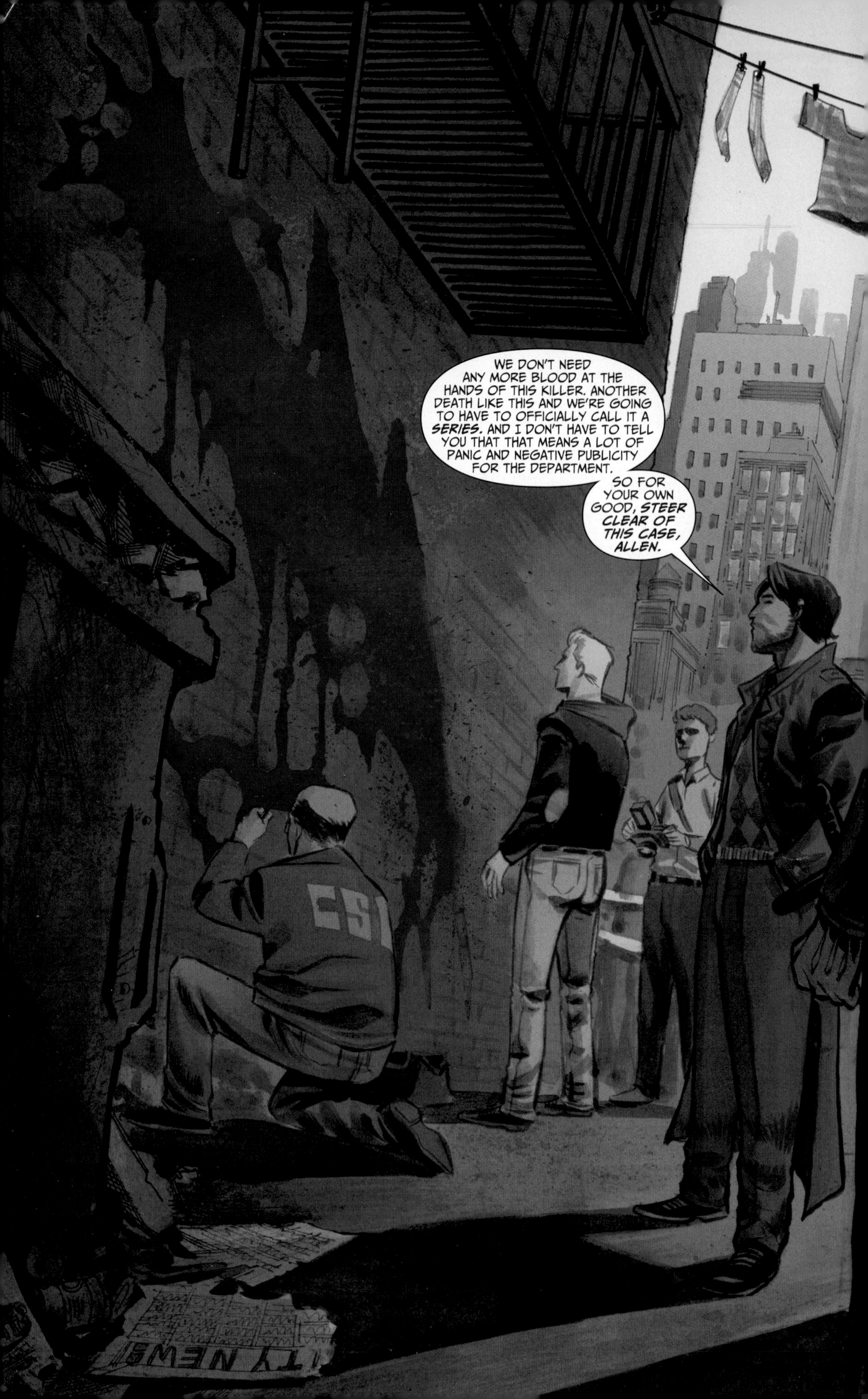
WE DON'T NEED ANY MORE BLOOD AT THE HANDS OF THIS KILLER. ANOTHER DEATH LIKE THIS AND WE'RE GOING TO HAVE TO OFFICIALLY CALL IT A SERIES. AND I DON'T HAVE TO TELL YOU THAT THAT MEANS A LOT OF PANIC AND NEGATIVE PUBLICITY FOR THE DEPARTMENT.
SO FOR YOUR OWN GOOD, STEER CLEAR OF THIS CASE, ALLEN.
TY NEWS

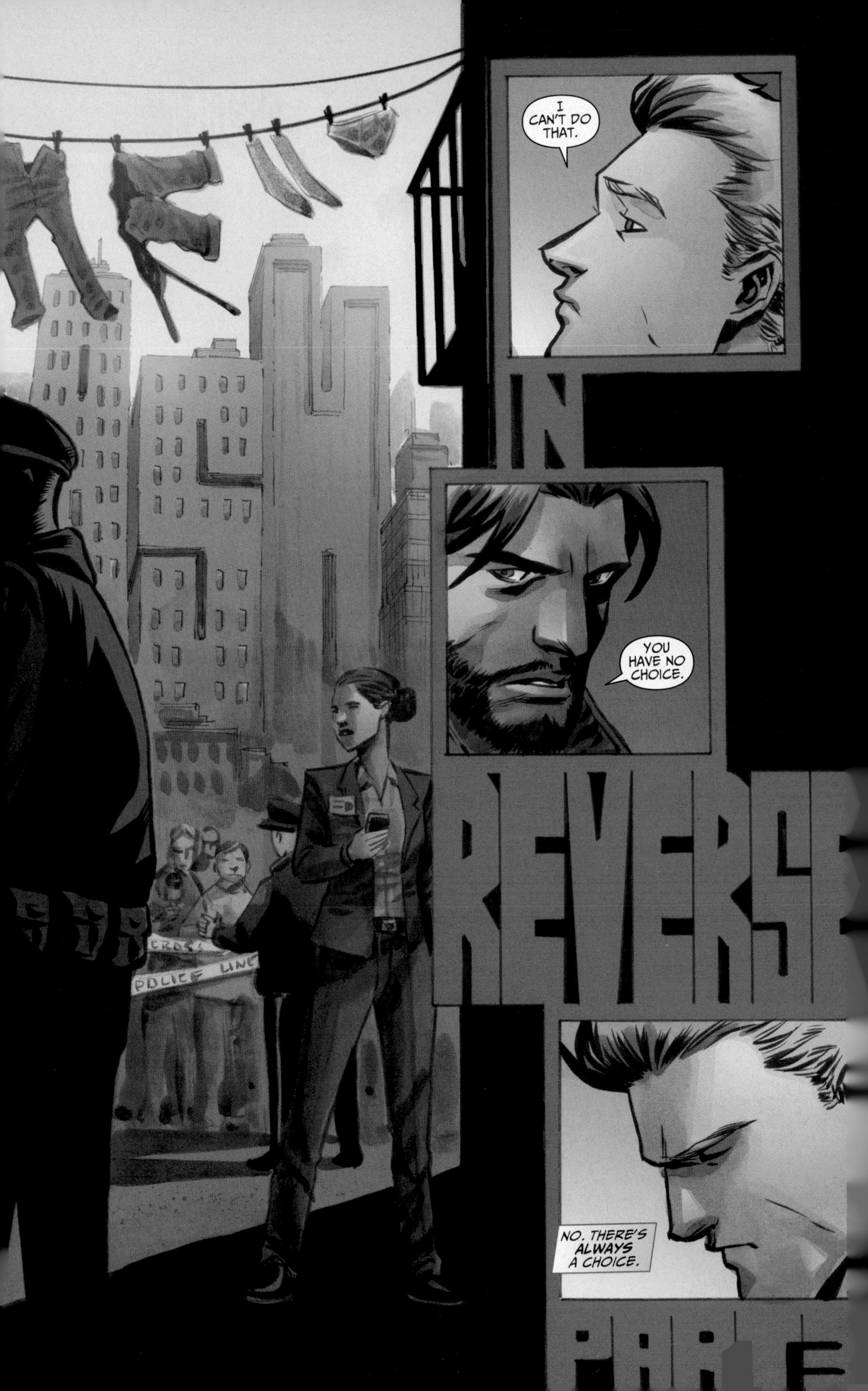
I CAN'T DO THAT.
IN
YOU HAVE NO CHOICE.
REVERSE
NO. THERE'S ALWAYS A CHOICE.

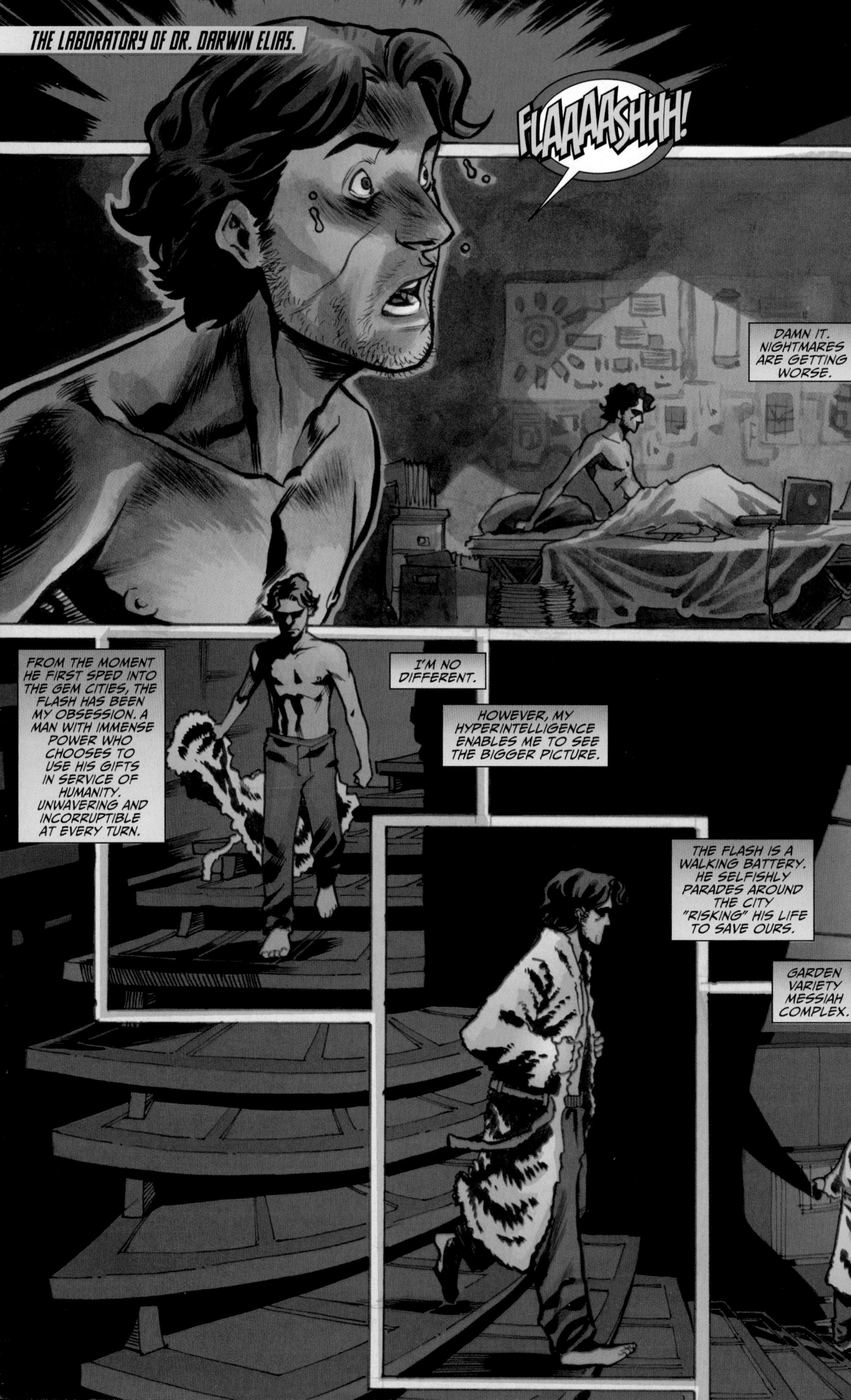
THE LABORATORY OF DR. DARWIN ELIAS.
FLAAAASHHH!
DAMN IT. NIGHTMARES ARE GETTING WORSE.
FROM THE MOMENT HE FIRST SPED INTO THE GEM CITIES, THE FLASH HAS BEEN MY OBSESSION. A MAN WITH IMMENSE POWER WHO CHOOSES TO USE HIS GIFTS IN SERVICE OF HUMANITY. UNWAVERING AND INCORRUPTIBLE AT EVERY TURN.
I'M NO DIFFERENT.
HOWEVER, MY HYPERINTELLIGENCE ENABLES ME TO SEE THE BIGGER PICTURE.
THE FLASH IS A WALKING BATTERY. HE SELFISHLY PARADES AROUND THE CITY "RISKING" HIS LIFE TO SAVE OURS.
GARDEN VARIETY MESSIAH COMPLEX.

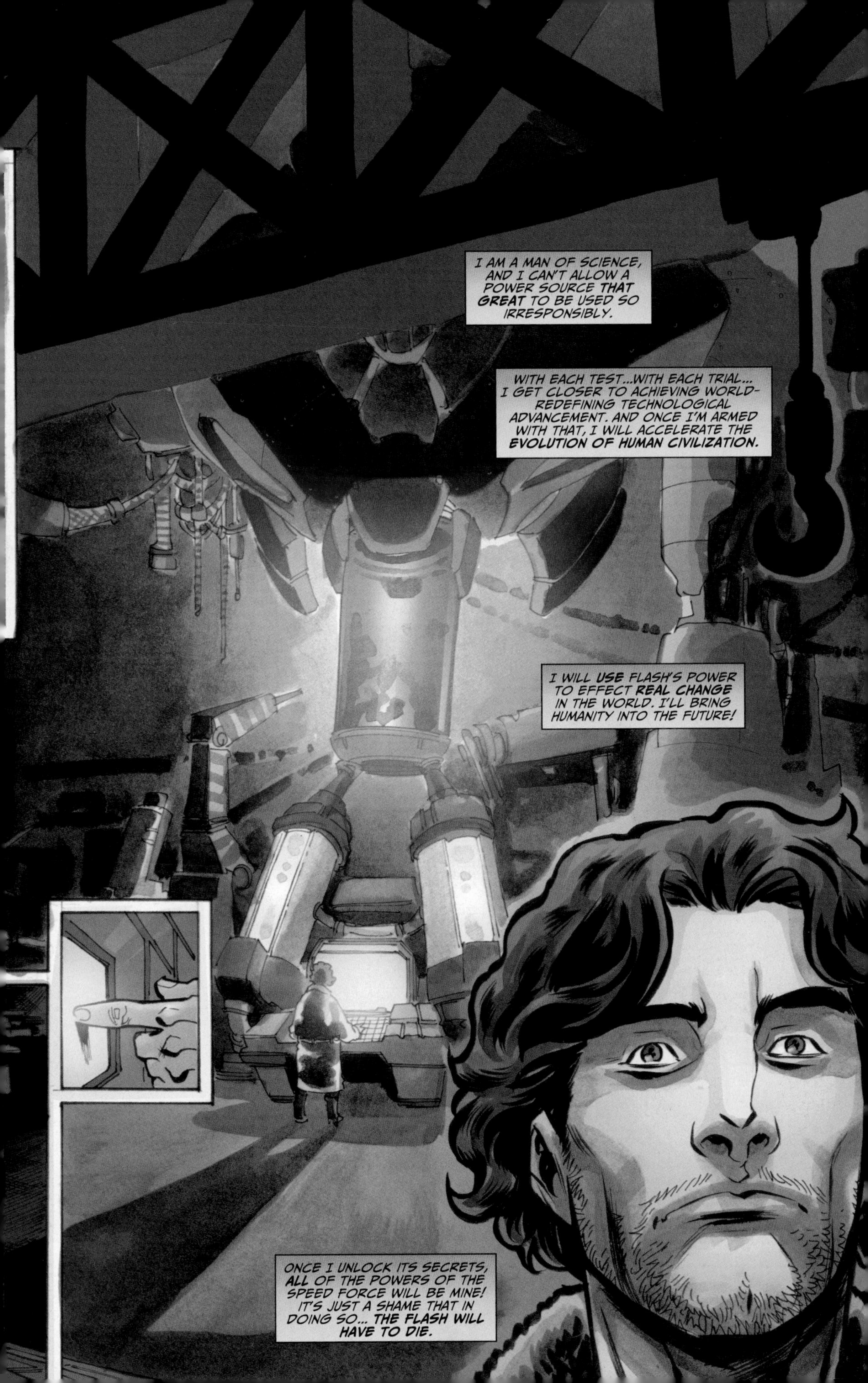
I AM A MAN OF SCIENCE, AND I CAN'T ALLOW A POWER SOURCE THAT GREAT TO BE USED SO IRRESPONSIBLY.
WITH EACH TEST...WITH EACH TRIAL... I GET CLOSER TO ACHIEVING WORLD-REDEFINING TECHNOLOGICAL ADVANCEMENT. AND ONCE I'M ARMED WITH THAT, I WILL ACCELERATE THE EVOLUTION OF HUMAN CIVILIZATION.
I WILL USE FLASH'S POWER TO EFFECT REAL CHANGE IN THE WORLD. I'LL BRING HUMANITY INTO THE FUTURE!
ONCE I UNLOCK ITS SECRETS, ALL OF THE POWERS OF THE SPEED FORCE WILL BE MINE! IT'S JUST A SHAME THAT IN DOING SO... THE FLASH WILL HAVE TO DIE.

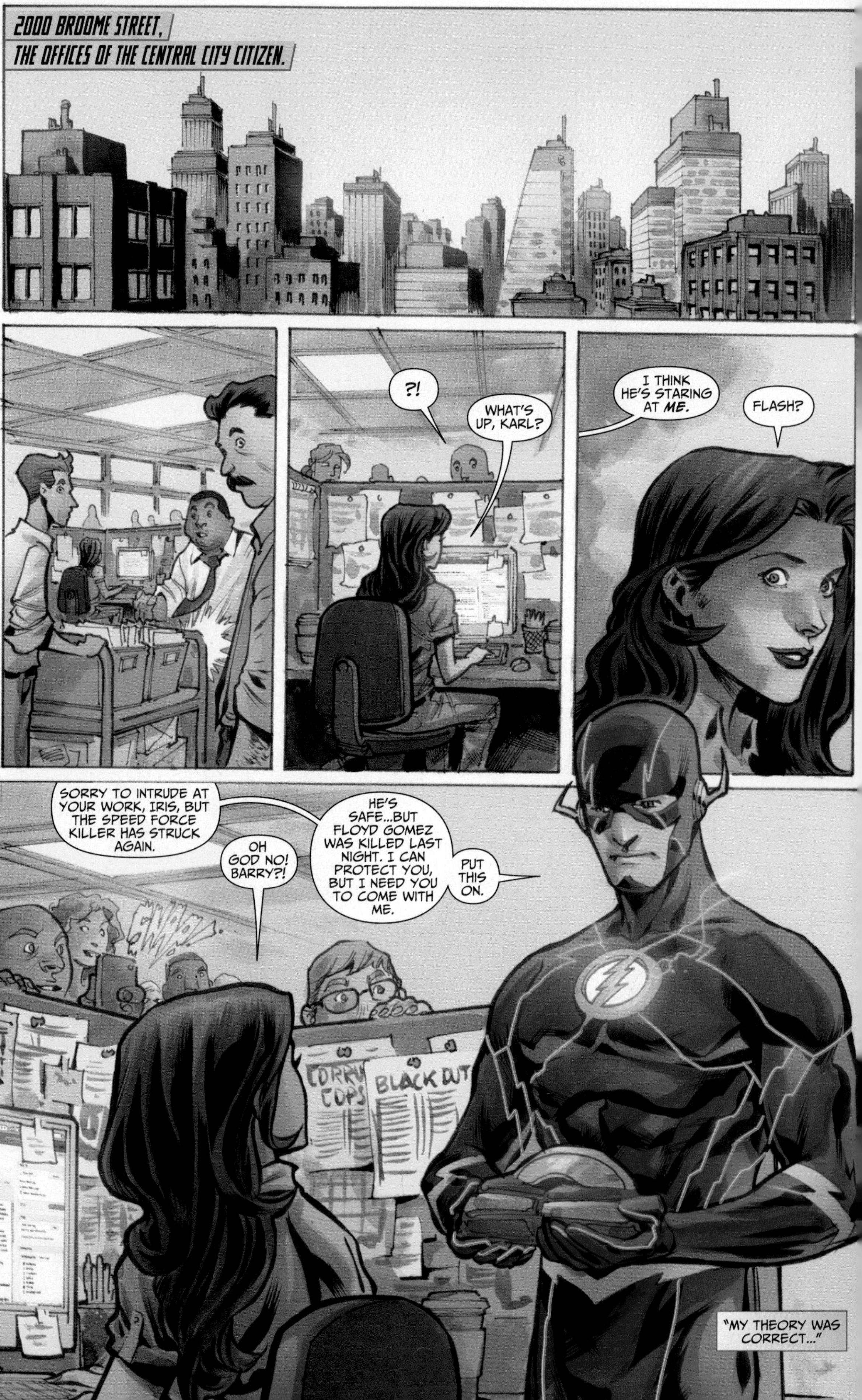
2000 BROOME STREET,
THE OFFICES OF THE CENTRAL CITY CITIZEN.
?!
WHAT'S UP, KARL?
I THINK HE'S STARING AT *ME*.
FLASH?
SORRY TO INTRUDE AT YOUR WORK, IRIS, BUT THE SPEED FORCE KILLER HAS STRUCK AGAIN.
OH GOD NO! BARRY?!
HE'S SAFE...BUT FLOYD GOMEZ WAS KILLED LAST NIGHT. I CAN PROTECT YOU, BUT I NEED YOU TO COME WITH ME.
PUT THIS ON.
BLACK OUT
"MY THEORY WAS CORRECT..."

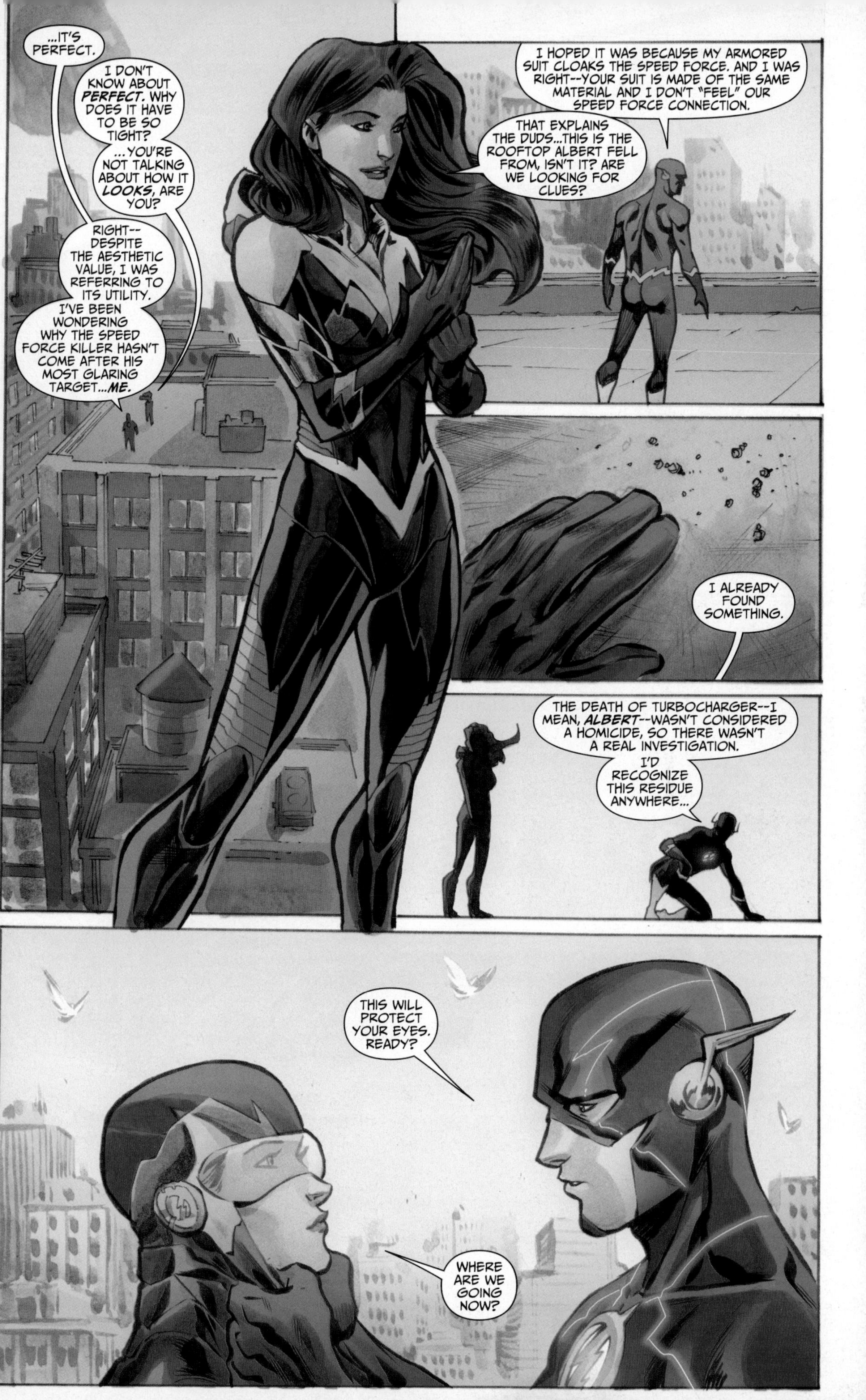
...IT'S PERFECT.
I DON'T KNOW ABOUT PERFECT. WHY DOES IT HAVE TO BE SO TIGHT?
...YOU'RE NOT TALKING ABOUT HOW IT LOOKS, ARE YOU?
RIGHT--DESPITE THE AESTHETIC VALUE, I WAS REFERRING TO ITS UTILITY.
I'VE BEEN WONDERING WHY THE SPEED FORCE KILLER HASN'T COME AFTER HIS MOST GLARING TARGET...ME.
I HOPED IT WAS BECAUSE MY ARMORED SUIT CLOAKS THE SPEED FORCE. AND I WAS RIGHT--YOUR SUIT IS MADE OF THE SAME MATERIAL AND I DON'T "FEEL" OUR SPEED FORCE CONNECTION.
THAT EXPLAINS THE DUDS...THIS IS THE ROOFTOP ALBERT FELL FROM, ISN'T IT? ARE WE LOOKING FOR CLUES?
I ALREADY FOUND SOMETHING.
THE DEATH OF TURBOCHARGER--I MEAN, ALBERT--WASN'T CONSIDERED A HOMICIDE, SO THERE WASN'T A REAL INVESTIGATION.
I'D RECOGNIZE THIS RESIDUE ANYWHERE...
THIS WILL PROTECT YOUR EYES. READY?
WHERE ARE WE GOING NOW?

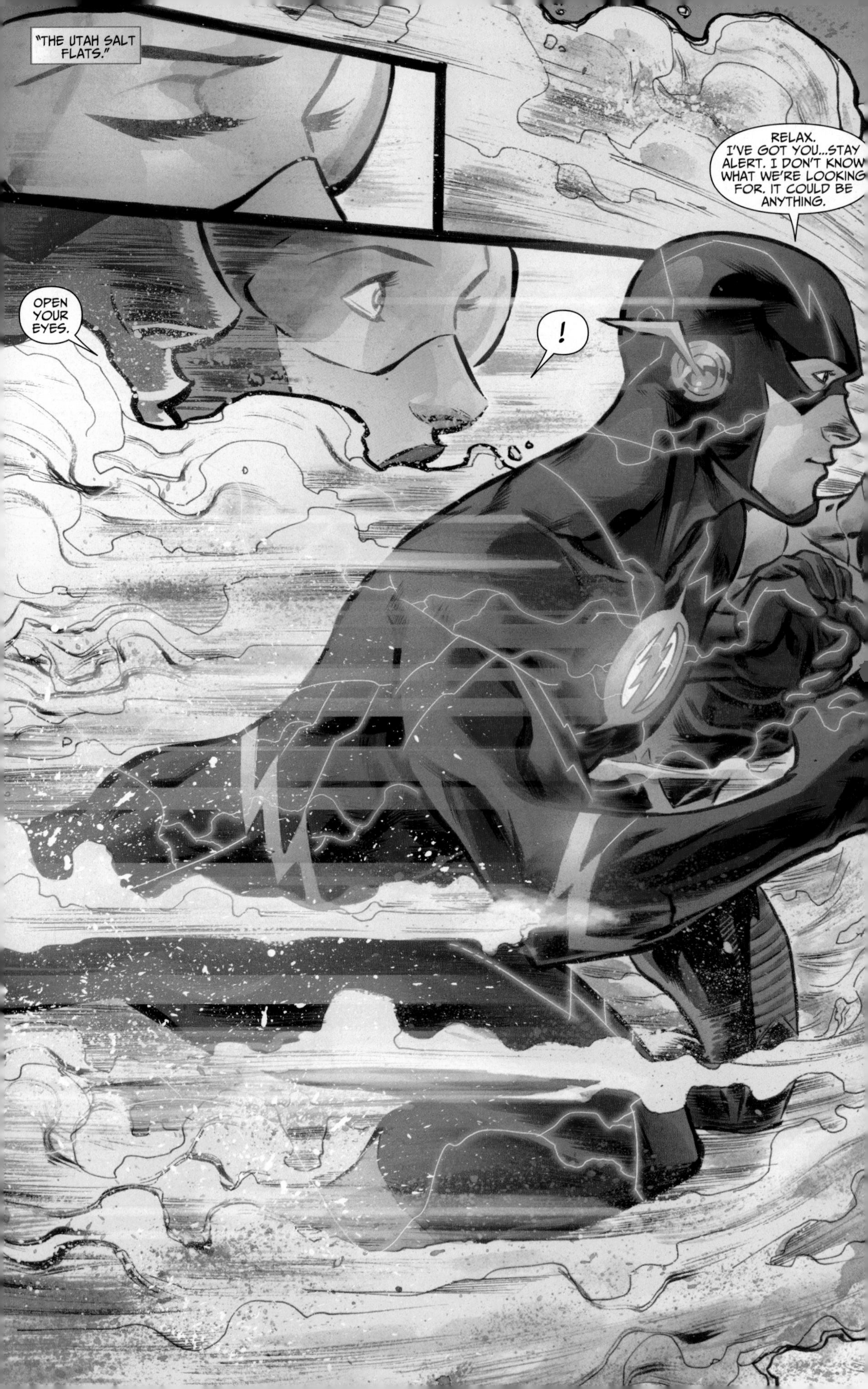
"THE UTAH SALT FLATS."
RELAX. I'VE GOT YOU...STAY ALERT. I DON'T KNOW WHAT WE'RE LOOKING FOR. IT COULD BE ANYTHING.
OPEN YOUR EYES.
!

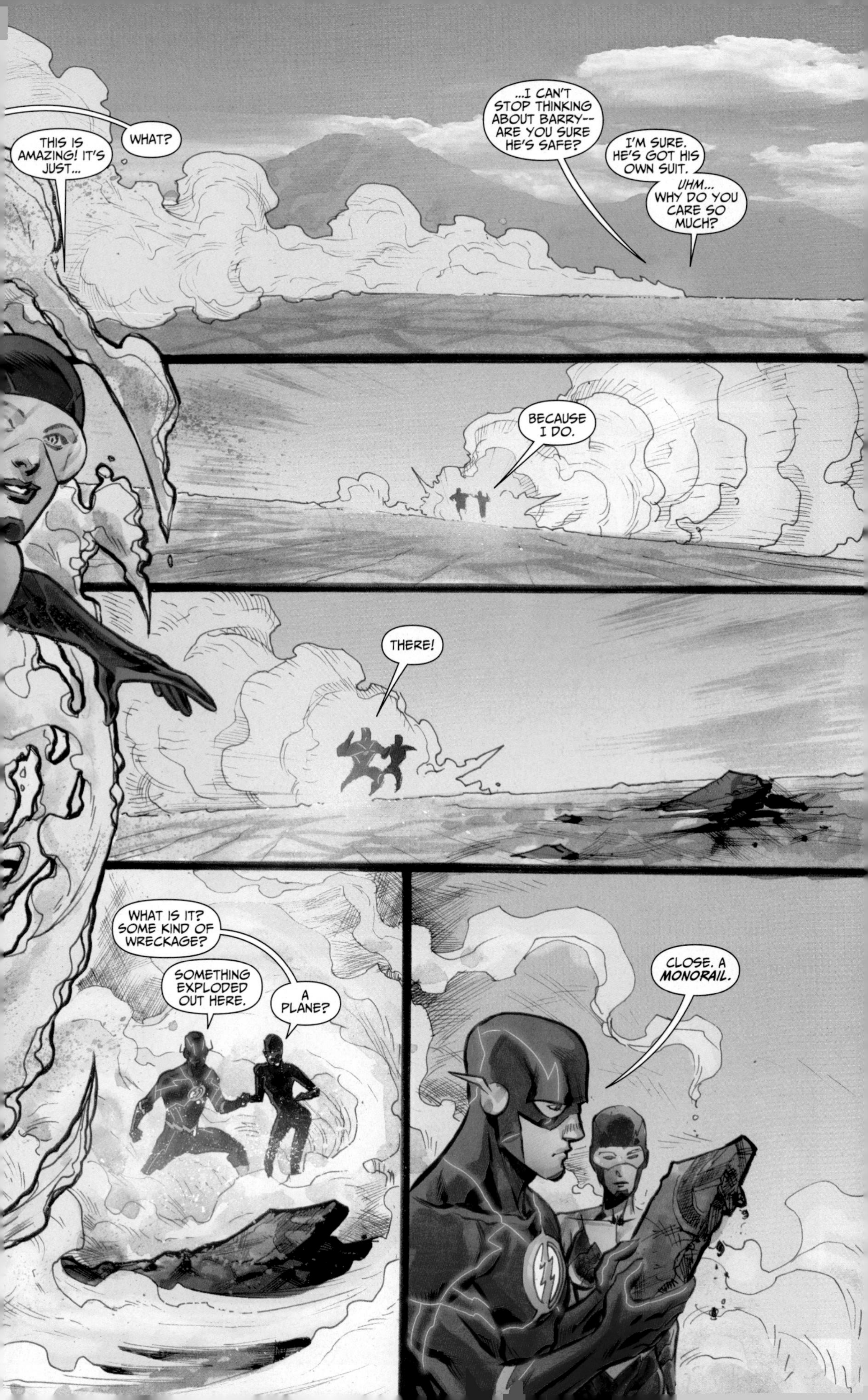
WHAT?
THIS IS AMAZING! IT'S JUST...
...I CAN'T STOP THINKING ABOUT BARRY-- ARE YOU SURE HE'S SAFE?
I'M SURE. HE'S GOT HIS OWN SUIT.
UHM... WHY DO YOU CARE SO MUCH?
BECAUSE I DO.
THERE!
WHAT IS IT? SOME KIND OF WRECKAGE?
SOMETHING EXPLODED OUT HERE.
A PLANE?
CLOSE. A MONORAIL.

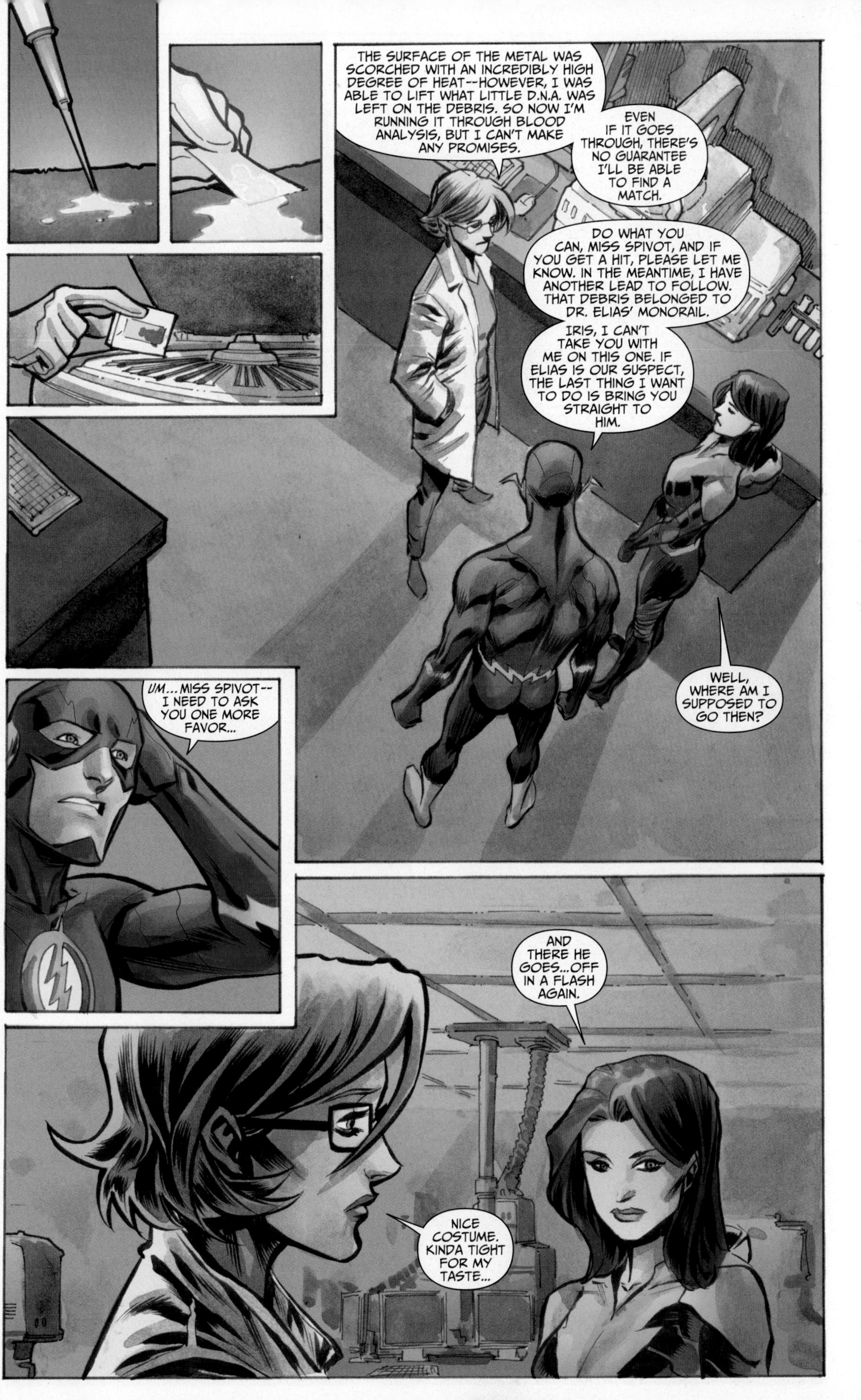
THE SURFACE OF THE METAL WAS SCORCHED WITH AN INCREDIBLY HIGH DEGREE OF HEAT--HOWEVER, I WAS ABLE TO LIFT WHAT LITTLE D.N.A. WAS LEFT ON THE DEBRIS. SO NOW I'M RUNNING IT THROUGH BLOOD ANALYSIS, BUT I CAN'T MAKE ANY PROMISES.
EVEN IF IT GOES THROUGH, THERE'S NO GUARANTEE I'LL BE ABLE TO FIND A MATCH.
DO WHAT YOU CAN, MISS SPIVOT, AND IF YOU GET A HIT, PLEASE LET ME KNOW. IN THE MEANTIME, I HAVE ANOTHER LEAD TO FOLLOW. THAT DEBRIS BELONGED TO DR. ELIAS' MONORAIL.
IRIS, I CAN'T TAKE YOU WITH ME ON THIS ONE. IF ELIAS IS OUR SUSPECT, THE LAST THING I WANT TO DO IS BRING YOU STRAIGHT TO HIM.
WELL, WHERE AM I SUPPOSED TO GO THEN?
UM... MISS SPIVOT-- I NEED TO ASK YOU ONE MORE FAVOR...
AND THERE HE GOES...OFF IN A FLASH AGAIN.
NICE COSTUME. KINDA TIGHT FOR MY TASTE...

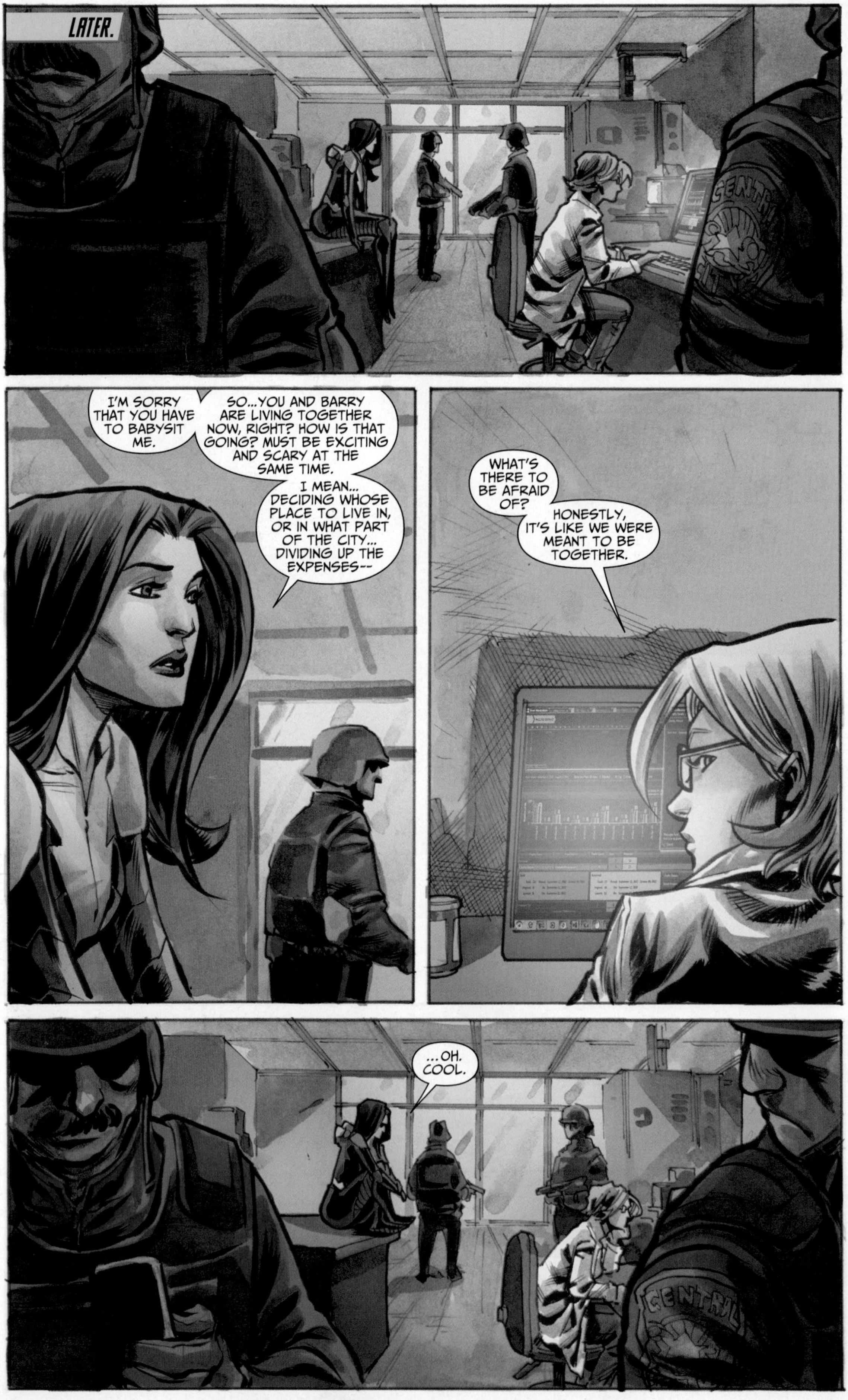
LATER.
I'M SORRY THAT YOU HAVE TO BABYSIT ME.
SO...YOU AND BARRY ARE LIVING TOGETHER NOW, RIGHT? HOW IS THAT GOING? MUST BE EXCITING AND SCARY AT THE SAME TIME.
I MEAN... DECIDING WHOSE PLACE TO LIVE IN, OR IN WHAT PART OF THE CITY... DIVIDING UP THE EXPENSES--
WHAT'S THERE TO BE AFRAID OF?
HONESTLY, IT'S LIKE WE WERE MEANT TO BE TOGETHER.
...OH. COOL.

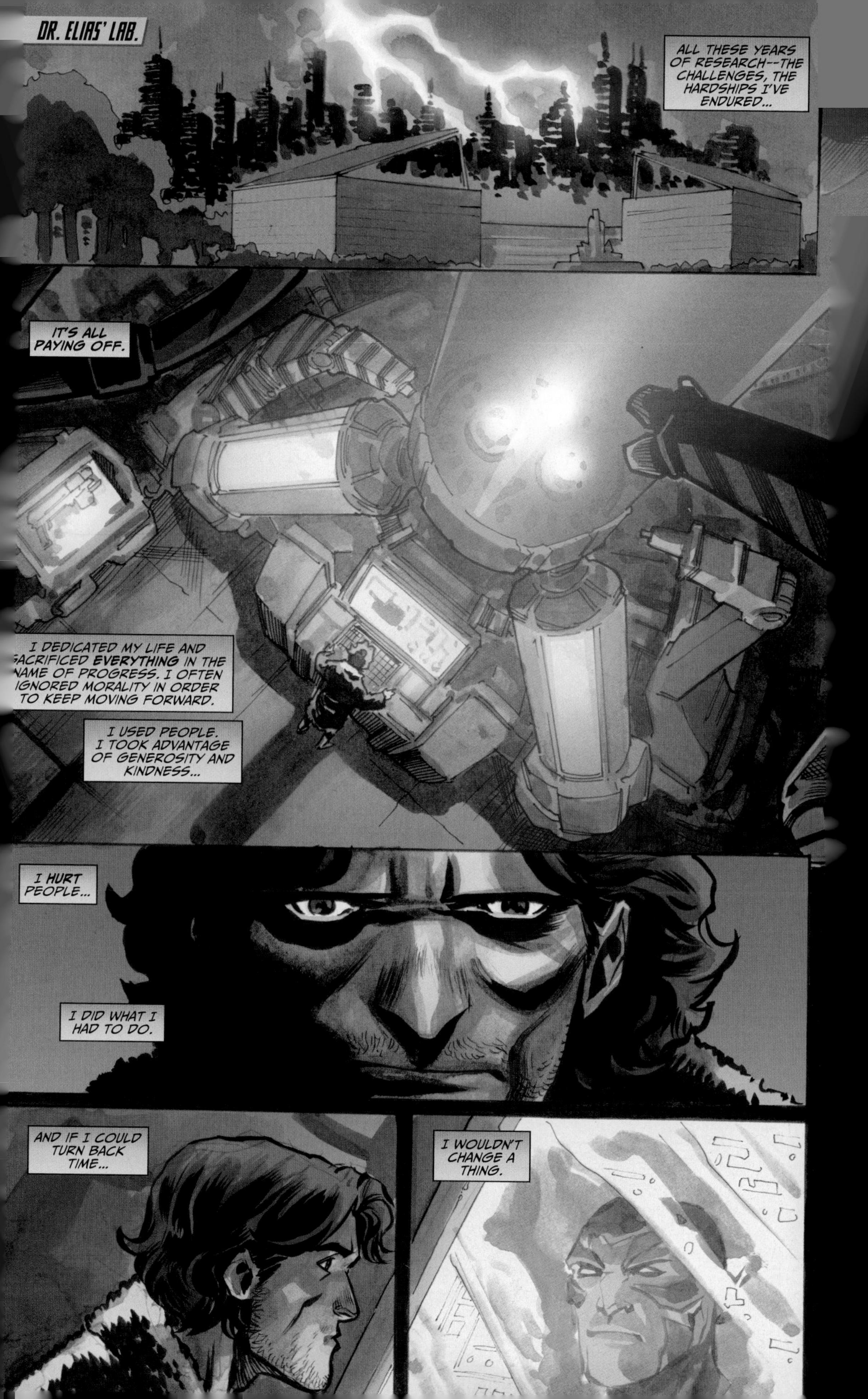
DR. ELIAS' LAB.
ALL THESE YEARS OF RESEARCH--THE CHALLENGES, THE HARDSHIPS I'VE ENDURED...
IT'S ALL PAYING OFF.
I DEDICATED MY LIFE AND SACRIFICED EVERYTHING IN THE NAME OF PROGRESS. I OFTEN IGNORED MORALITY IN ORDER TO KEEP MOVING FORWARD.
I USED PEOPLE. I TOOK ADVANTAGE OF GENEROSITY AND KINDNESS...
I HURT PEOPLE...
I DID WHAT I HAD TO DO.
AND IF I COULD TURN BACK TIME...
I WOULDN'T CHANGE A THING.

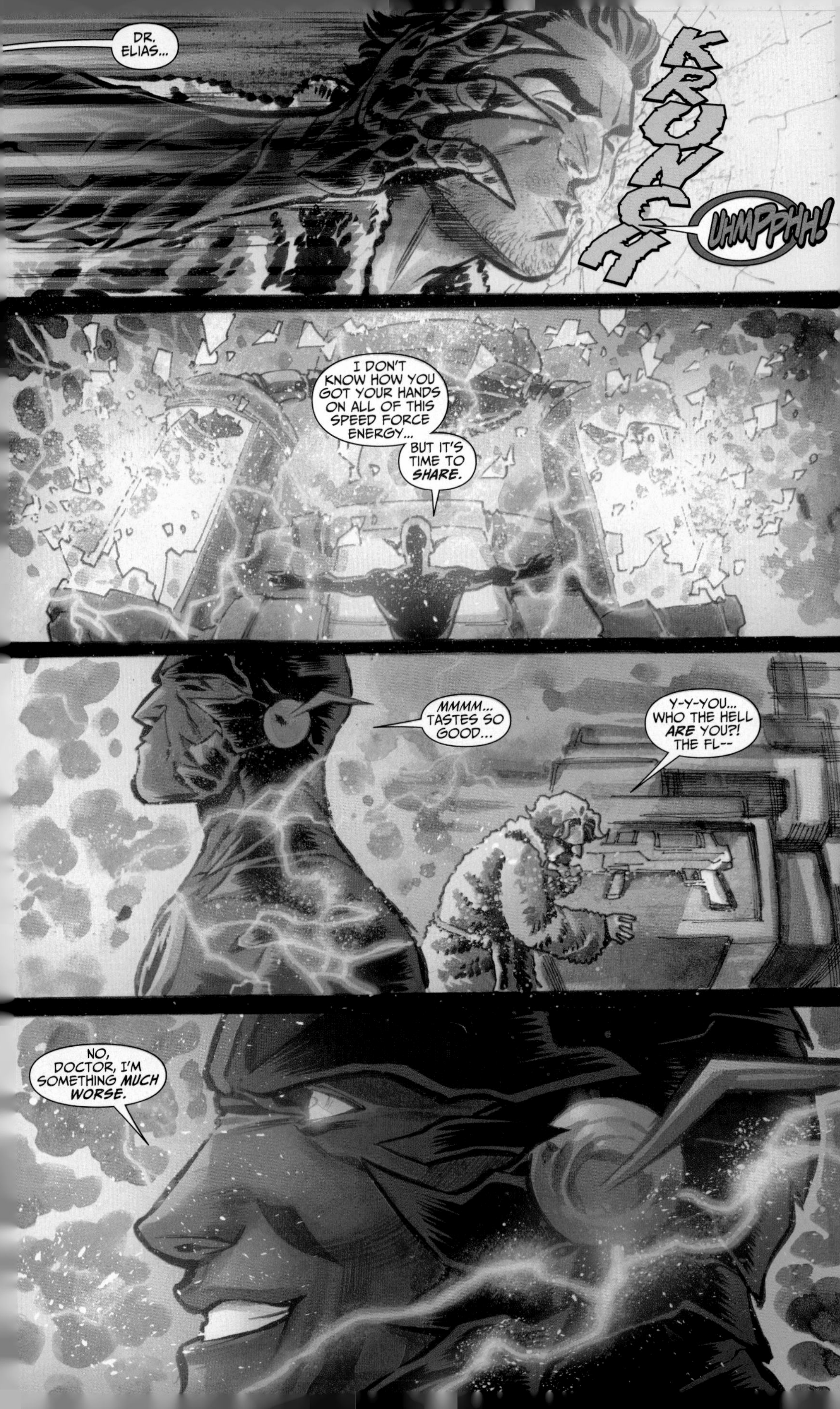
DR. ELIAS...
KRUNCH
UHMPPHH!
I DON'T KNOW HOW YOU GOT YOUR HANDS ON ALL OF THIS SPEED FORCE ENERGY...
BUT IT'S TIME TO *SHARE.*
MMMM... TASTES SO GOOD...
Y-Y-YOU... WHO THE HELL *ARE* YOU?! THE FL--
NO, DOCTOR, I'M SOMETHING *MUCH WORSE.*

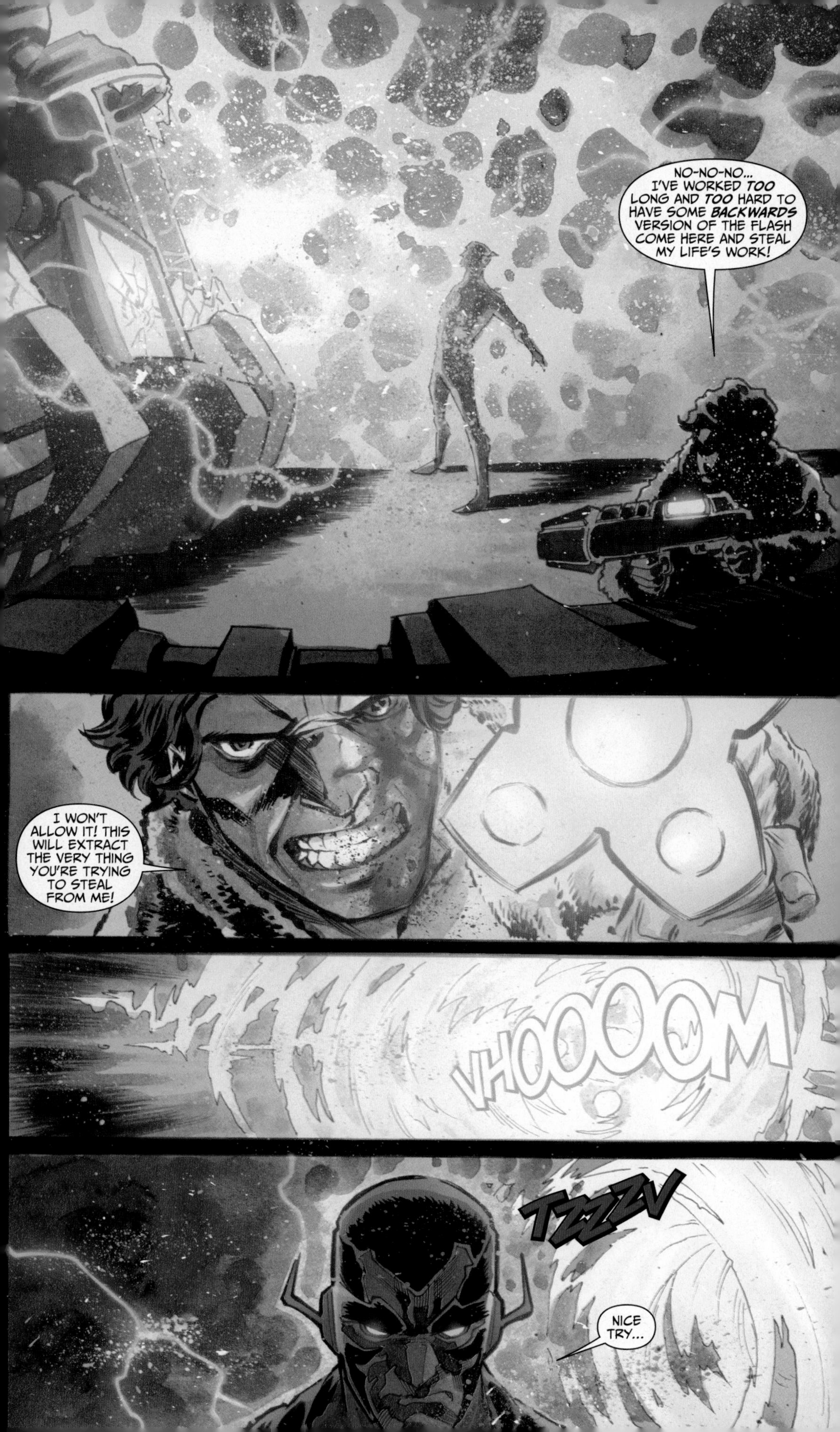
NO-NO-NO... I'VE WORKED TOO LONG AND TOO HARD TO HAVE SOME BACKWARDS VERSION OF THE FLASH COME HERE AND STEAL MY LIFE'S WORK!
I WON'T ALLOW IT! THIS WILL EXTRACT THE VERY THING YOU'RE TRYING TO STEAL FROM ME!
VHOOOOM
TZZZV
NICE TRY...

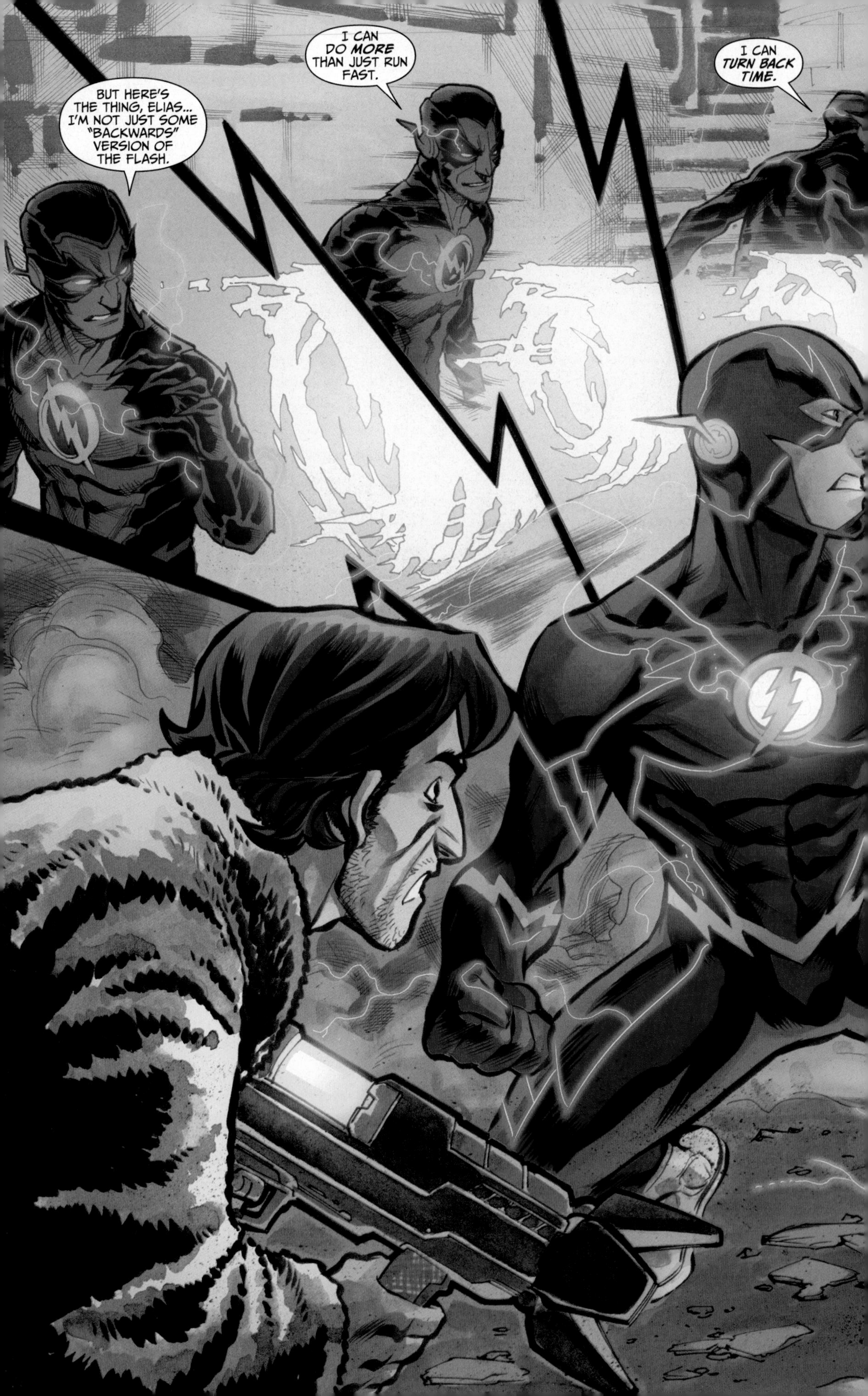
BUT HERE'S THE THING, ELIAS... I'M NOT JUST SOME "BACKWARDS" VERSION OF THE FLASH.
I CAN DO *MORE* THAN JUST RUN FAST.
I CAN *TURN BACK TIME.*

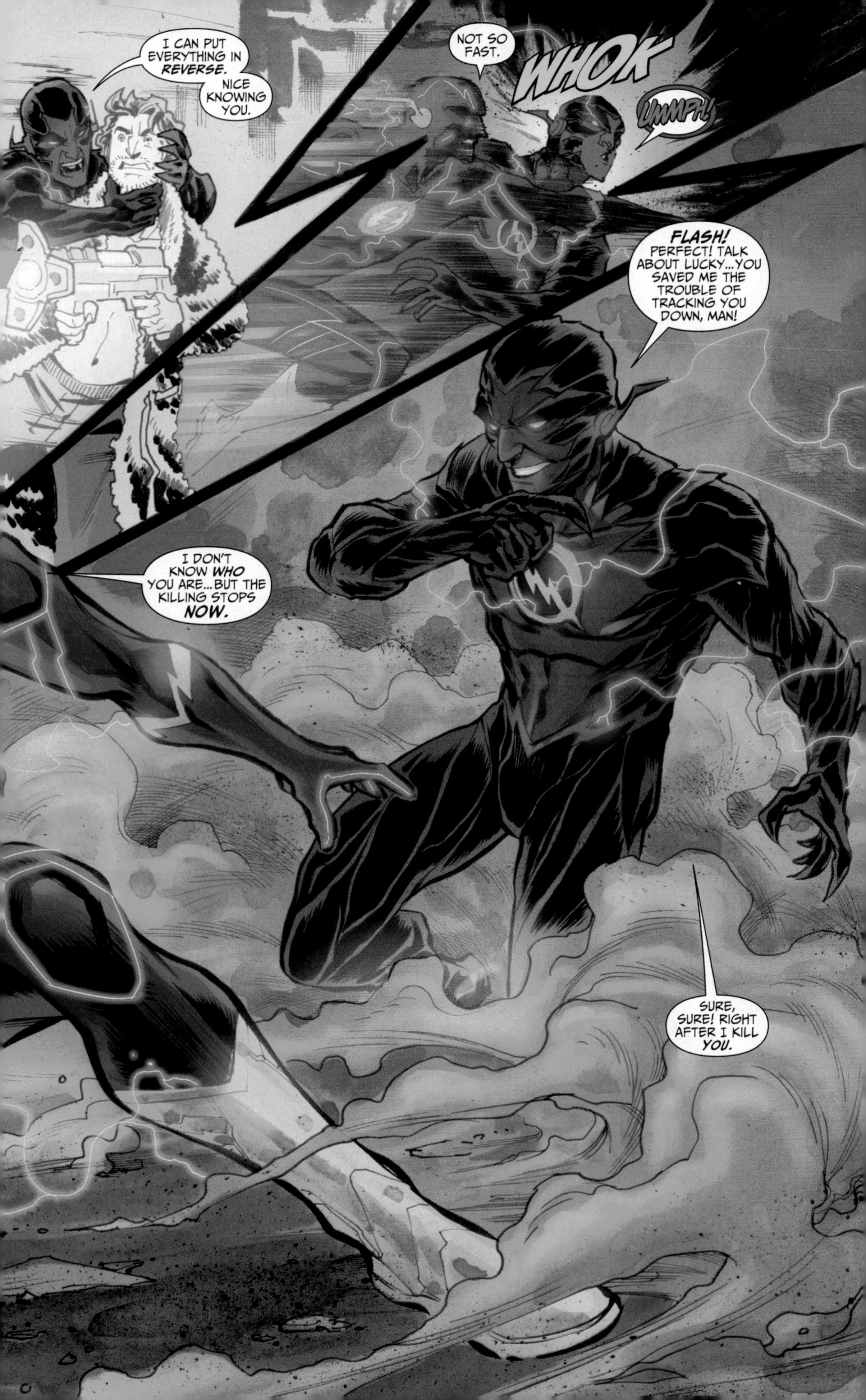
I CAN PUT EVERYTHING IN REVERSE.
NICE KNOWING YOU.
NOT SO FAST.
WHOK
UMMPH!
FLASH! PERFECT! TALK ABOUT LUCKY...YOU SAVED ME THE TROUBLE OF TRACKING YOU DOWN, MAN!
I DON'T KNOW WHO YOU ARE...BUT THE KILLING STOPS NOW.
SURE, SURE! RIGHT AFTER I KILL YOU.

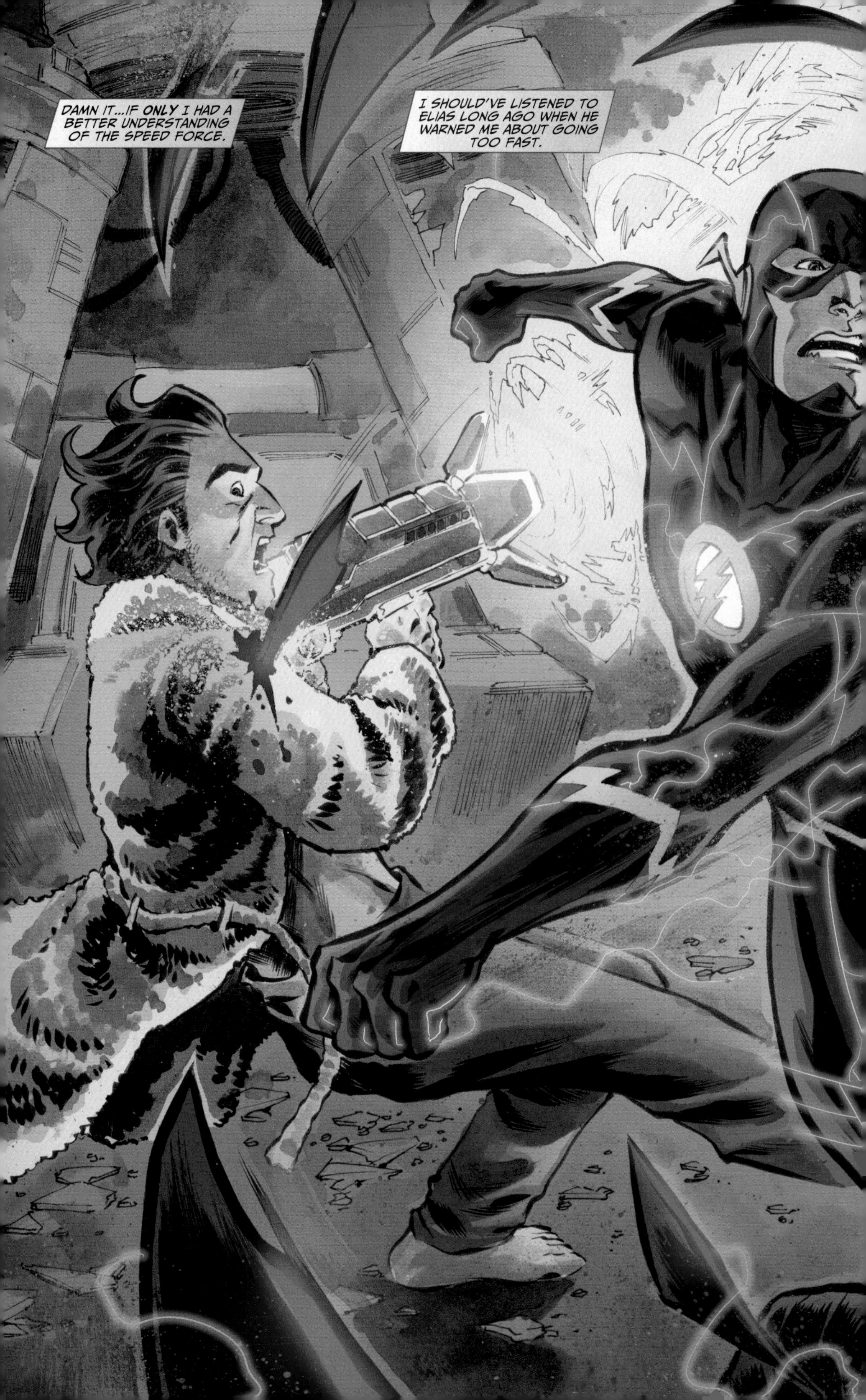
DAMN IT...IF ONLY I HAD A BETTER UNDERSTANDING OF THE SPEED FORCE.
I SHOULD'VE LISTENED TO ELIAS LONG AGO WHEN HE WARNED ME ABOUT GOING TOO FAST.

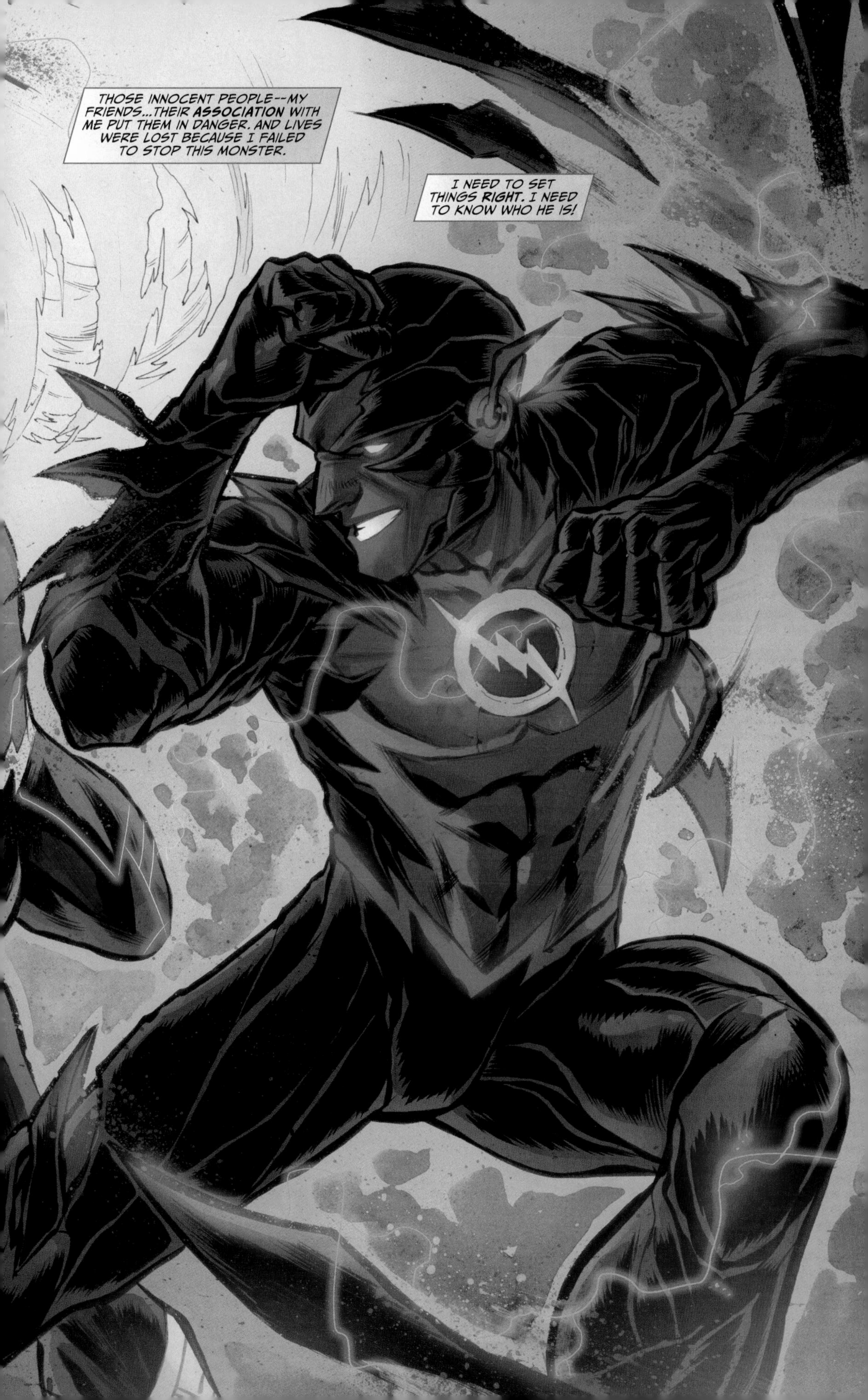
THOSE INNOCENT PEOPLE--MY FRIENDS...THEIR **ASSOCIATION** WITH ME PUT THEM IN DANGER. AND LIVES WERE LOST BECAUSE I FAILED TO STOP THIS MONSTER.
I NEED TO SET THINGS **RIGHT**. I NEED TO KNOW WHO HE IS!

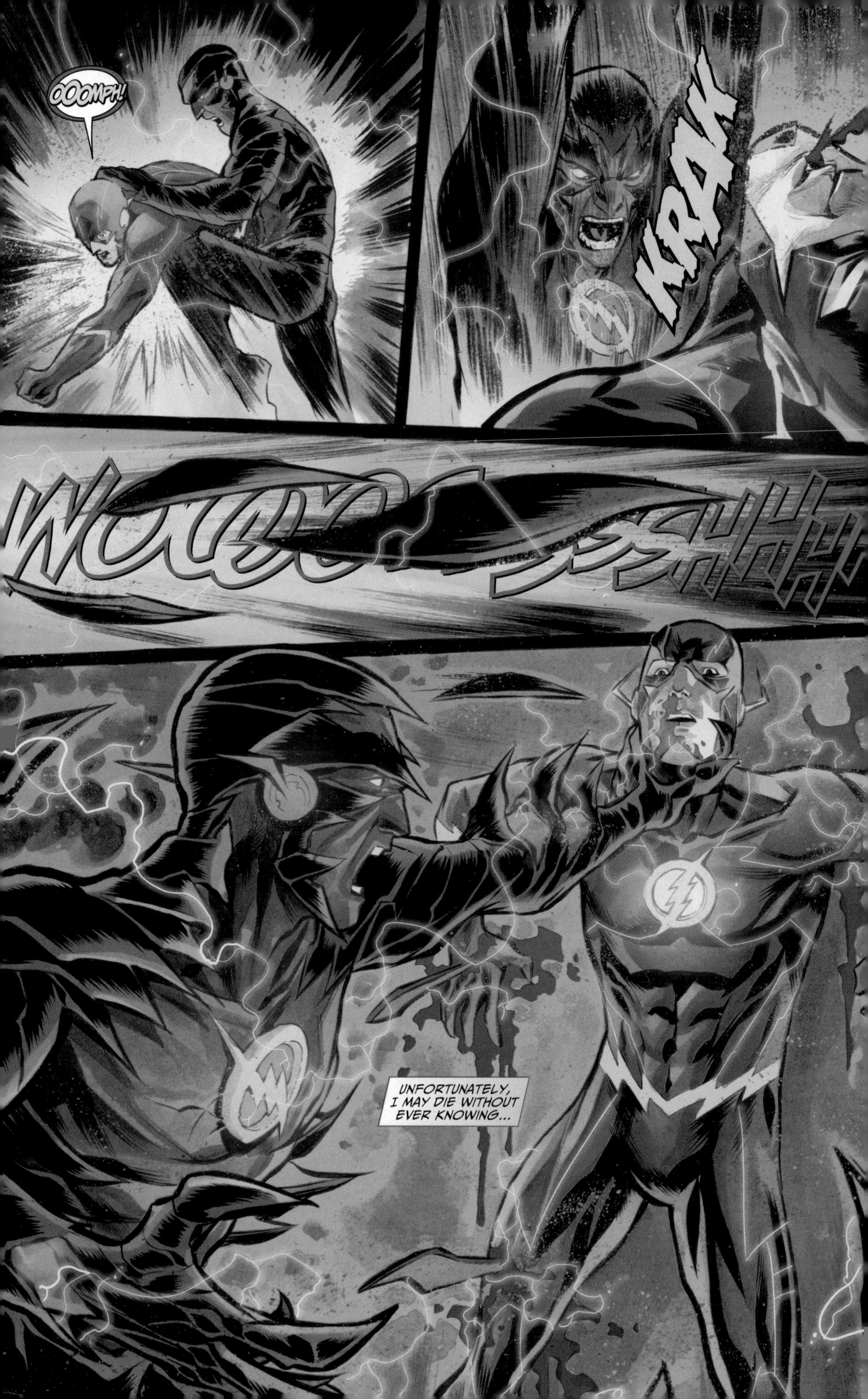
OOOMPH!
KRAK
WOOOOSSSHHH!
UNFORTUNATELY, I MAY DIE WITHOUT EVER KNOWING...

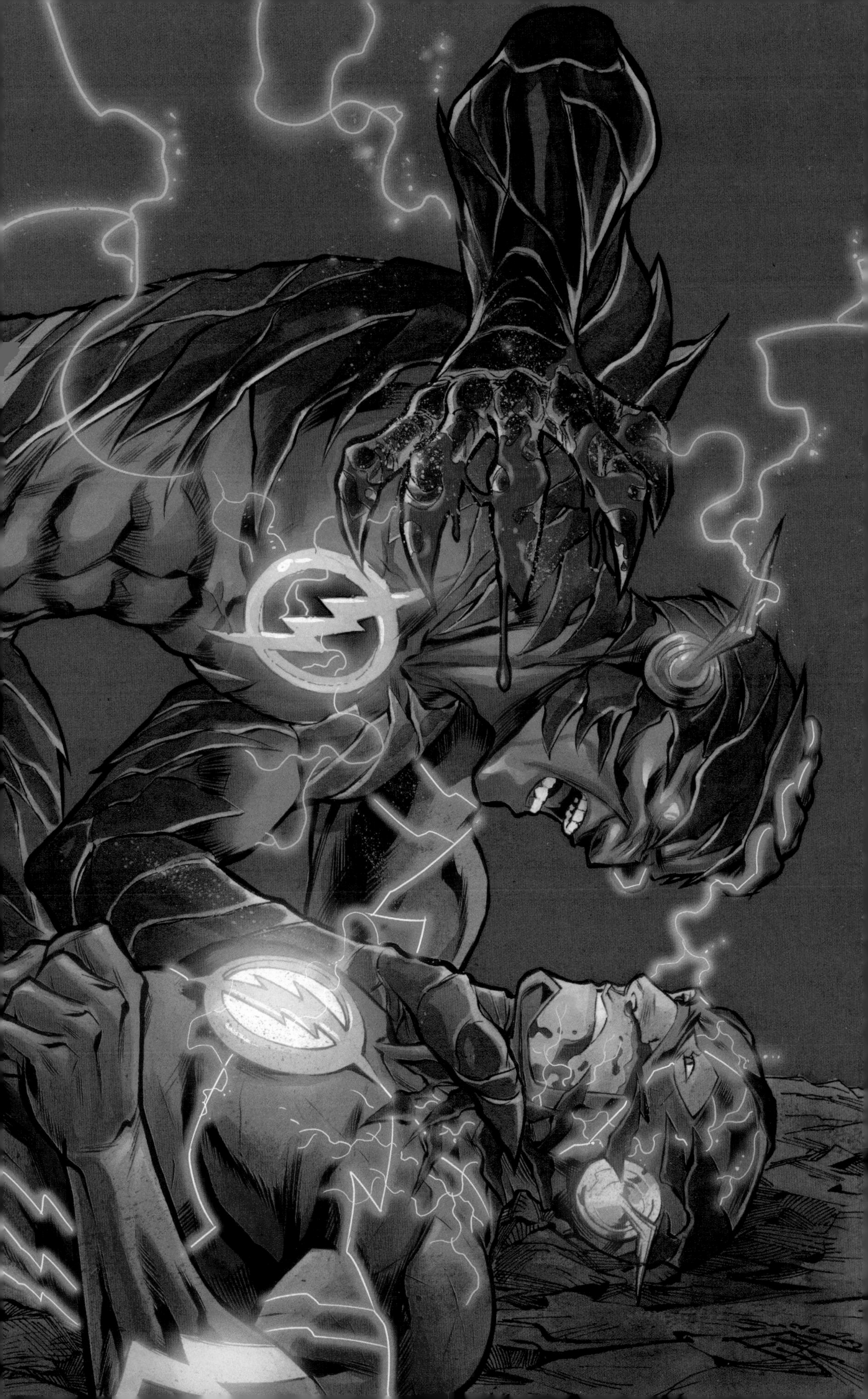

FRANCIS MANAPUL & BRIAN BUCCELLATO writers FRANCIS MANAPUL artist

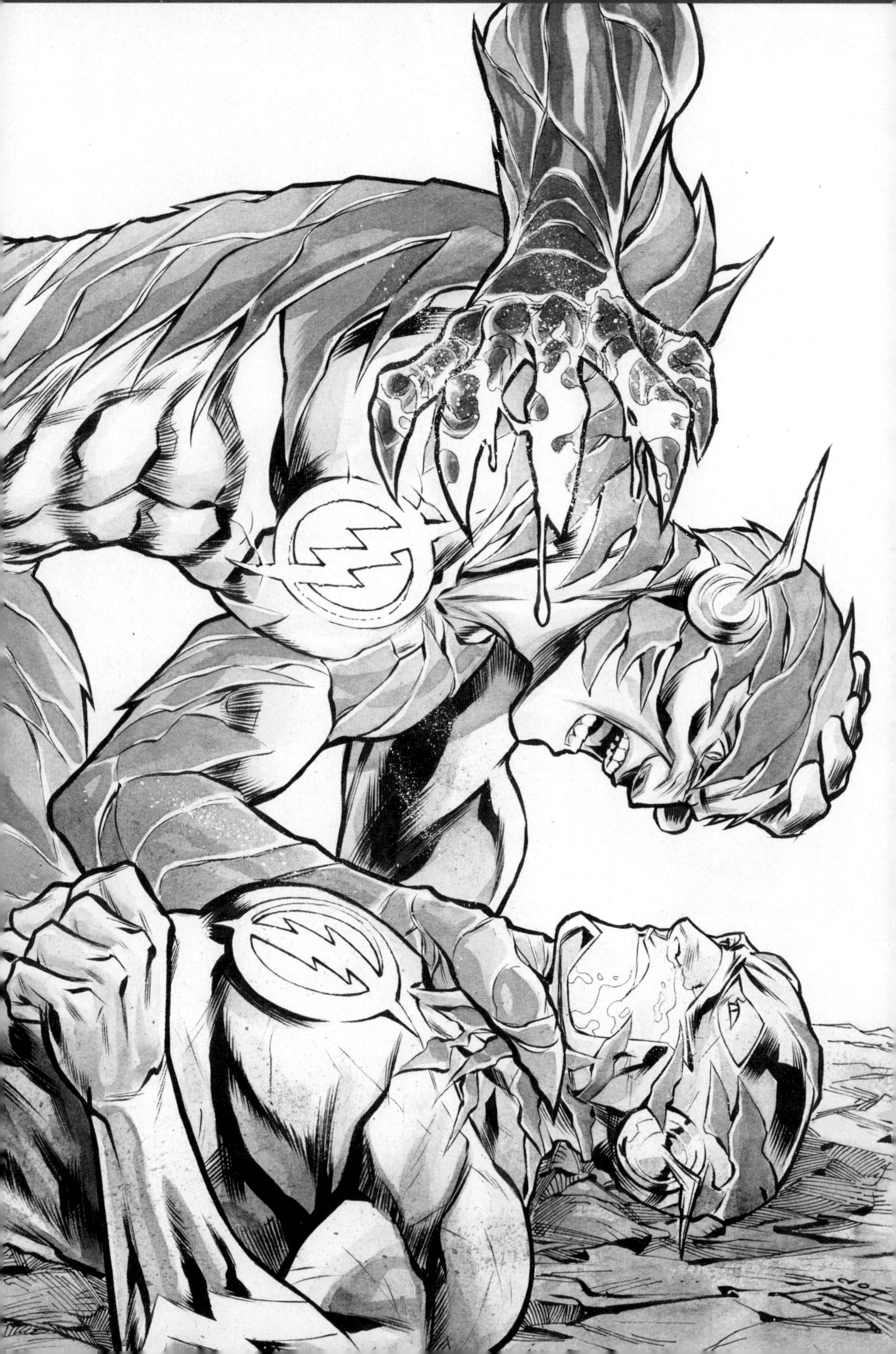

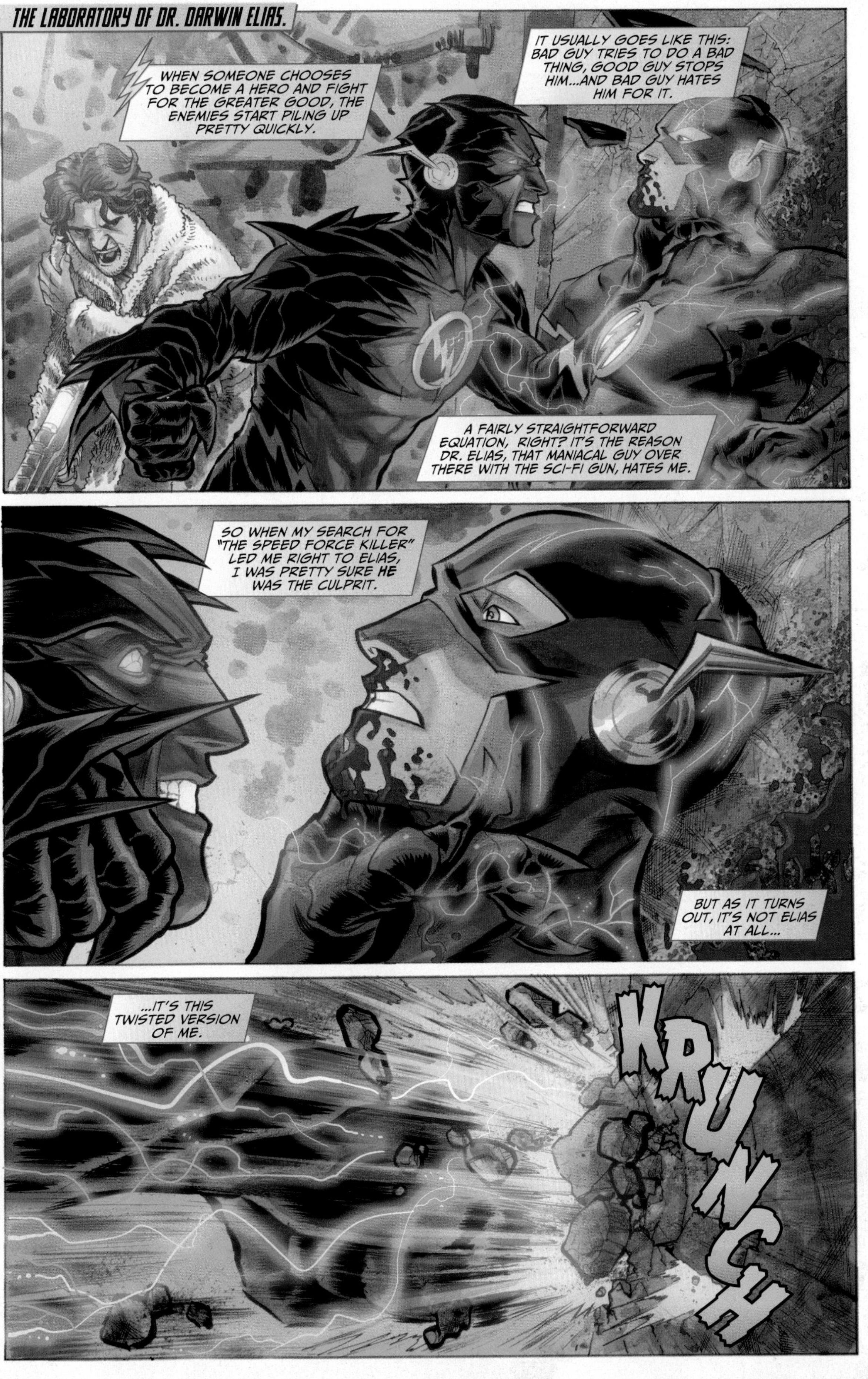
THE LABORATORY OF DR. DARWIN ELIAS.
WHEN SOMEONE CHOOSES TO BECOME A HERO AND FIGHT FOR THE GREATER GOOD, THE ENEMIES START PILING UP PRETTY QUICKLY.
IT USUALLY GOES LIKE THIS: BAD GUY TRIES TO DO A BAD THING, GOOD GUY STOPS HIM...AND BAD GUY HATES HIM FOR IT.
A FAIRLY STRAIGHTFORWARD EQUATION, RIGHT? IT'S THE REASON DR. ELIAS, THAT MANIACAL GUY OVER THERE WITH THE SCI-FI GUN, HATES ME.
SO WHEN MY SEARCH FOR "THE SPEED FORCE KILLER" LED ME RIGHT TO ELIAS, I WAS PRETTY SURE HE WAS THE CULPRIT.
BUT AS IT TURNS OUT, IT'S NOT ELIAS AT ALL...
...IT'S THIS TWISTED VERSION OF ME.
KRUNCH

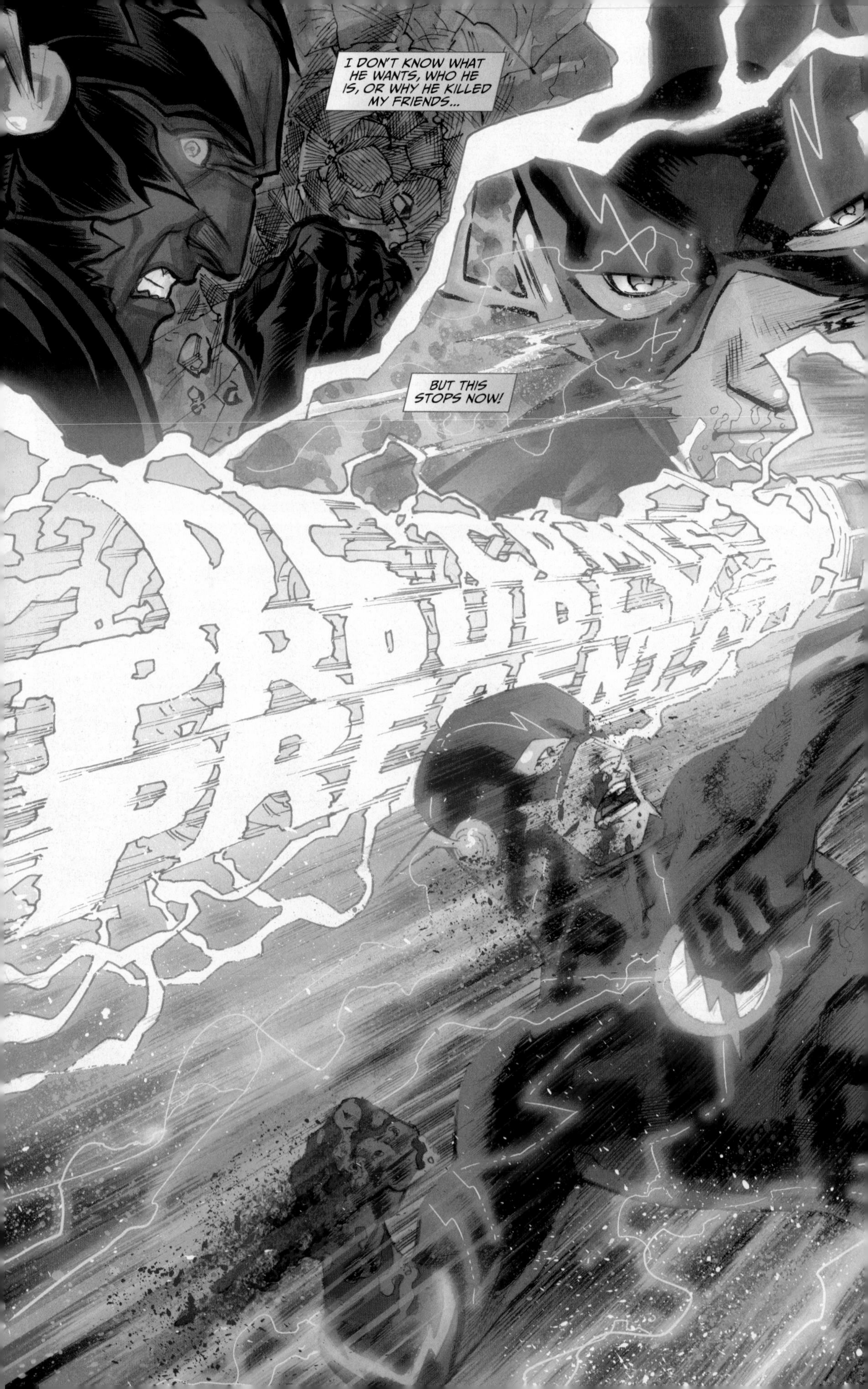
I DON'T KNOW WHAT HE WANTS, WHO HE IS, OR WHY HE KILLED MY FRIENDS...
BUT THIS STOPS NOW!

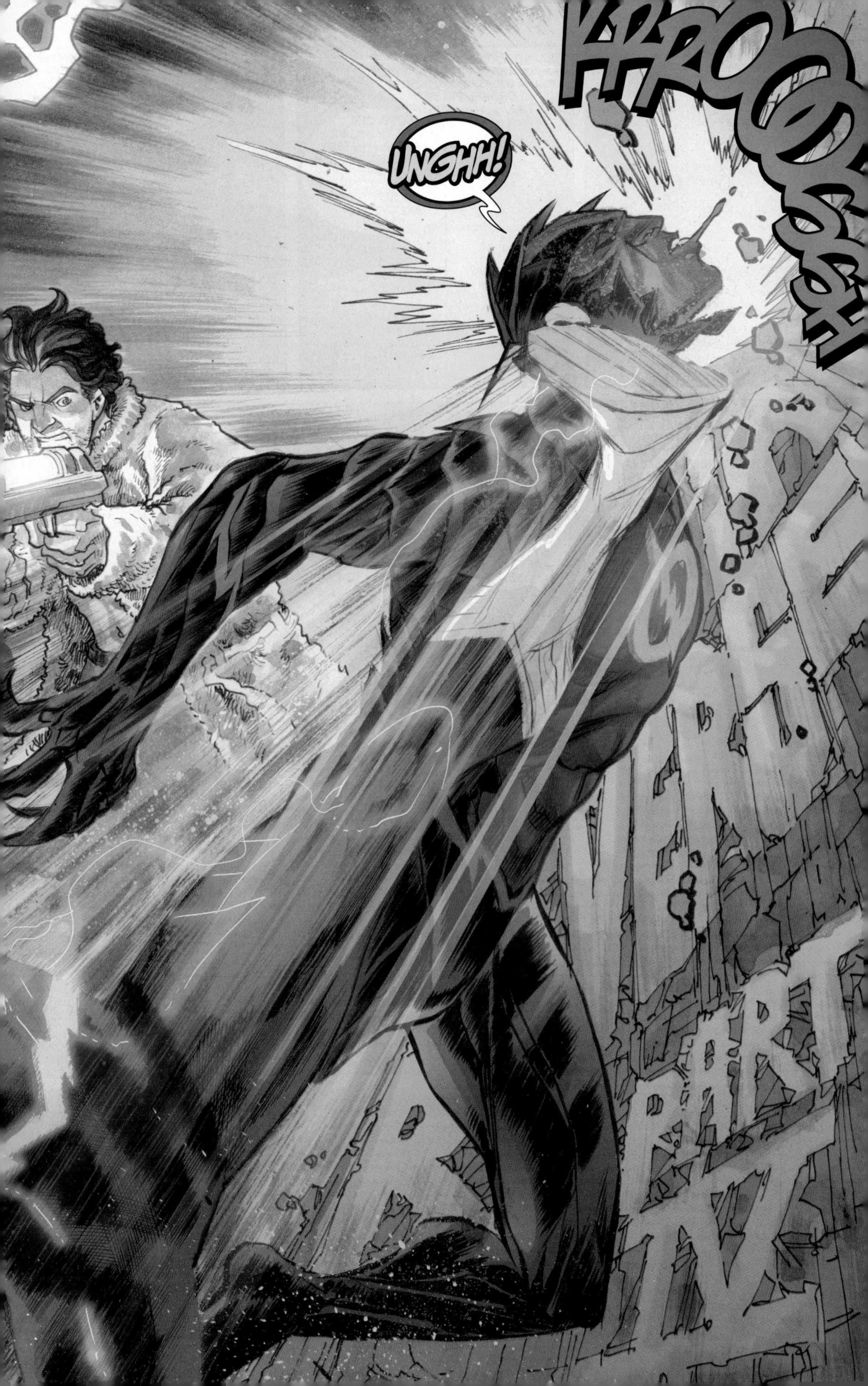
KRROOOSSH!
UNGHH!
PART IV

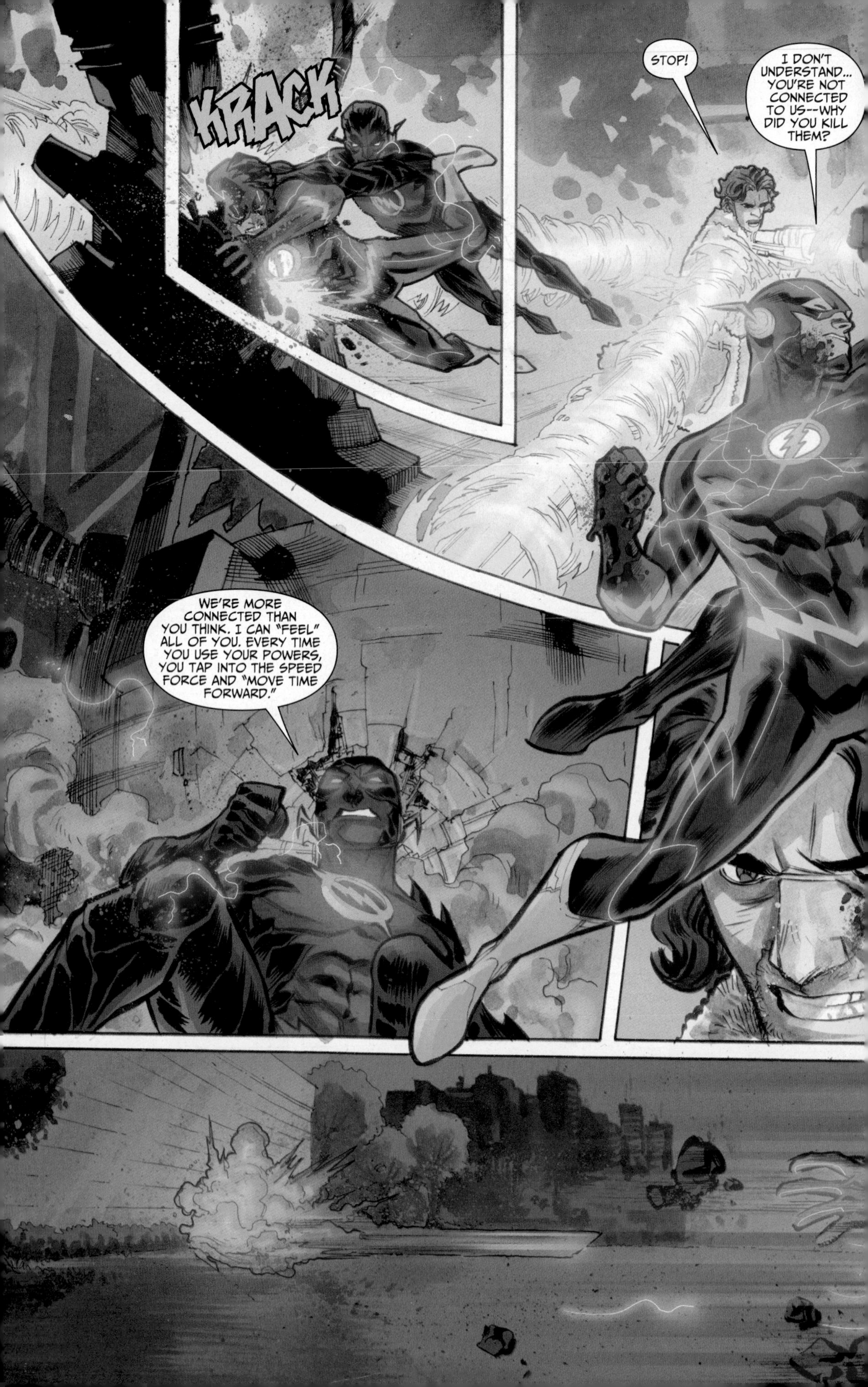
KRACK
STOP!
I DON'T UNDERSTAND... YOU'RE NOT CONNECTED TO US--WHY DID YOU KILL THEM?
WE'RE MORE CONNECTED THAN YOU THINK. I CAN "FEEL" ALL OF YOU. EVERY TIME YOU USE YOUR POWERS, YOU TAP INTO THE SPEED FORCE AND "MOVE TIME FORWARD."

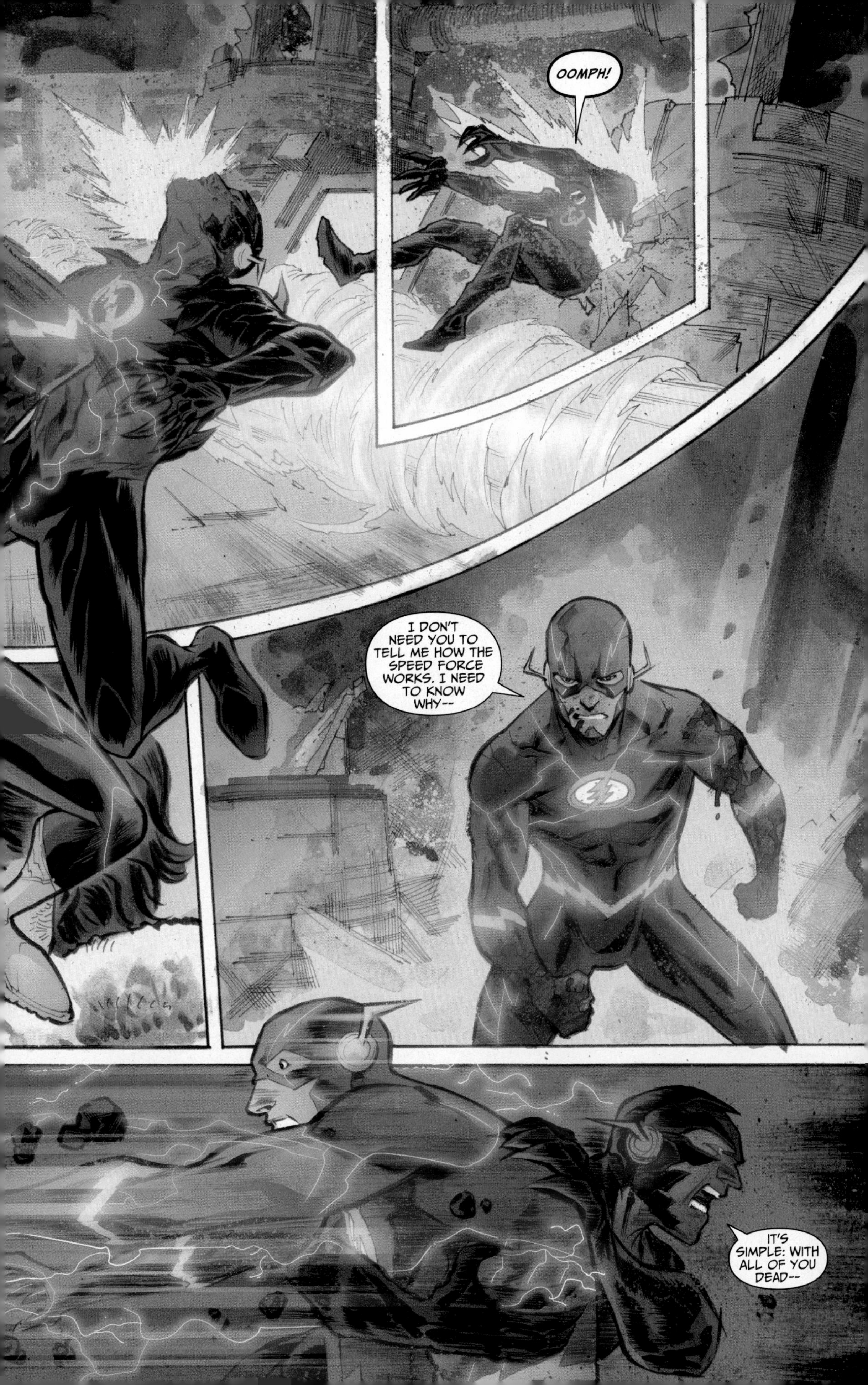
OOMPH!
I DON'T NEED YOU TO TELL ME HOW THE SPEED FORCE WORKS. I NEED TO KNOW WHY--
IT'S SIMPLE: WITH ALL OF YOU DEAD--

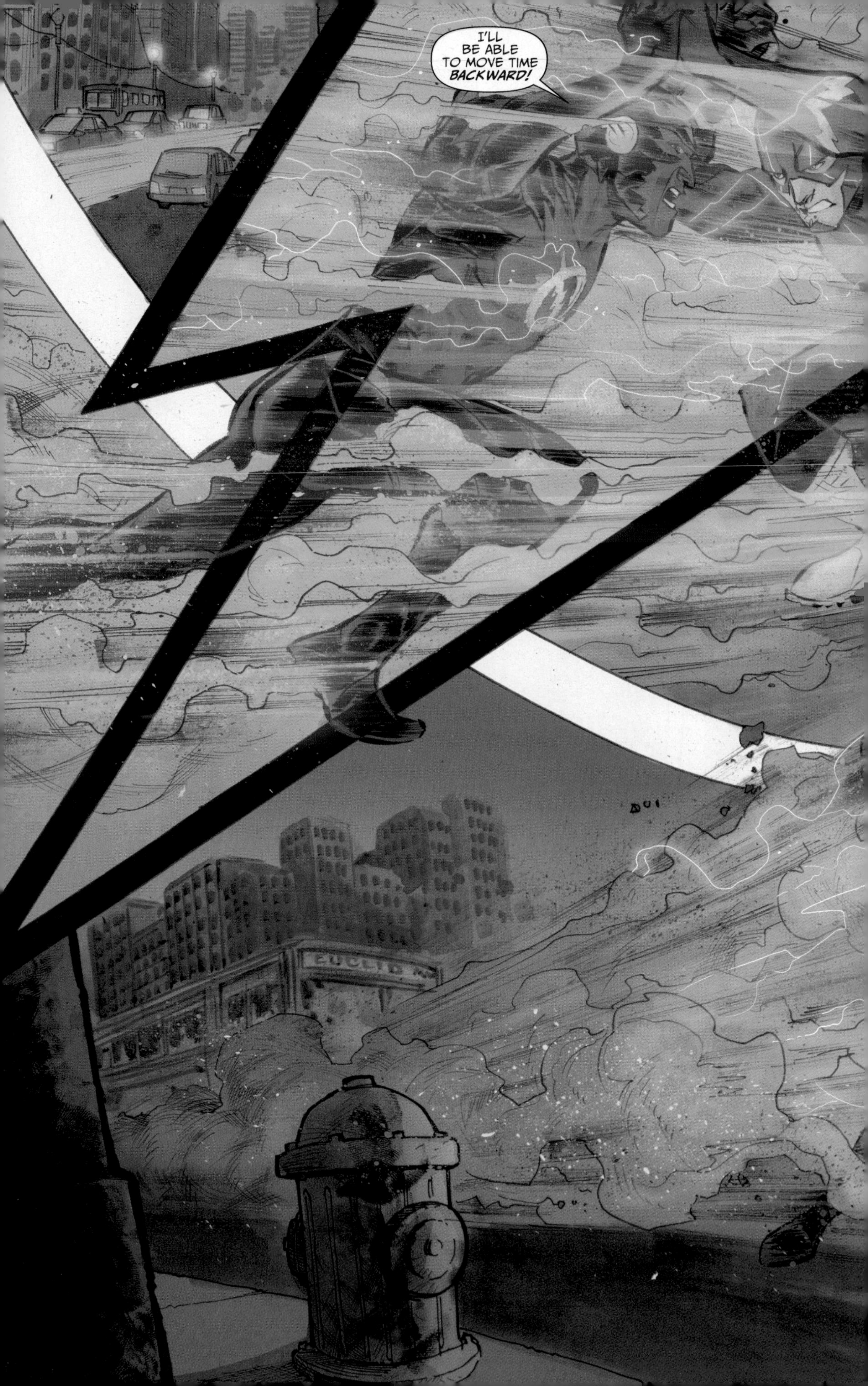
I'LL BE ABLE TO MOVE TIME BACKWARD!

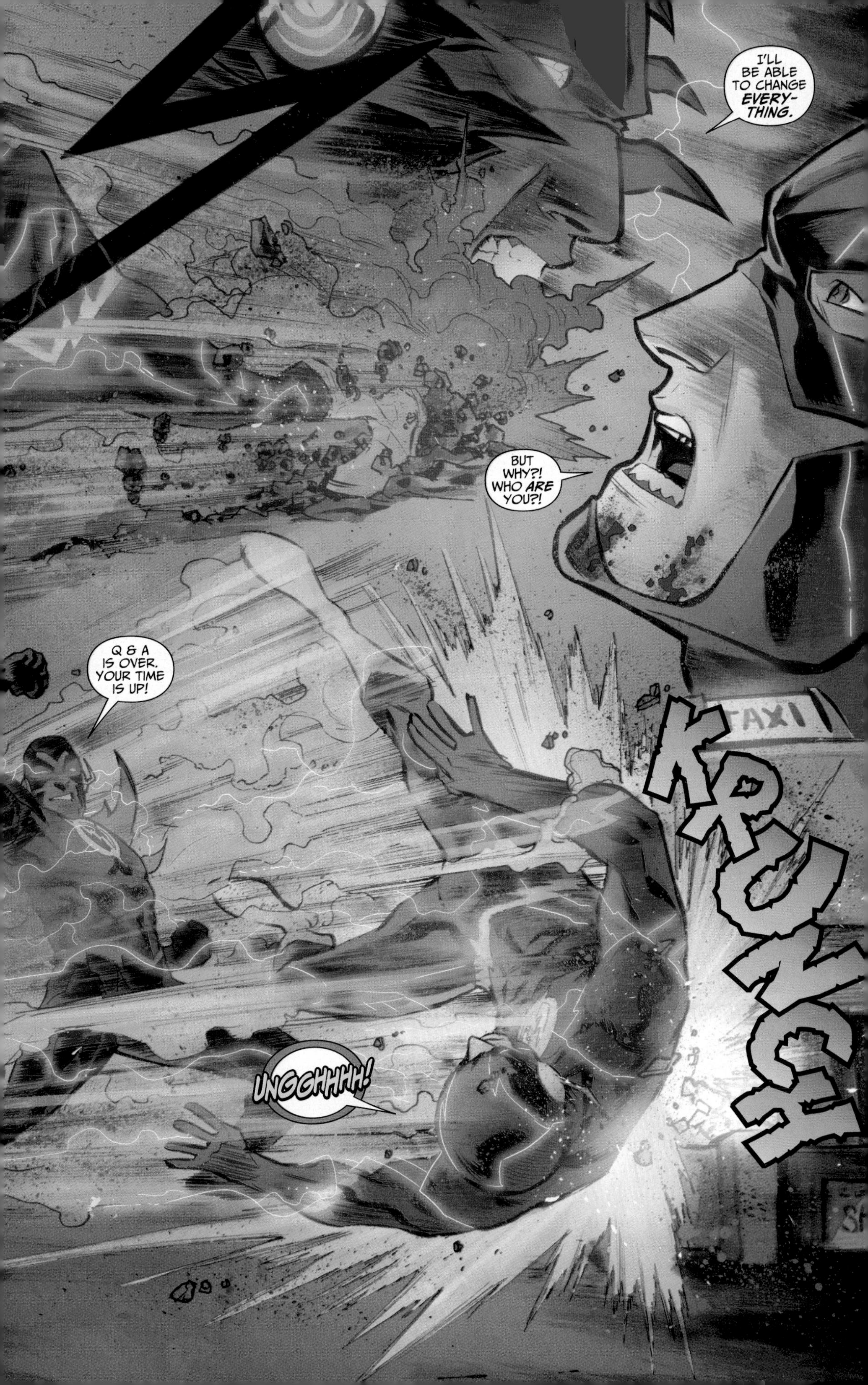
I'LL BE ABLE TO CHANGE EVERY-THING.
BUT WHY?! WHO ARE YOU?!
Q & A IS OVER. YOUR TIME IS UP!
TAXI
KRUNCH
UNGGHHHH!

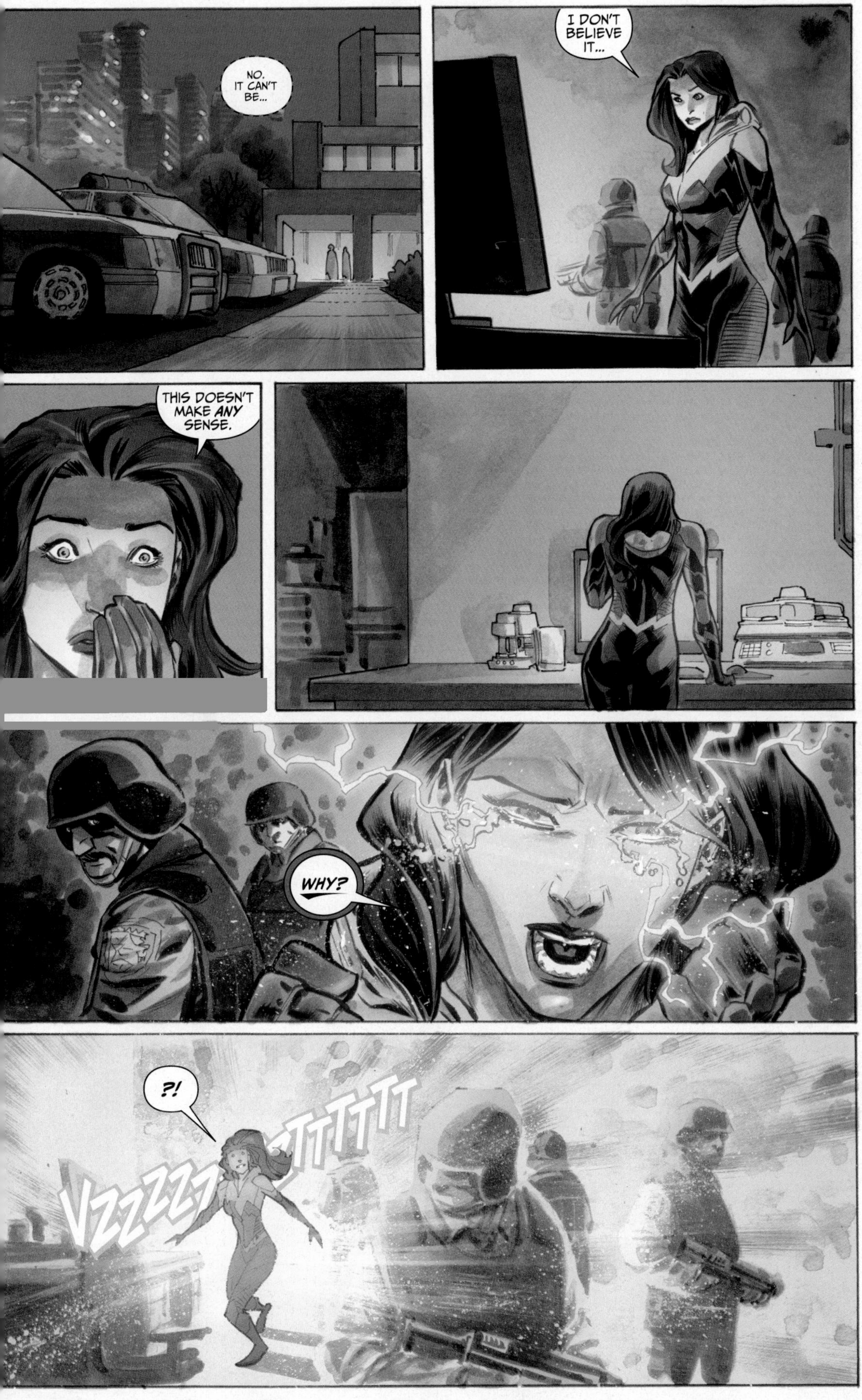
NO. IT CAN'T BE...
I DON'T BELIEVE IT...
THIS DOESN'T MAKE *ANY* SENSE.
WHY?
?!
VZZZZZTTTTTTT

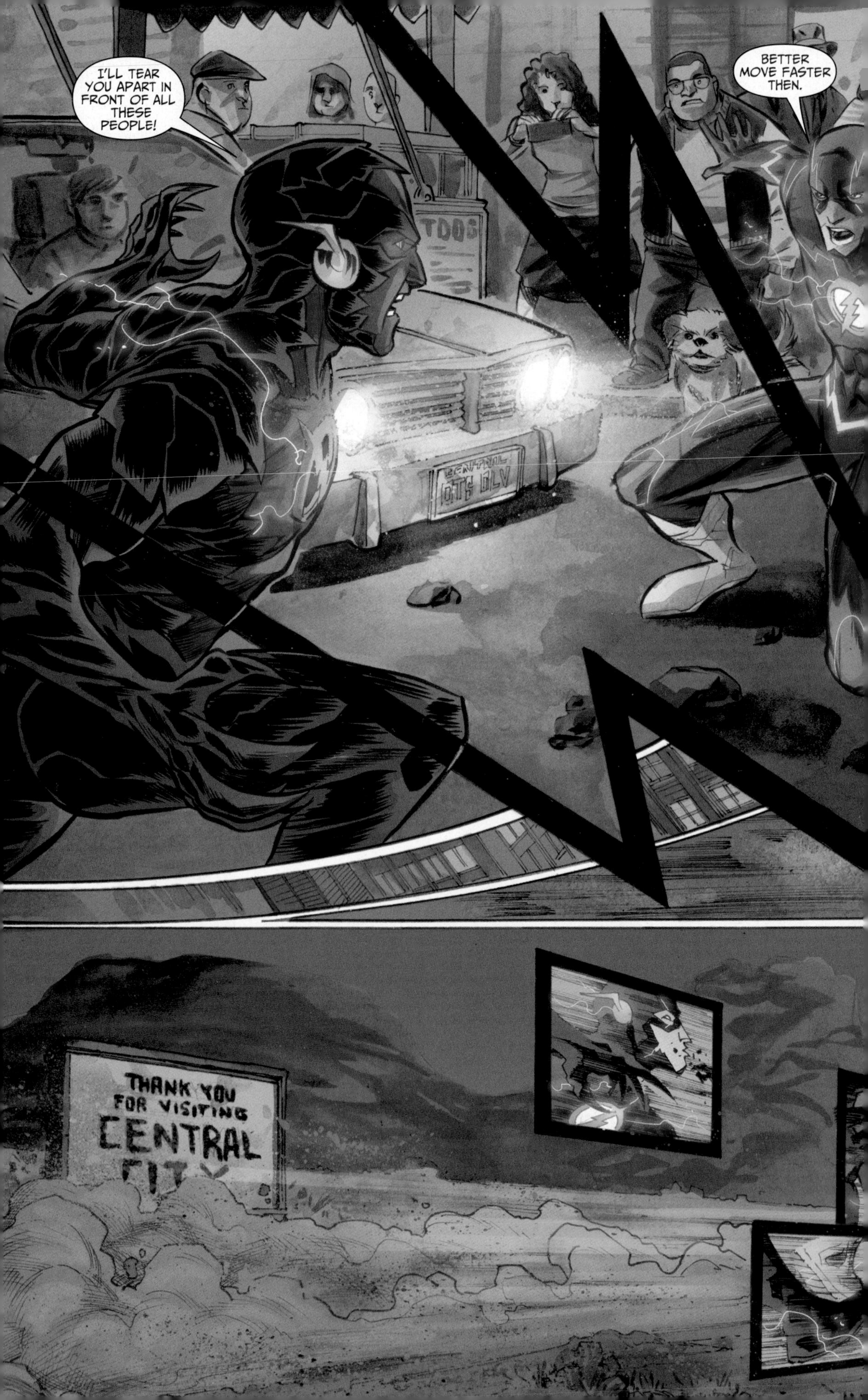
I'LL TEAR YOU APART IN FRONT OF ALL THESE PEOPLE!
BETTER MOVE FASTER THEN.
THANK YOU FOR VISITING CENTRAL

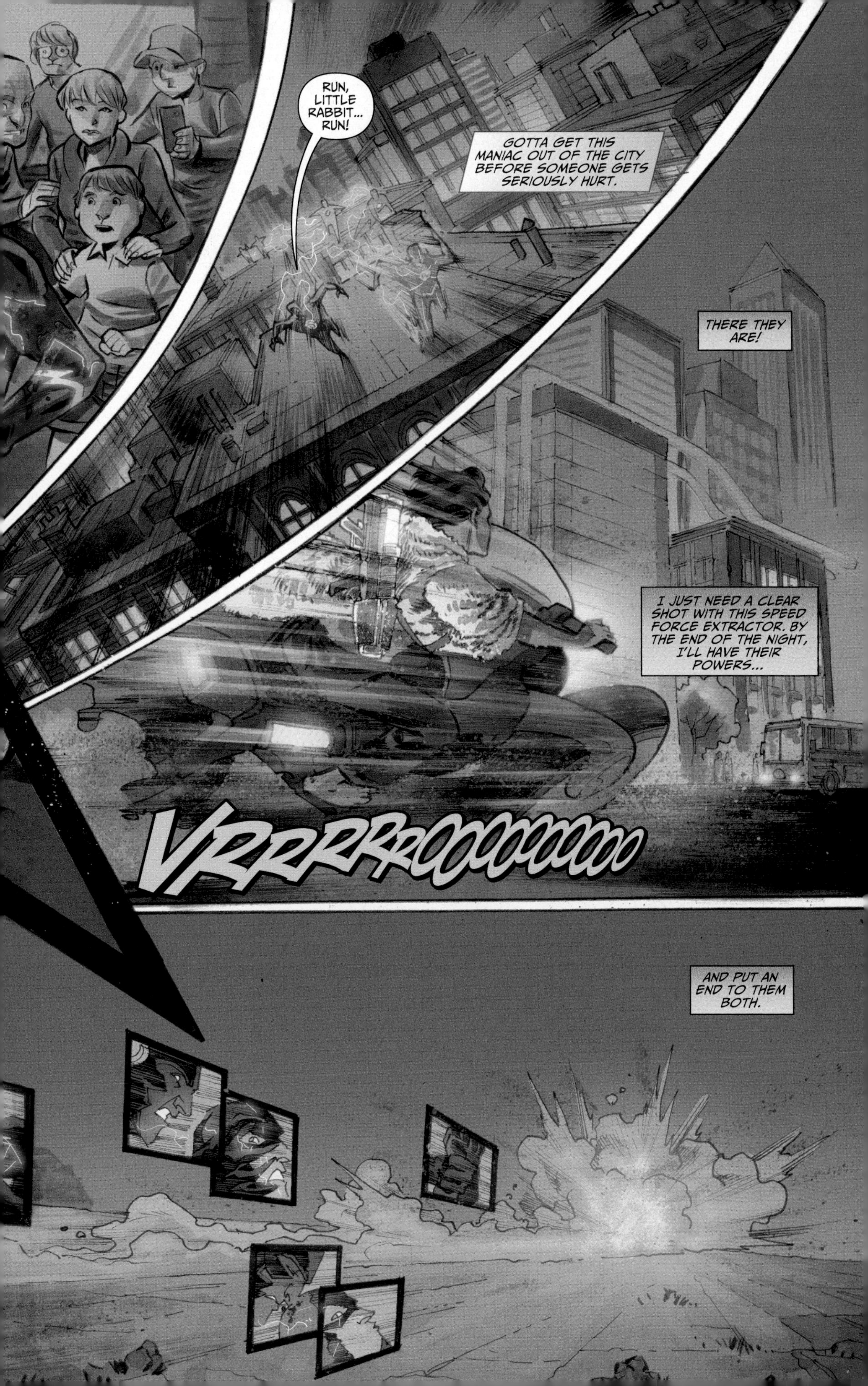
RUN, LITTLE RABBIT... RUN!
GOTTA GET THIS MANIAC OUT OF THE CITY BEFORE SOMEONE GETS SERIOUSLY HURT.
THERE THEY ARE!
I JUST NEED A CLEAR SHOT WITH THIS SPEED FORCE EXTRACTOR. BY THE END OF THE NIGHT, I'LL HAVE THEIR POWERS...
VRRRRROOOOOOOOOO
AND PUT AN END TO THEM BOTH.

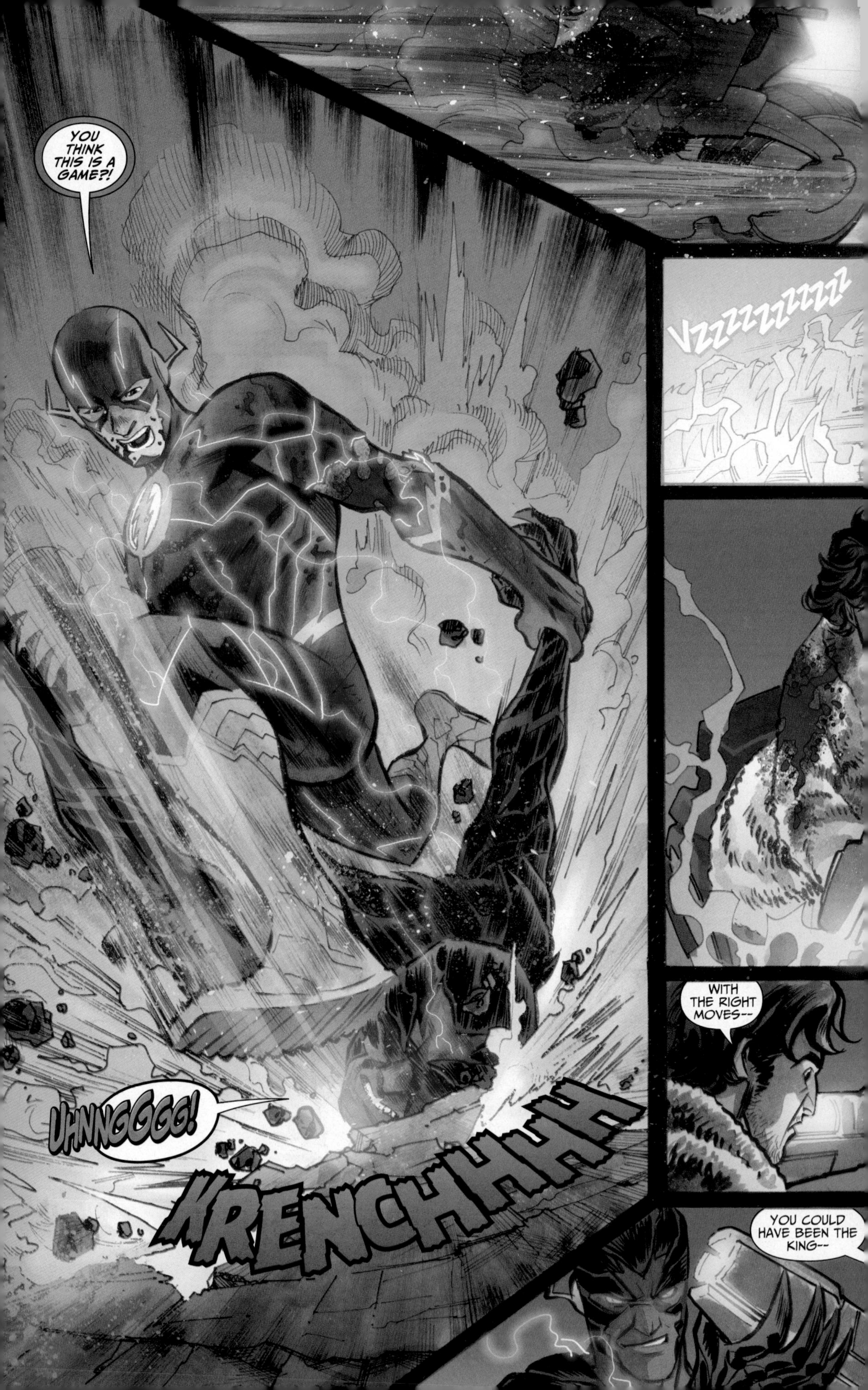
YOU THINK THIS IS A GAME?!
VZZZZZZZZZZZ
UHNNGGGG!
KRENCHHHH
WITH THE RIGHT MOVES--
YOU COULD HAVE BEEN THE KING--

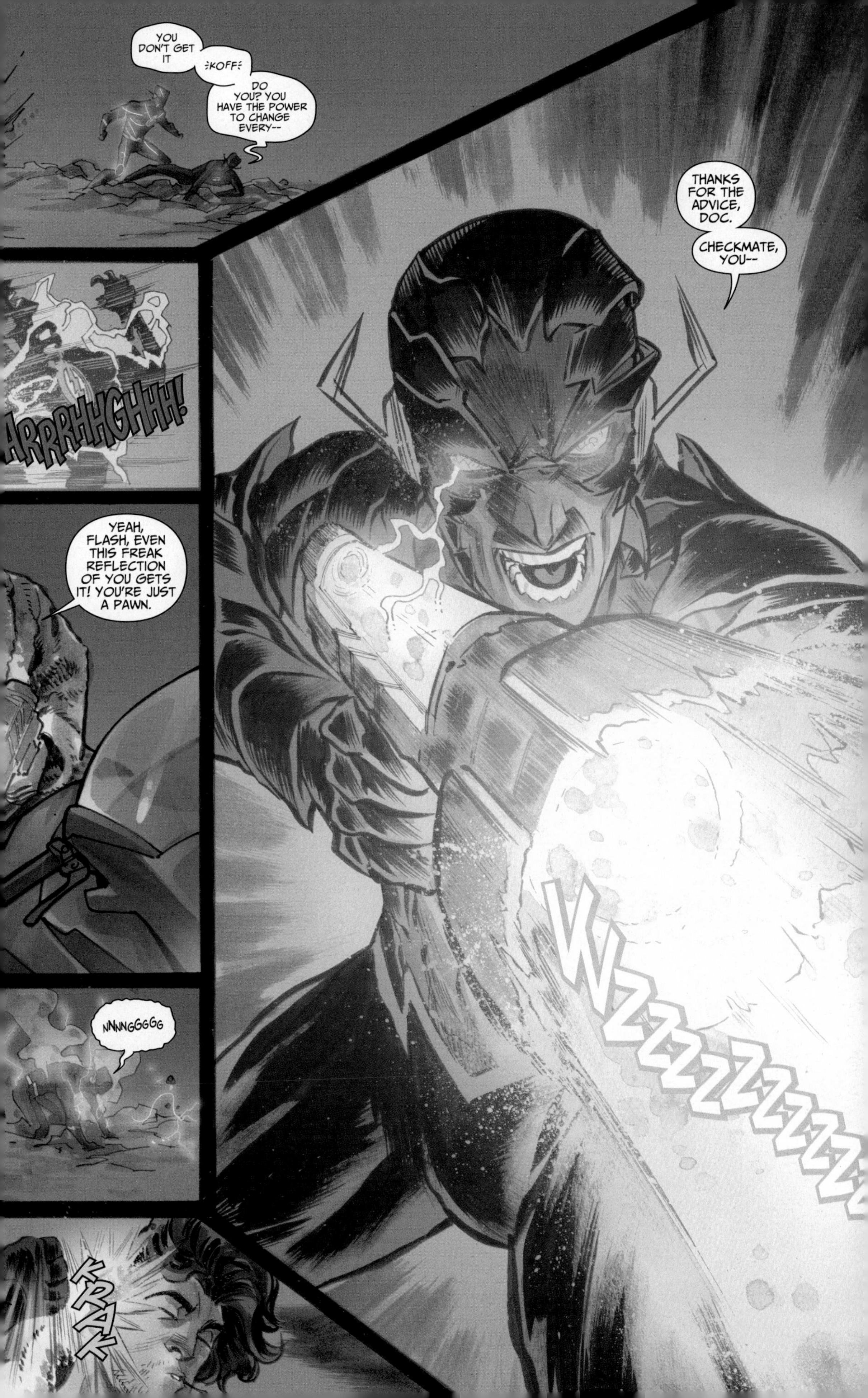
YOU DON'T GET IT
KOFF
DO YOU? YOU HAVE THE POWER TO CHANGE EVERY--
THANKS FOR THE ADVICE, DOC.
CHECKMATE, YOU--
ARRRHHGHHH!
YEAH, FLASH, EVEN THIS FREAK REFLECTION OF YOU GETS IT! YOU'RE JUST A PAWN.
NNNNGGGG
WZZZZZZZZ
KRAK

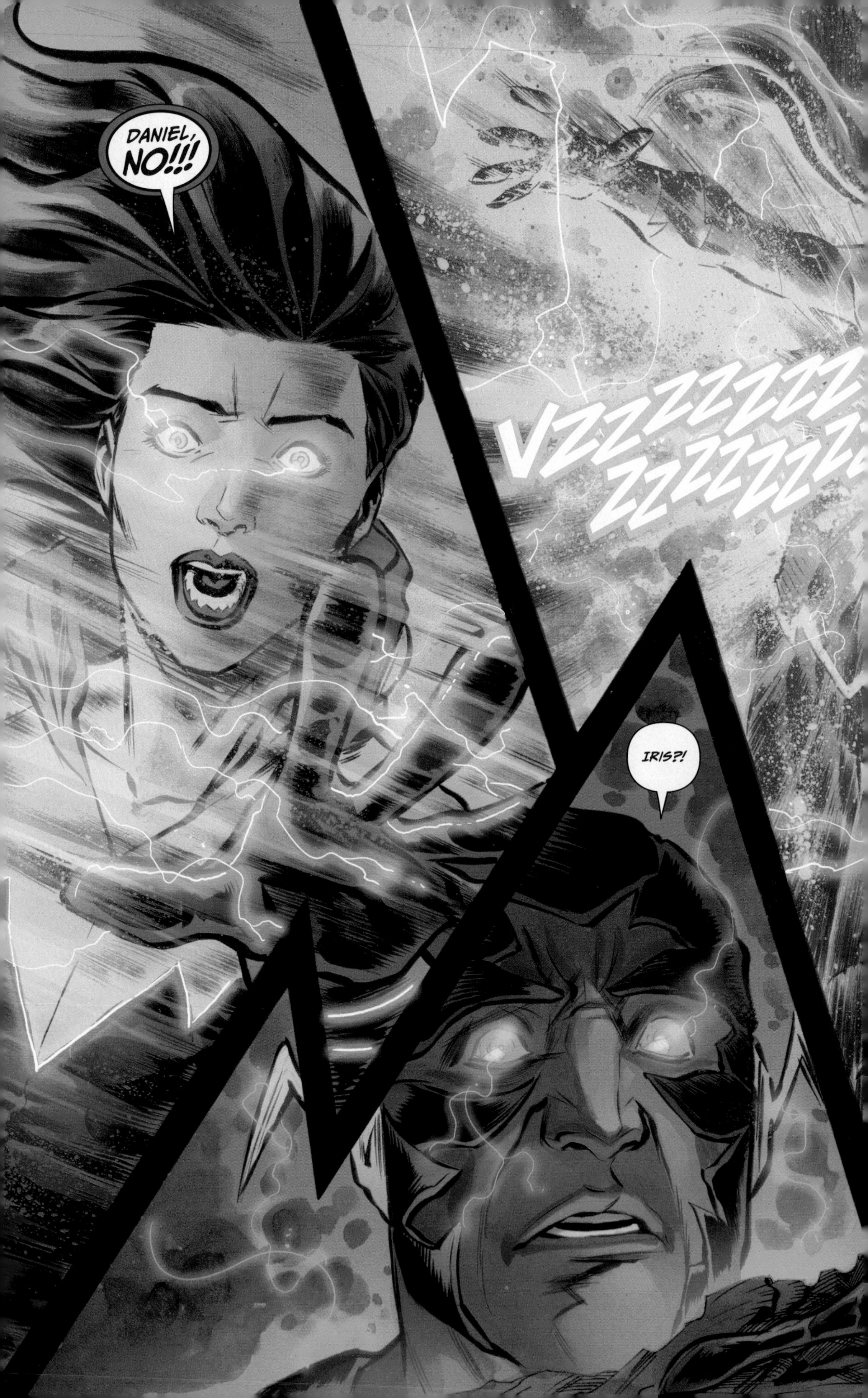
DANIEL, NO!!!
VZZZZZZ
ZZZZZZ
IRIS?!

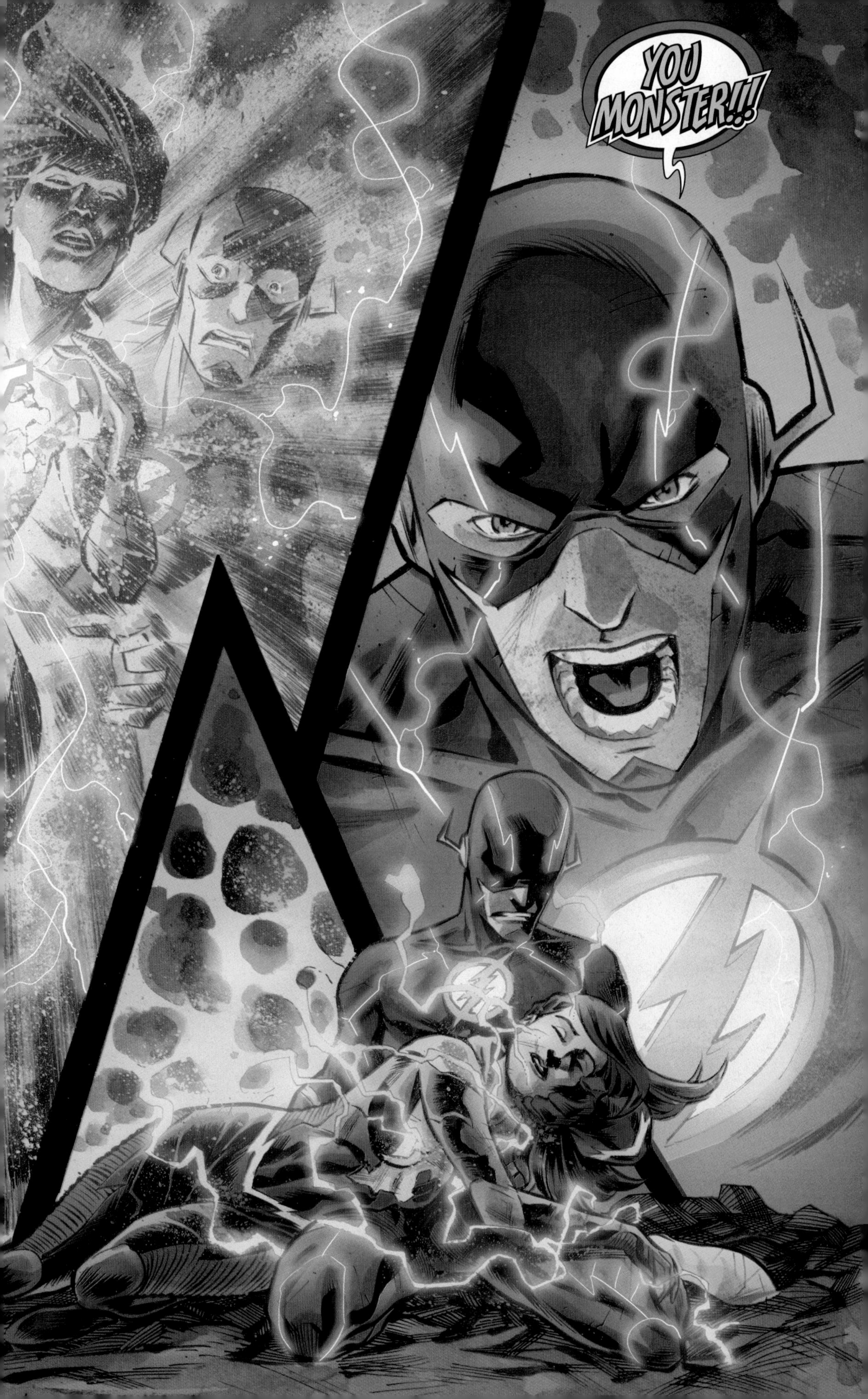
YOU MONSTER!!!

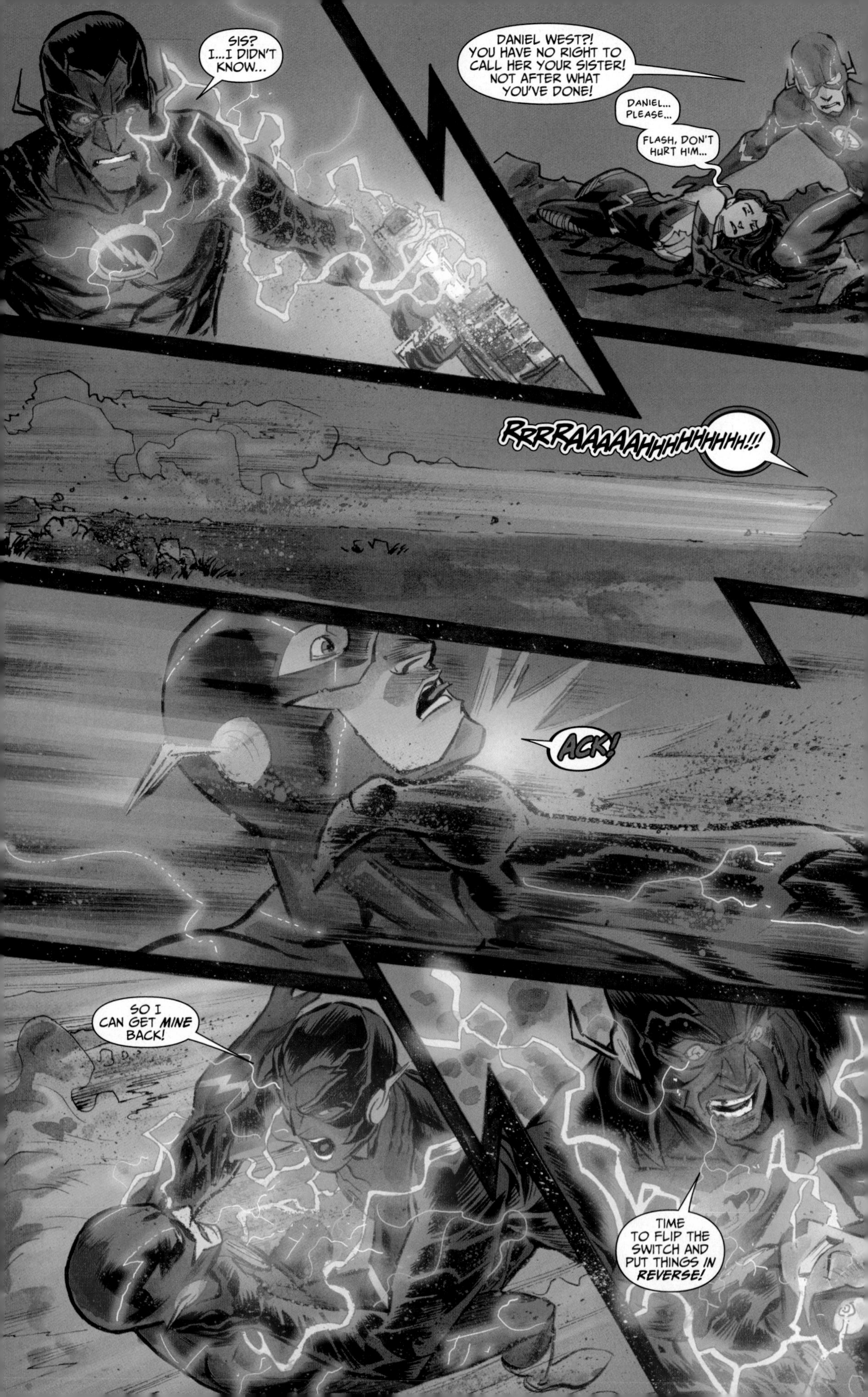

SIS? I...I DIDN'T KNOW...
DANIEL WEST?! YOU HAVE NO RIGHT TO CALL HER YOUR SISTER! NOT AFTER WHAT YOU'VE DONE!
DANIEL... PLEASE...
FLASH, DON'T HURT HIM...
RRRRAAAAAHHHHHHHH!!!
ACK!
SO I CAN GET MINE BACK!
TIME TO FLIP THE SWITCH AND PUT THINGS IN REVERSE!

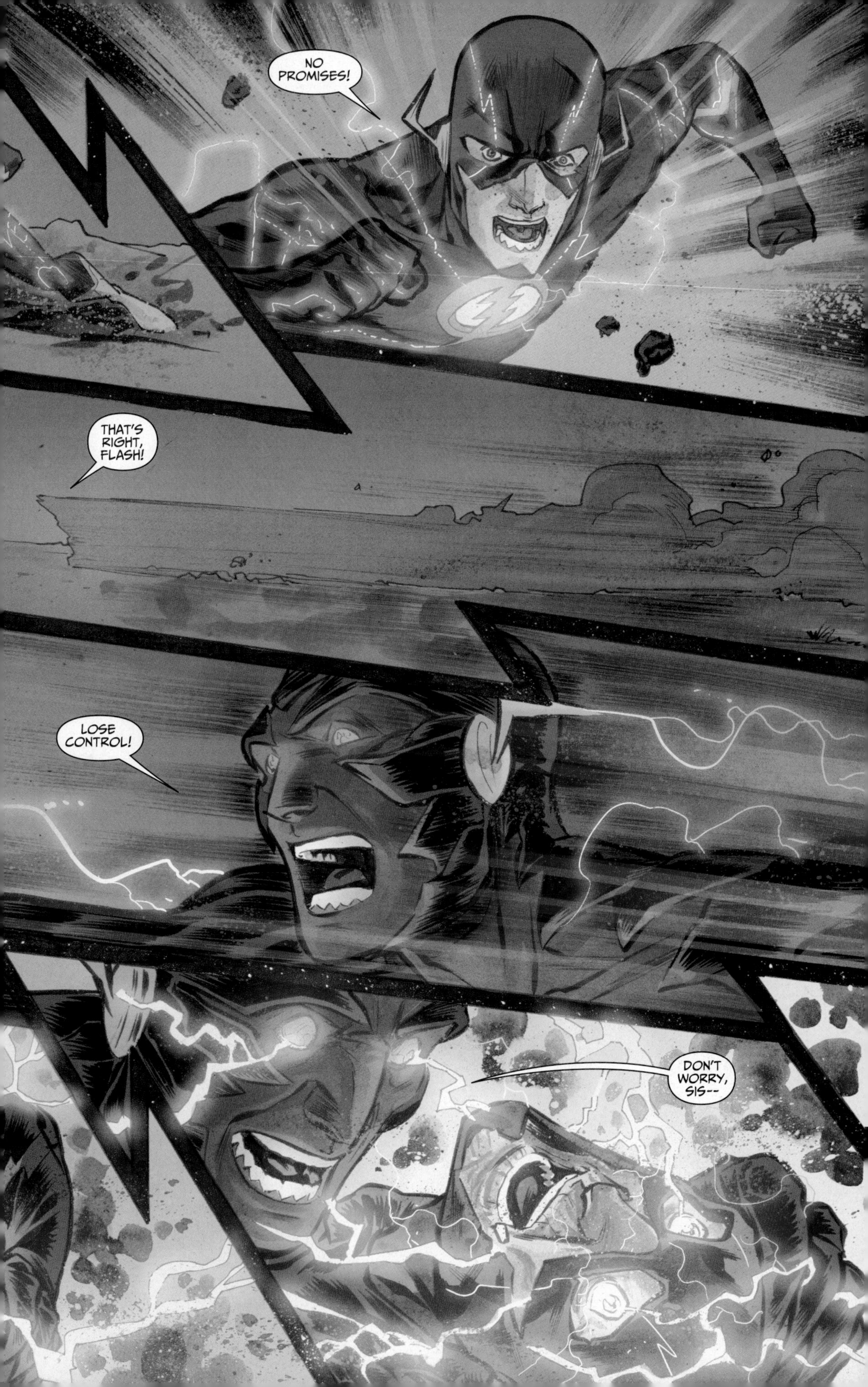
NO PROMISES!
THAT'S RIGHT, FLASH!
LOSE CONTROL!
DON'T WORRY, SIS--

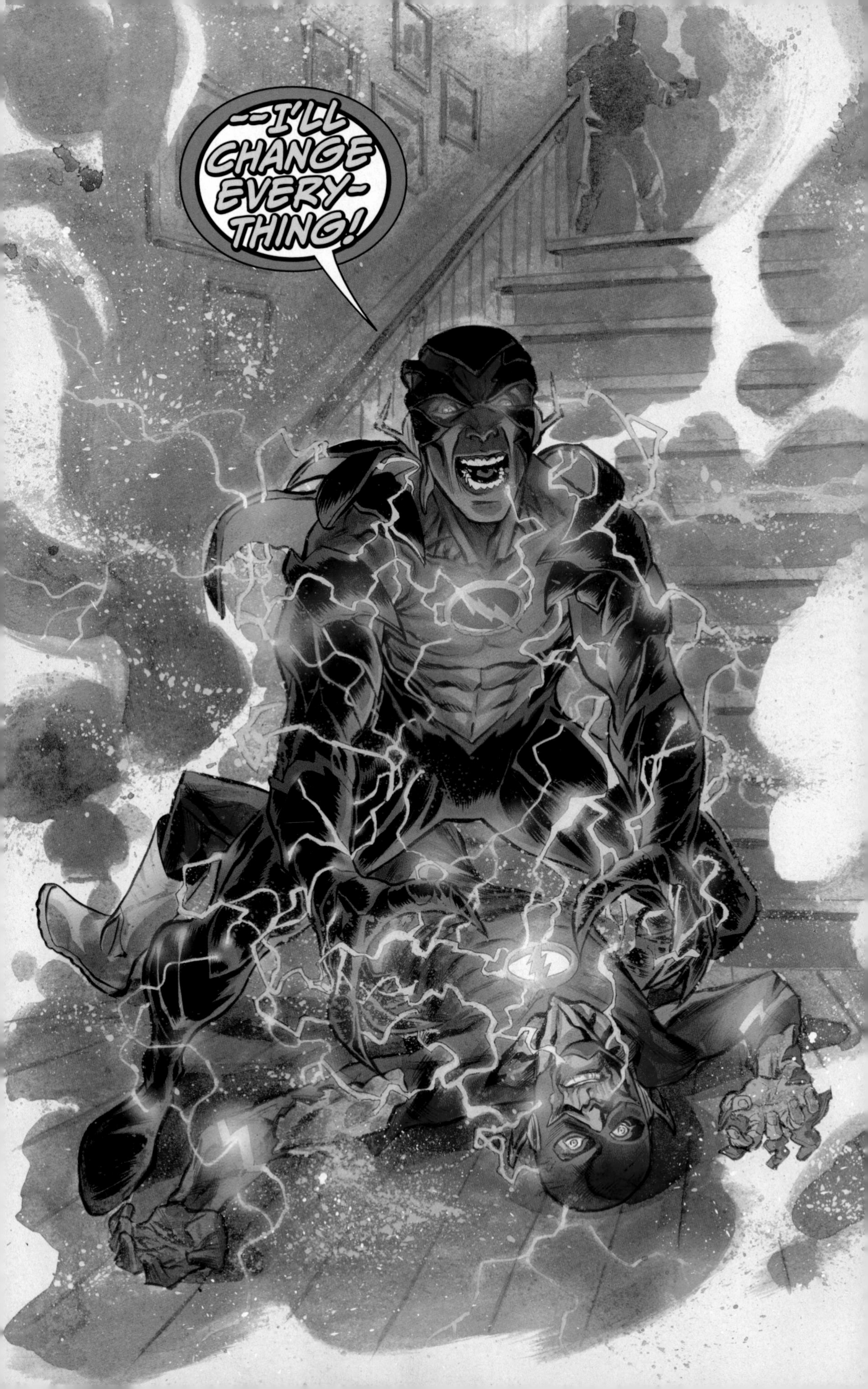
--I'LL CHANGE EVERY-THING!

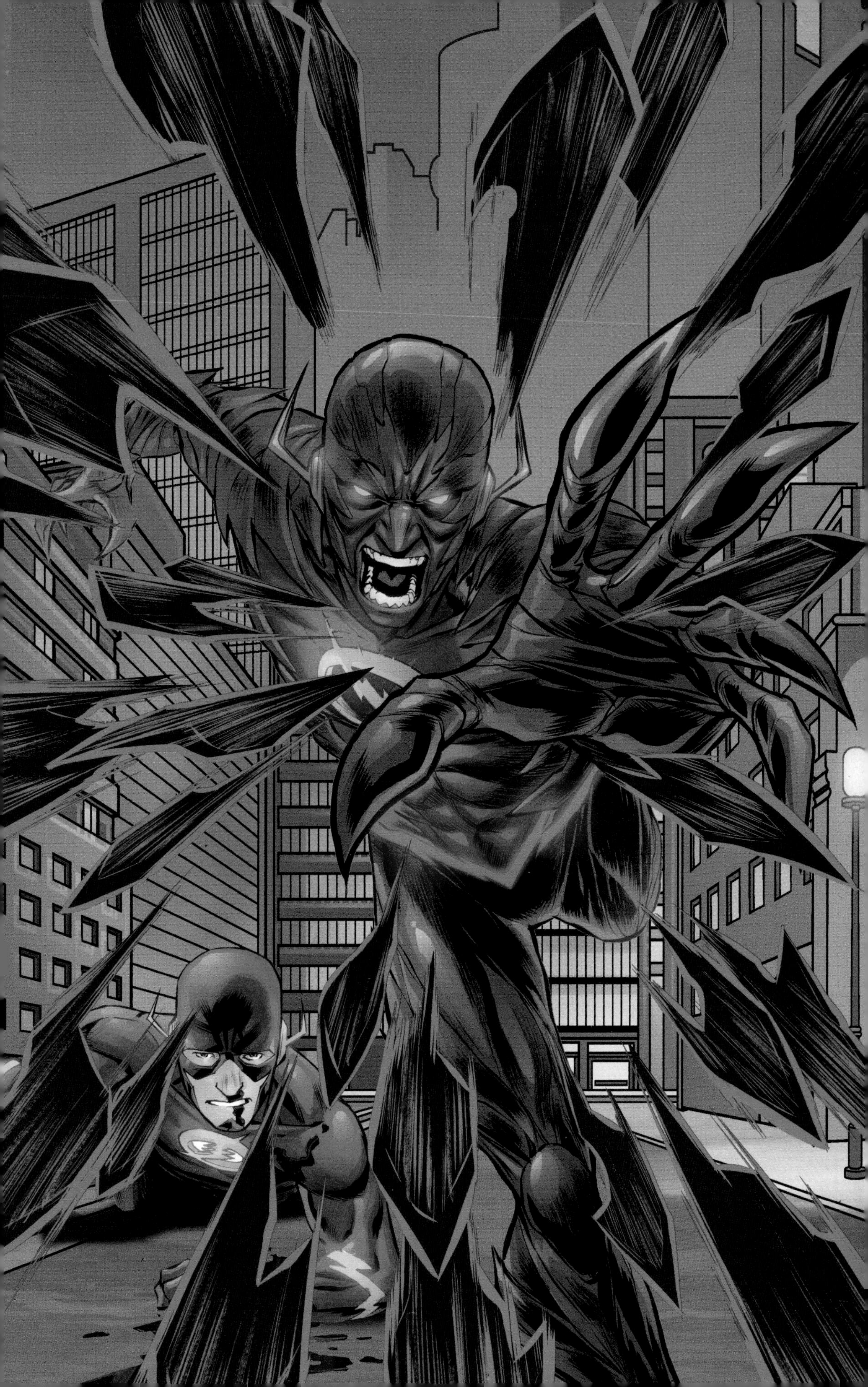

FRANCIS MANAPUL & BRIAN BUCCELLATO writers SCOTT HEPBURN artist

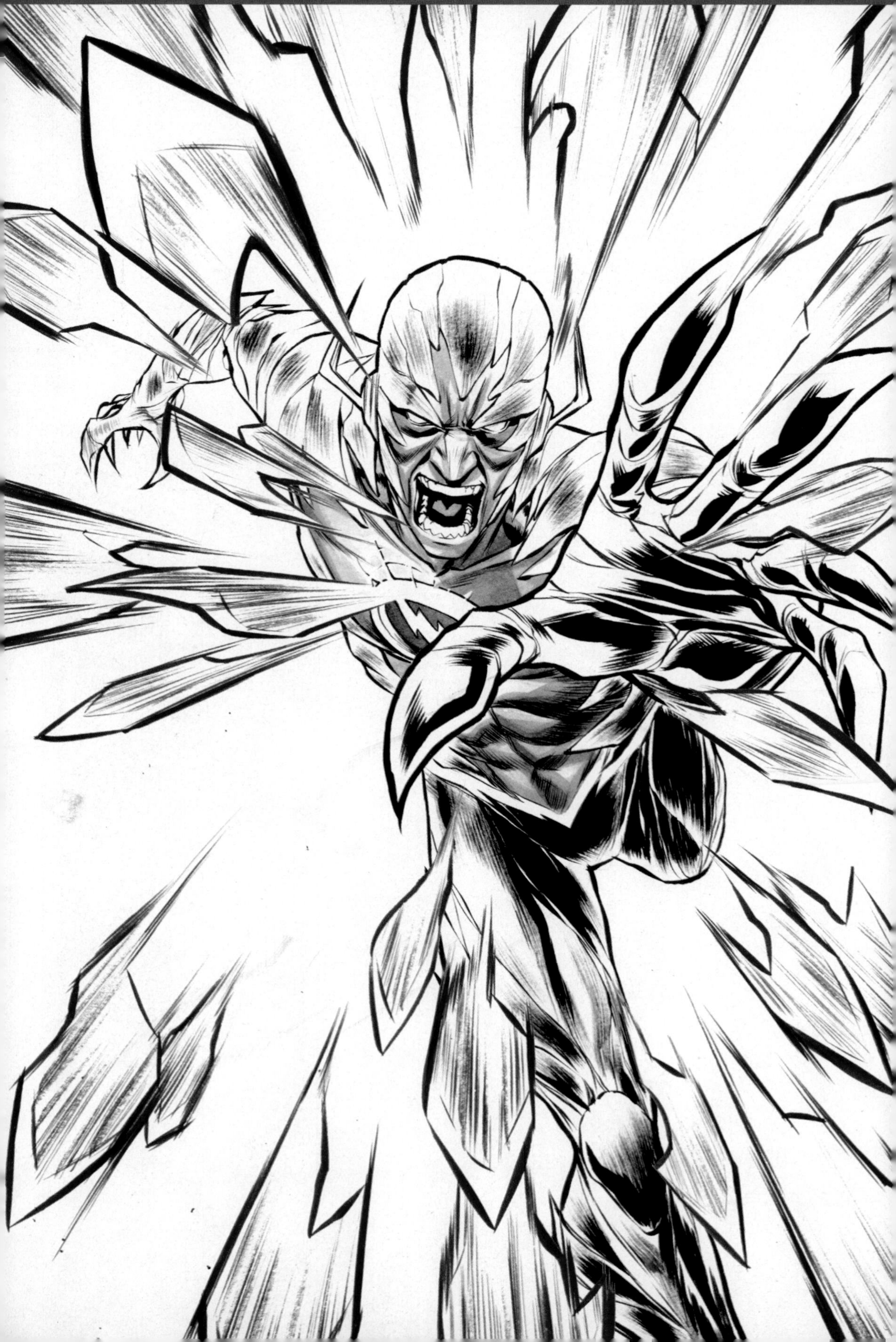

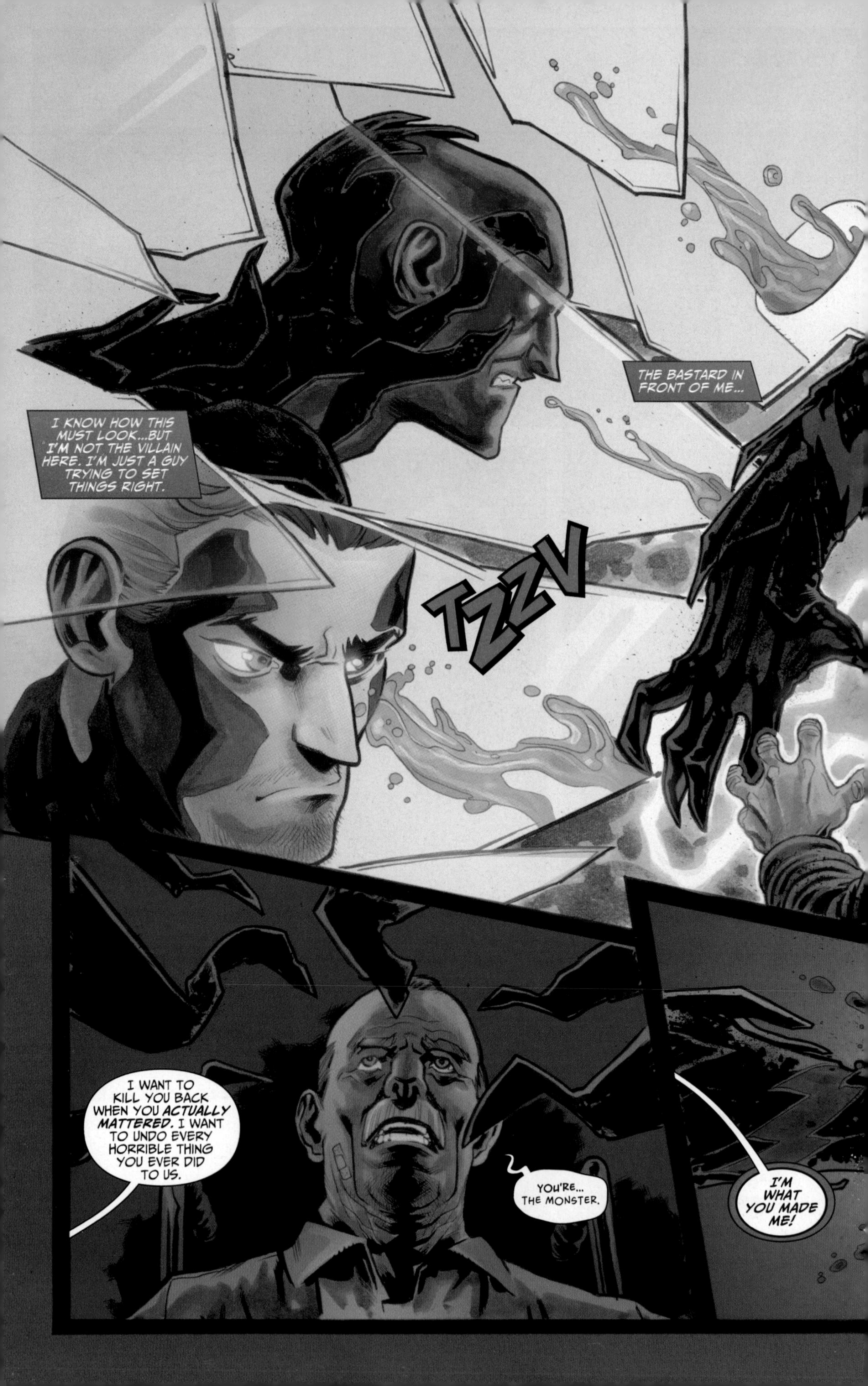
THE BASTARD IN FRONT OF ME...
I KNOW HOW THIS MUST LOOK...BUT I'M NOT THE VILLAIN HERE. I'M JUST A GUY TRYING TO SET THINGS RIGHT.
TZZV
I WANT TO KILL YOU BACK WHEN YOU ACTUALLY MATTERED. I WANT TO UNDO EVERY HORRIBLE THING YOU EVER DID TO US.
YOU'RE... THE MONSTER.
I'M WHAT YOU MADE ME!

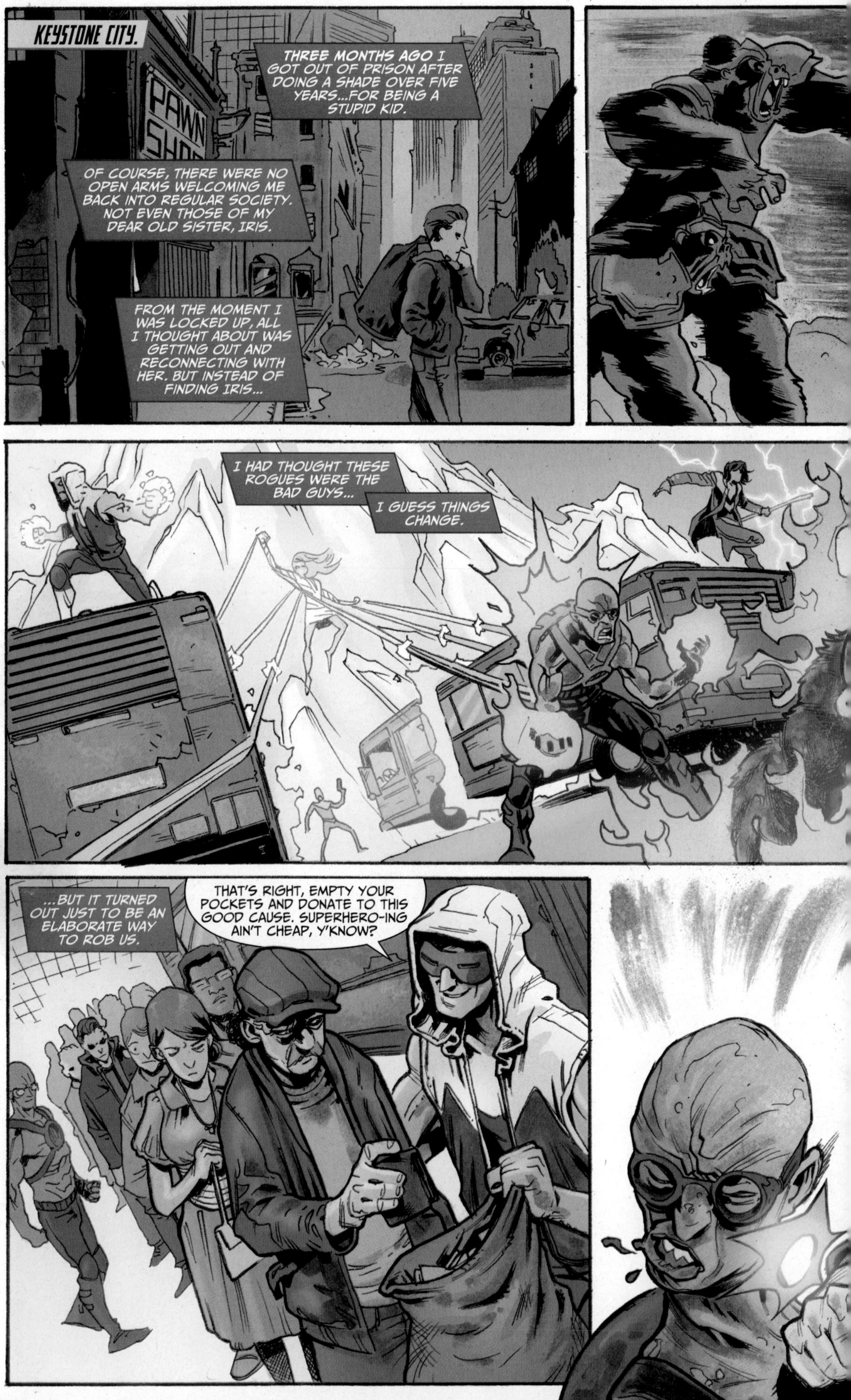
KEYSTONE CITY.
THREE MONTHS AGO I GOT OUT OF PRISON AFTER DOING A SHADE OVER FIVE YEARS...FOR BEING A STUPID KID.
PAWN SHOP
OF COURSE, THERE WERE NO OPEN ARMS WELCOMING ME BACK INTO REGULAR SOCIETY. NOT EVEN THOSE OF MY DEAR OLD SISTER, IRIS.
FROM THE MOMENT I WAS LOCKED UP, ALL I THOUGHT ABOUT WAS GETTING OUT AND RECONNECTING WITH HER. BUT INSTEAD OF FINDING IRIS...
I HAD THOUGHT THESE ROGUES WERE THE BAD GUYS...
I GUESS THINGS CHANGE.
...BUT IT TURNED OUT JUST TO BE AN ELABORATE WAY TO ROB US.
THAT'S RIGHT, EMPTY YOUR POCKETS AND DONATE TO THIS GOOD CAUSE. SUPERHERO-ING AIN'T CHEAP, Y'KNOW?

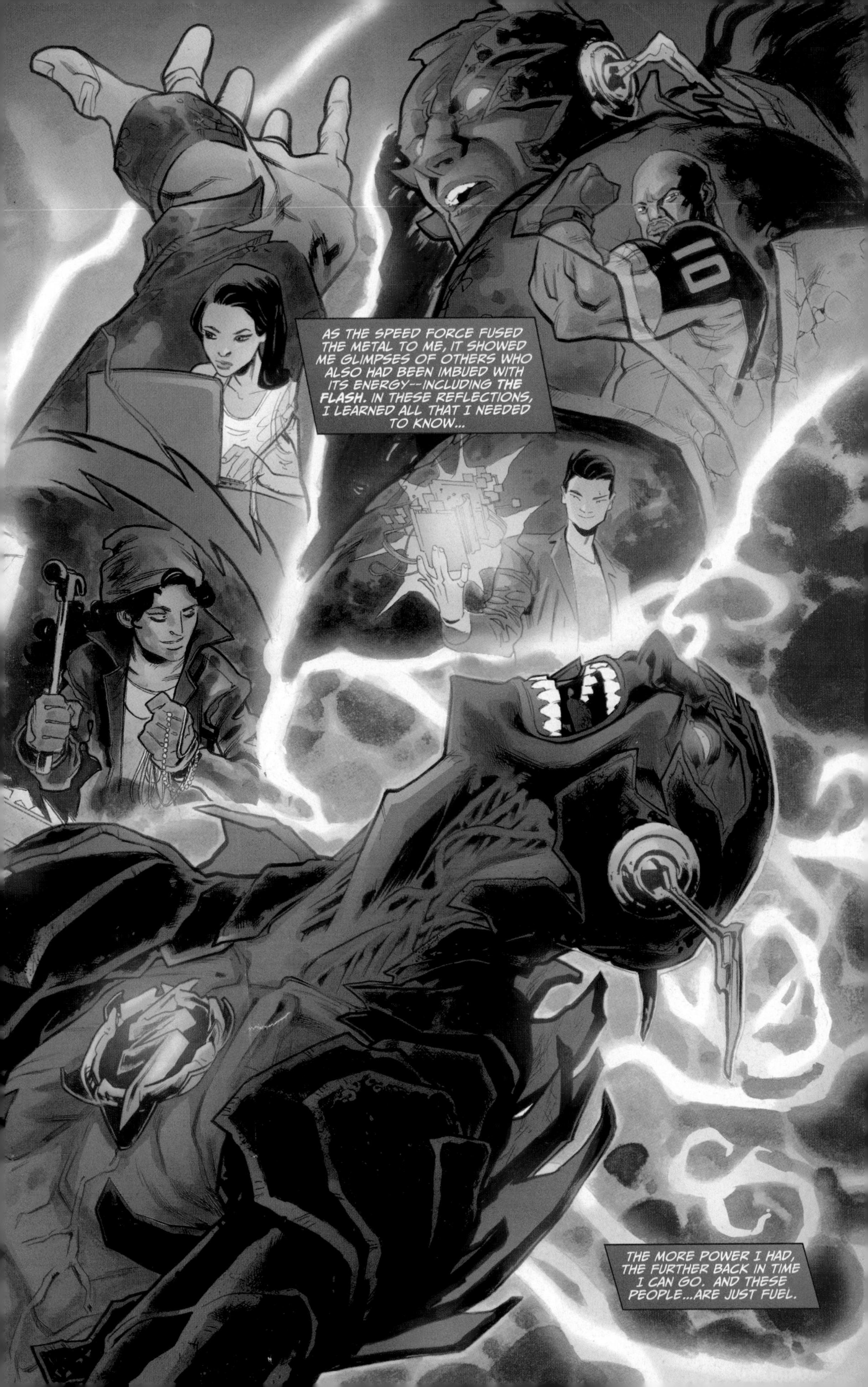
AS THE SPEED FORCE FUSED THE METAL TO ME, IT SHOWED ME GLIMPSES OF OTHERS WHO ALSO HAD BEEN IMBUED WITH ITS ENERGY--INCLUDING **THE FLASH.** IN THESE REFLECTIONS, I LEARNED ALL THAT I NEEDED TO KNOW...
THE MORE POWER I HAD, THE FURTHER BACK IN TIME I CAN GO. AND THESE PEOPLE...ARE JUST FUEL.
10

PRISON CHANGED ME SOME, SURE, BUT NOT AS MUCH AS WHAT HAPPENED *ELEVEN YEARS AGO*...WHEN MY LIFE CHANGED FOREVER...AND MY SISTER TURNED HER BACK ON ME.

BY THE TIME I WAS 12 I WAS USED TO DOING WITHOUT. MY DAD NEVER BOUGHT US TOYS OR GAMES...SO I HAD TO FIND OTHER WAYS TO ENTERTAIN MYSELF.

IRIS WAS ALWAYS GOOD AT MAKING FRIENDS, SO SHE GOT BY OKAY. ME...MY ONLY FRIENDS WERE THE CRICKETS I CAUGHT BEHIND THE HOUSE.

KRREEET

KRRREEEET

KRREEET

THEY WERE NOISY LITTLE BUGGERS, BUT THEIR CLICKING ACTUALLY HELPED ME FALL ASLEEP.

KRREEET
KRRREEEET
KRREEET

SSSS

THAT BASTARD DIDN'T AGREE.

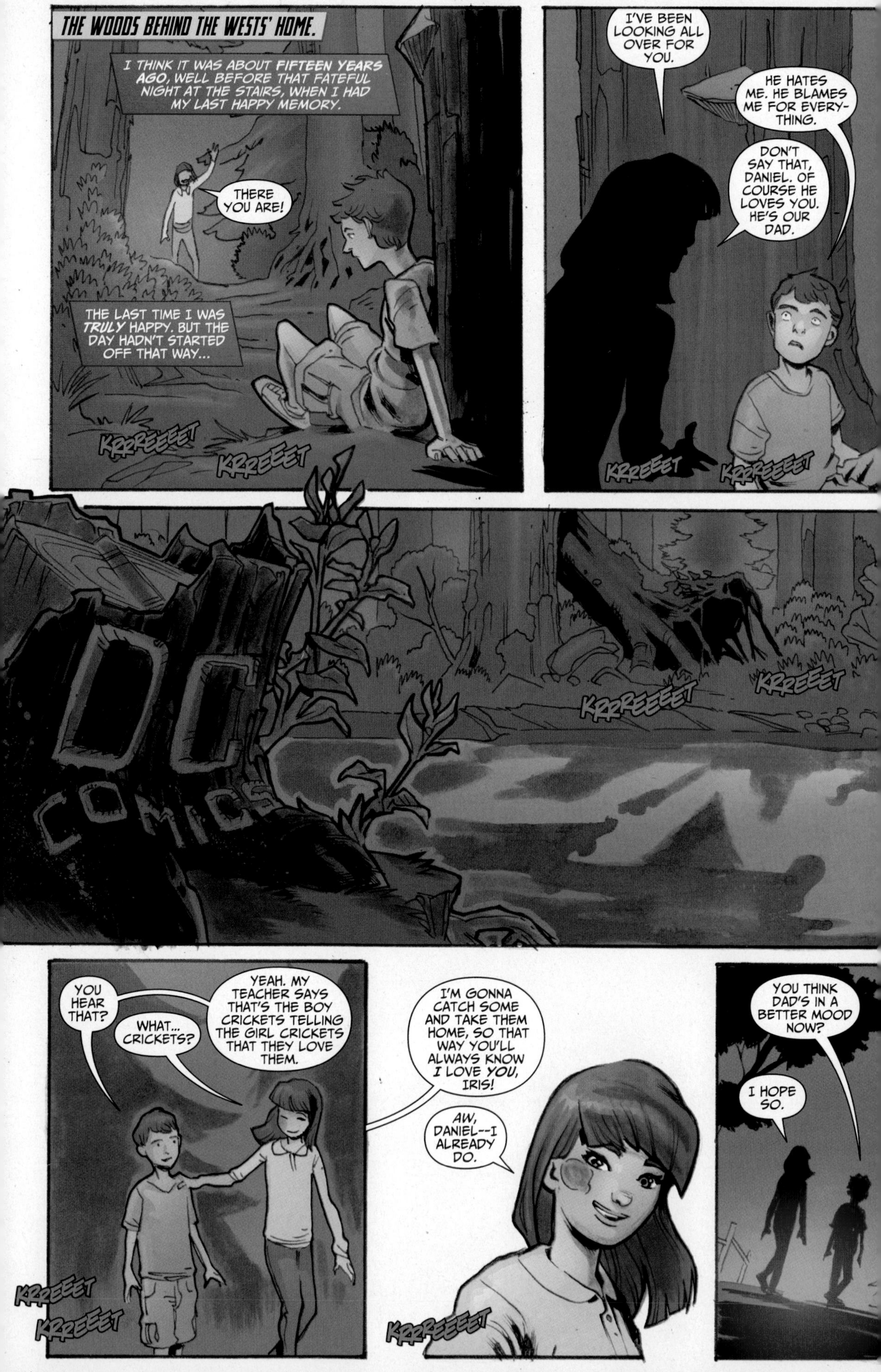
THE WOODS BEHIND THE WESTS' HOME.
I THINK IT WAS ABOUT FIFTEEN YEARS AGO, WELL BEFORE THAT FATEFUL NIGHT AT THE STAIRS, WHEN I HAD MY LAST HAPPY MEMORY.
THERE YOU ARE!
THE LAST TIME I WAS TRULY HAPPY. BUT THE DAY HADN'T STARTED OFF THAT WAY...
KRRREEEET
KRREEEET
I'VE BEEN LOOKING ALL OVER FOR YOU.
HE HATES ME. HE BLAMES ME FOR EVERYTHING.
DON'T SAY THAT, DANIEL. OF COURSE HE LOVES YOU. HE'S OUR DAD.
KRREEET
KRRREEEET
KRRREEEET
KRREEET
YOU HEAR THAT?
WHAT... CRICKETS?
YEAH. MY TEACHER SAYS THAT'S THE BOY CRICKETS TELLING THE GIRL CRICKETS THAT THEY LOVE THEM.
I'M GONNA CATCH SOME AND TAKE THEM HOME, SO THAT WAY YOU'LL ALWAYS KNOW I LOVE YOU, IRIS!
AW, DANIEL--I ALREADY DO.
KRRREEET
KRREEET
KRRREEEET
YOU THINK DAD'S IN A BETTER MOOD NOW?
I HOPE SO.

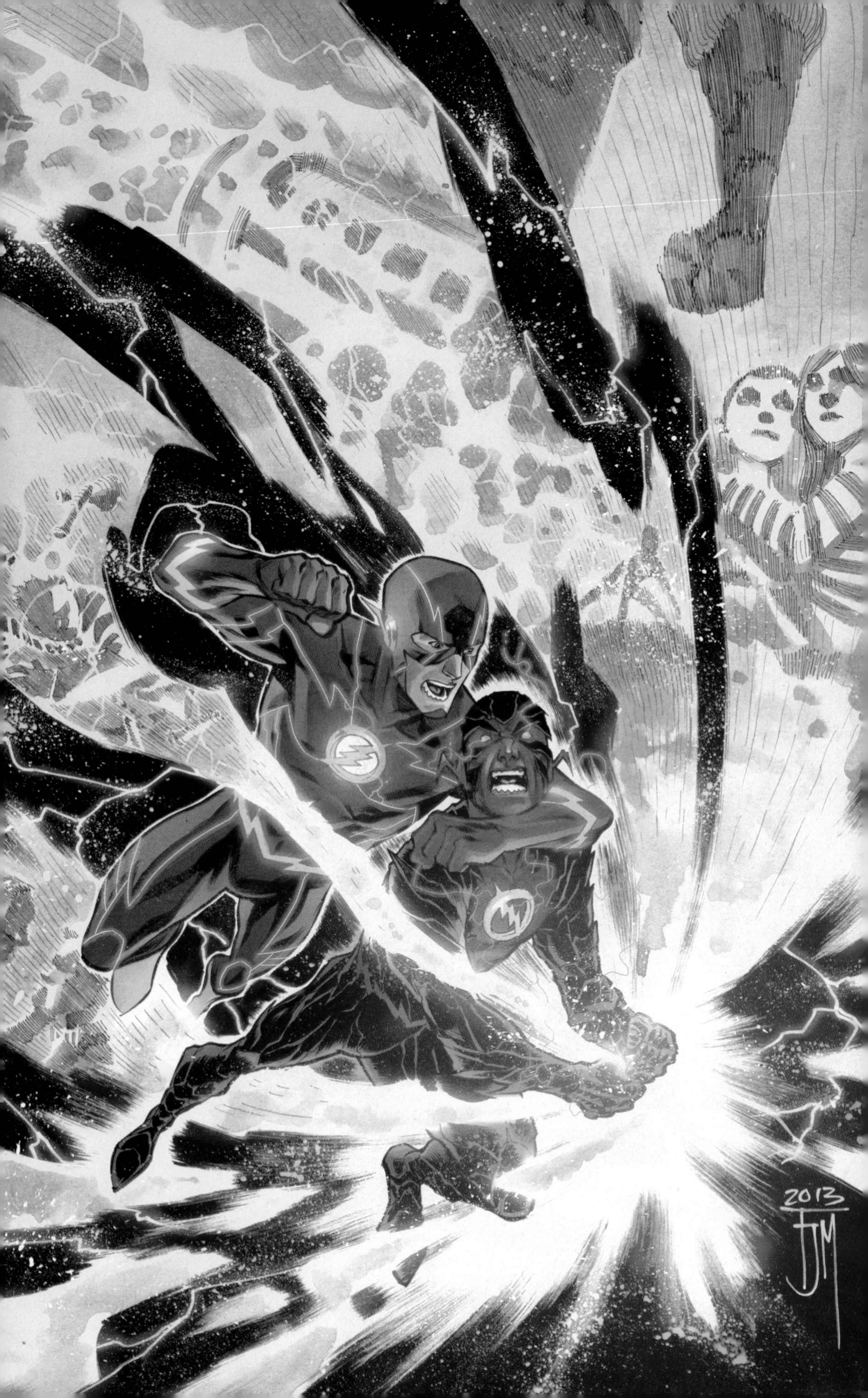
2013

FRANCIS MANAPUL & BRIAN BUCCELLATO writers **FRANCIS MANAPUL** artist

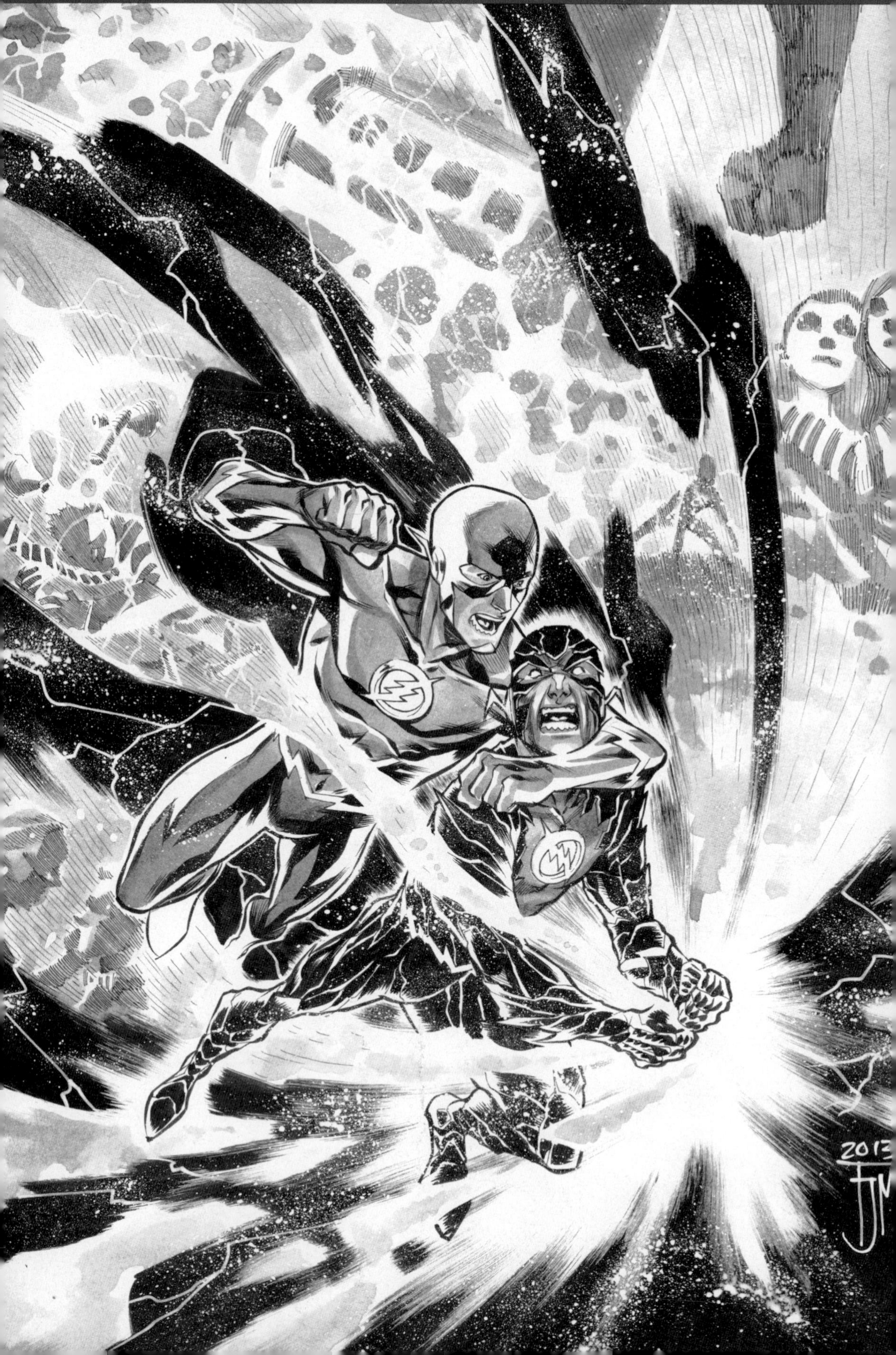
2013
FJM

POWER IS A STRANGE THING. IT GIVES YOU THE ABILITY TO CHANGE THINGS, TO MAKE A DIFFERENCE. I GOT MINE FROM A PLACE CALLED THE **SPEED FORCE.** I USED IT TO SAVE PEOPLE'S LIVES...BUT AFTER A MISTAKE I MADE, INNOCENT PEOPLE, INCLUDING **IRIS WEST,** GOT TRAPPED INSIDE IT. WHEN I FINALLY RESCUED THEM, THEY CAME BACK DIFFERENT.

THEY MANIFESTED POWERS FROM THE SPEED FORCE, WHICH PUT A TARGET ON THEIR BACK. ONE BY ONE THEY WERE MURDERED-- ALL BUT IRIS.

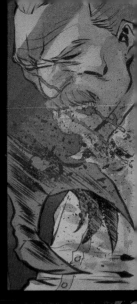

I FOLLOWED THE TRAIL OF THEIR KILLER. BUT WHEN I FOUND HIM, HE DRAGGED ME BACK IN TIME. I GUESS HE WANTED TO MAKE A DIFFERENCE TOO.

DC COMICS

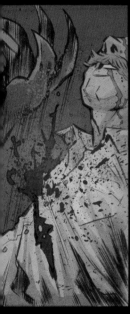

GIVEN THE OPPORTUNITY... WHAT WOULD YOU CHANGE?

PROUDLY PRESENTS

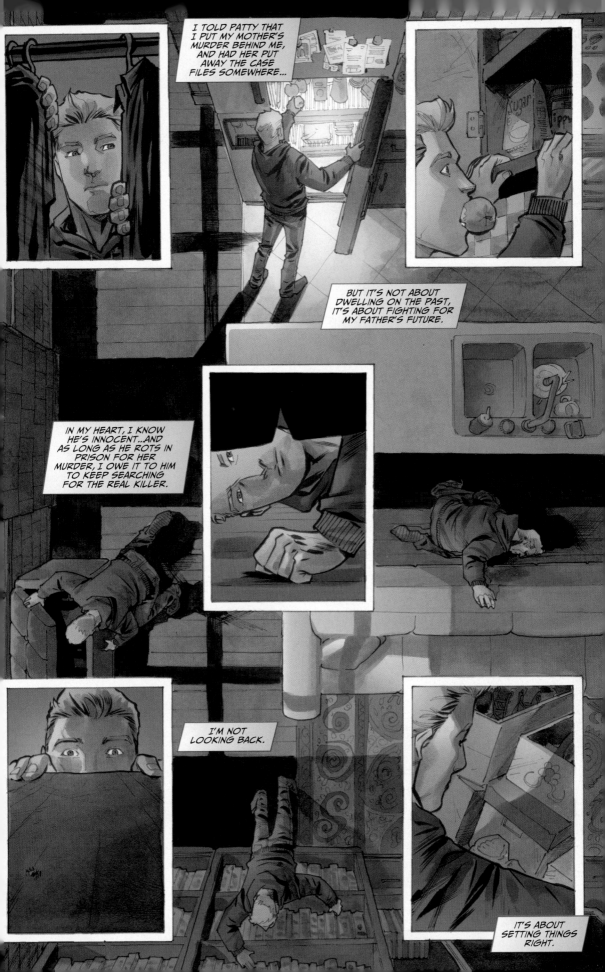

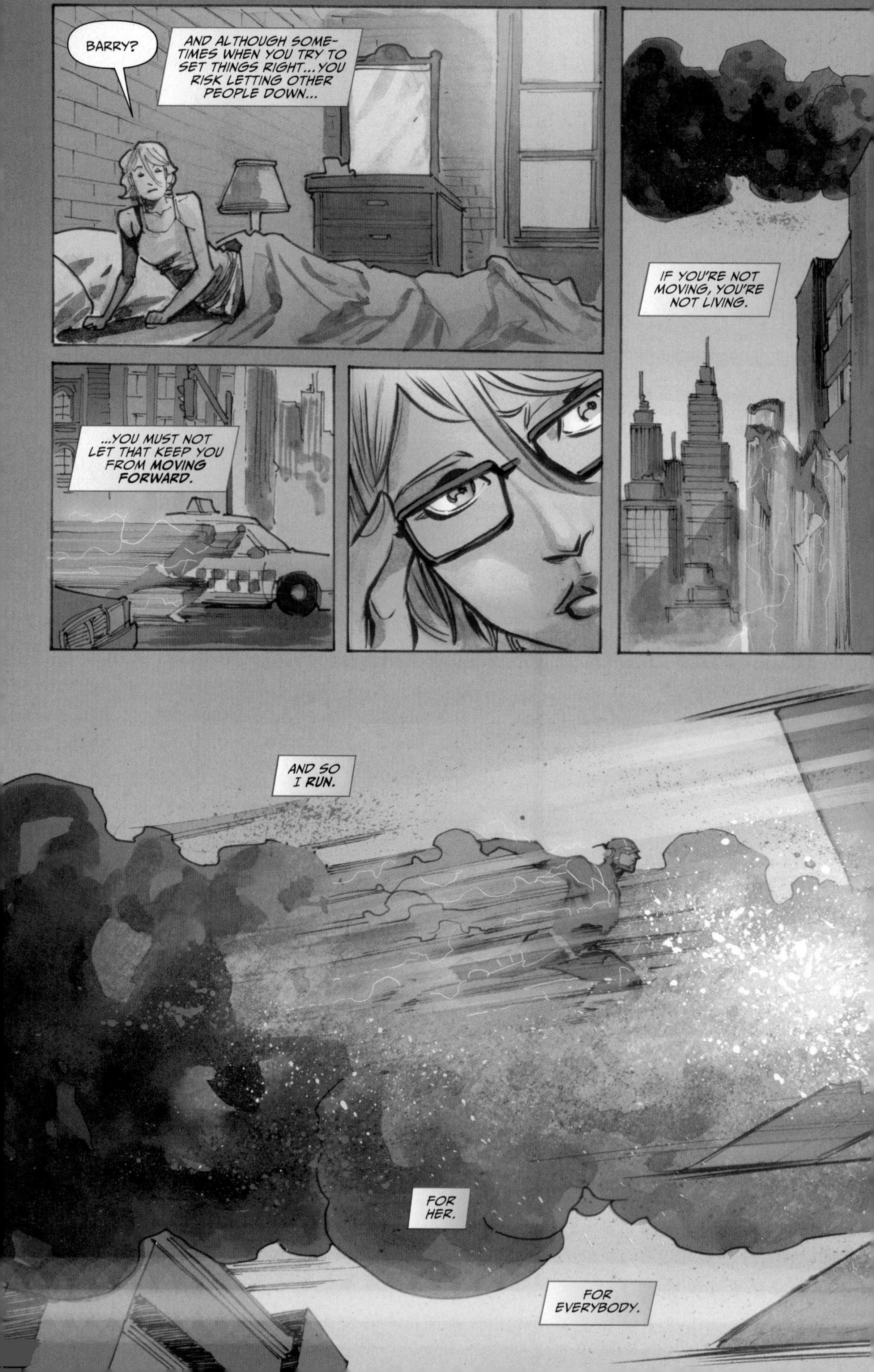
BARRY?
AND ALTHOUGH SOMETIMES WHEN YOU TRY TO SET THINGS RIGHT...YOU RISK LETTING OTHER PEOPLE DOWN...
...YOU MUST NOT LET THAT KEEP YOU FROM MOVING FORWARD.
IF YOU'RE NOT MOVING, YOU'RE NOT LIVING.
AND SO I RUN.
FOR HER.
FOR EVERYBODY.

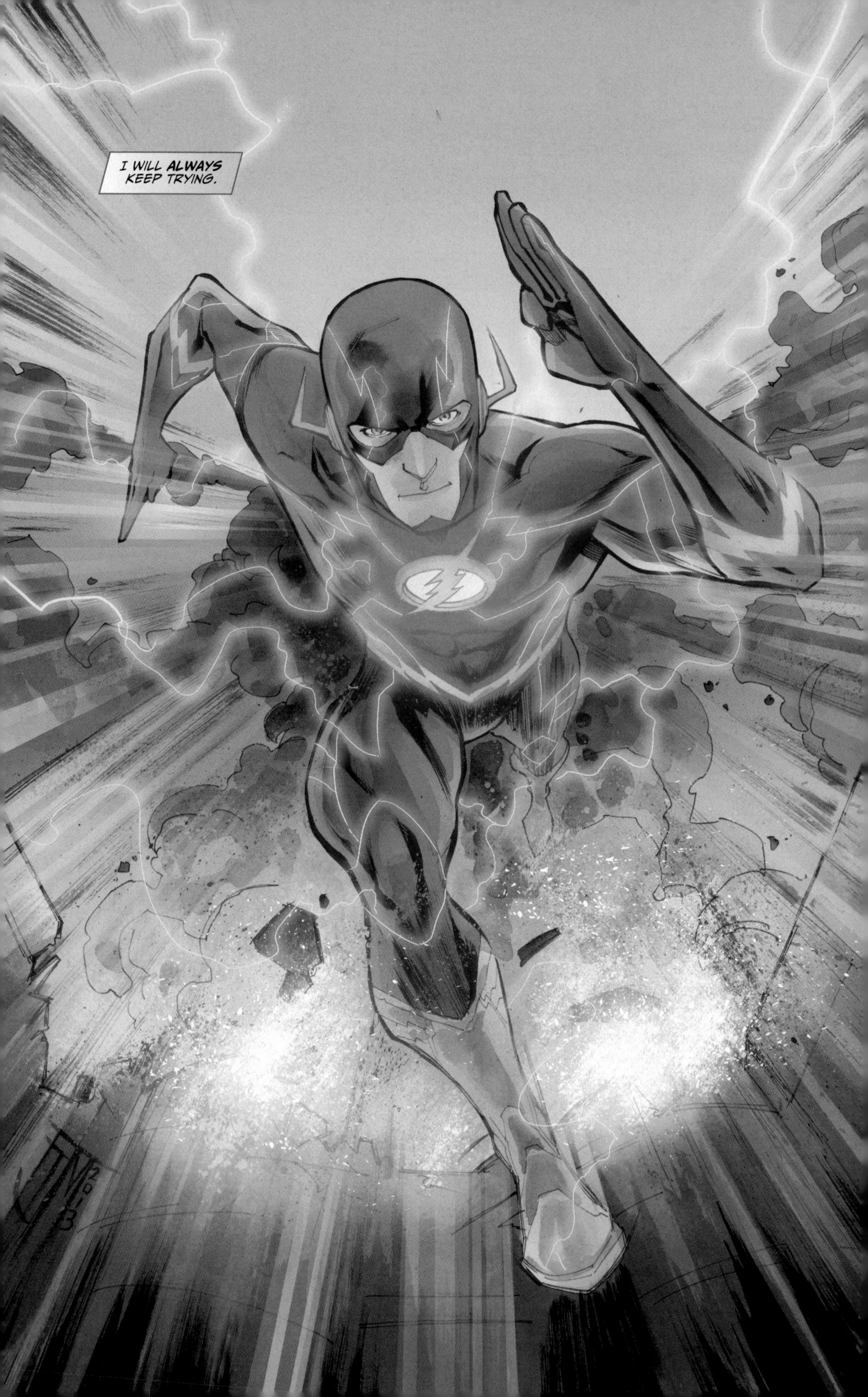
I WILL ALWAYS KEEP TRYING.

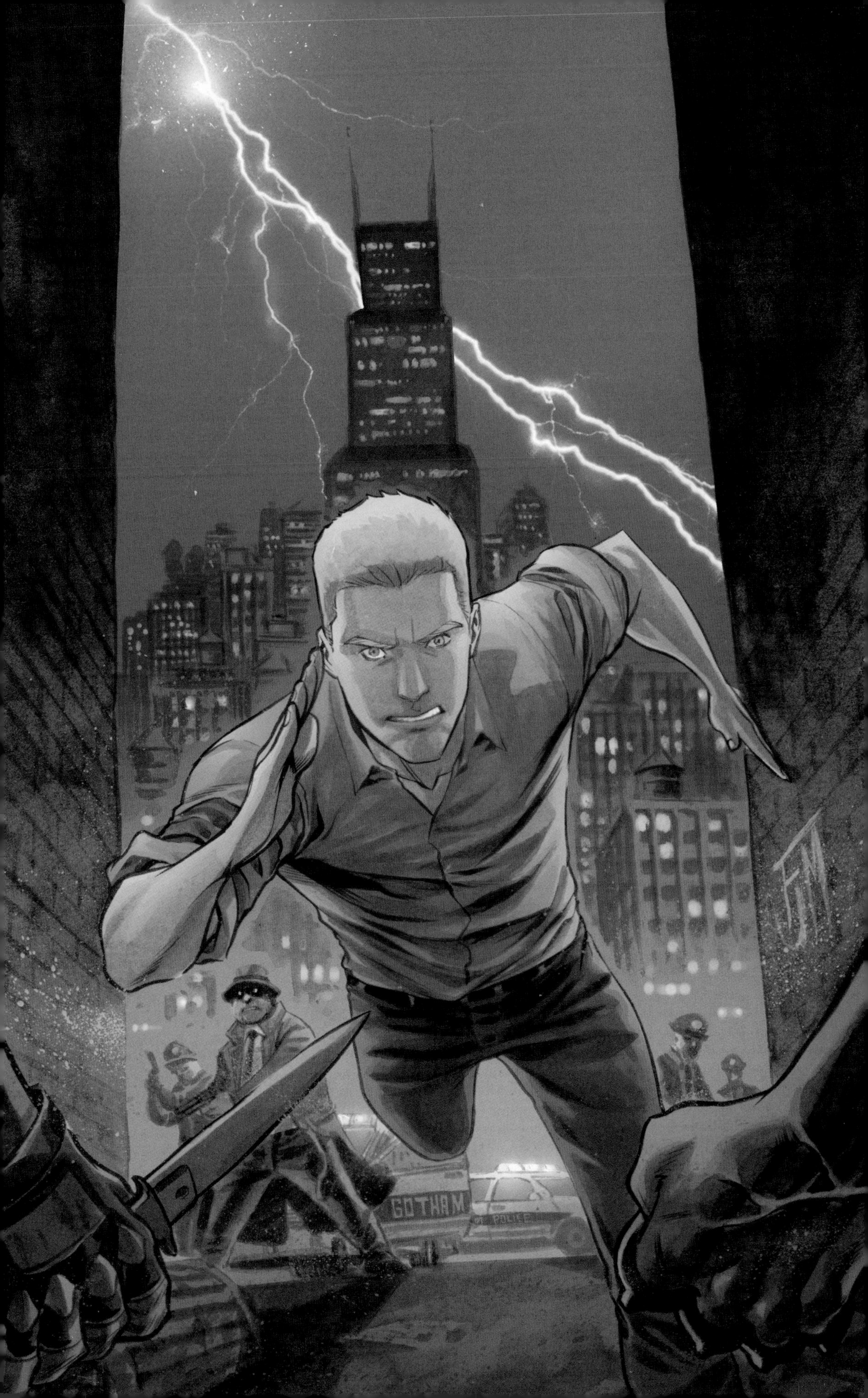
GOTHAM

FRANCIS MANAPUL & BRIAN BUCCELLATO writers   CHRIS SPROUSE, FRANCIS MANAPUL pencillers
KARL STORY, KEITH CHAMPAGNE, FRANCIS MANAPUL inkers

THIS GUY IS HOOKED ON SOME DANGEROUS NEW DRUG THAT APPEARED OUT OF NOWHERE...

YOU HEARD ME TELL HIM TO STAY PUT, RIGHT, HARVEY?

WE'RE LOSING THEM, SPENCER! KEEP UP!

BUT FOR SOME REASON, THE LOCAL COPS I'M WORKING WITH--OFFICERS HARVEY BULLOCK AND SPENCER THOMPSON--DON'T HAVE THE SAME SENSE OF URGENCY.

I GOT IC'RUS POWERS...

FREEZE! YOU'VE GOT NOWHERE ELSE TO GO!

I-I... DON'T NEED TO RUN NO MORE...

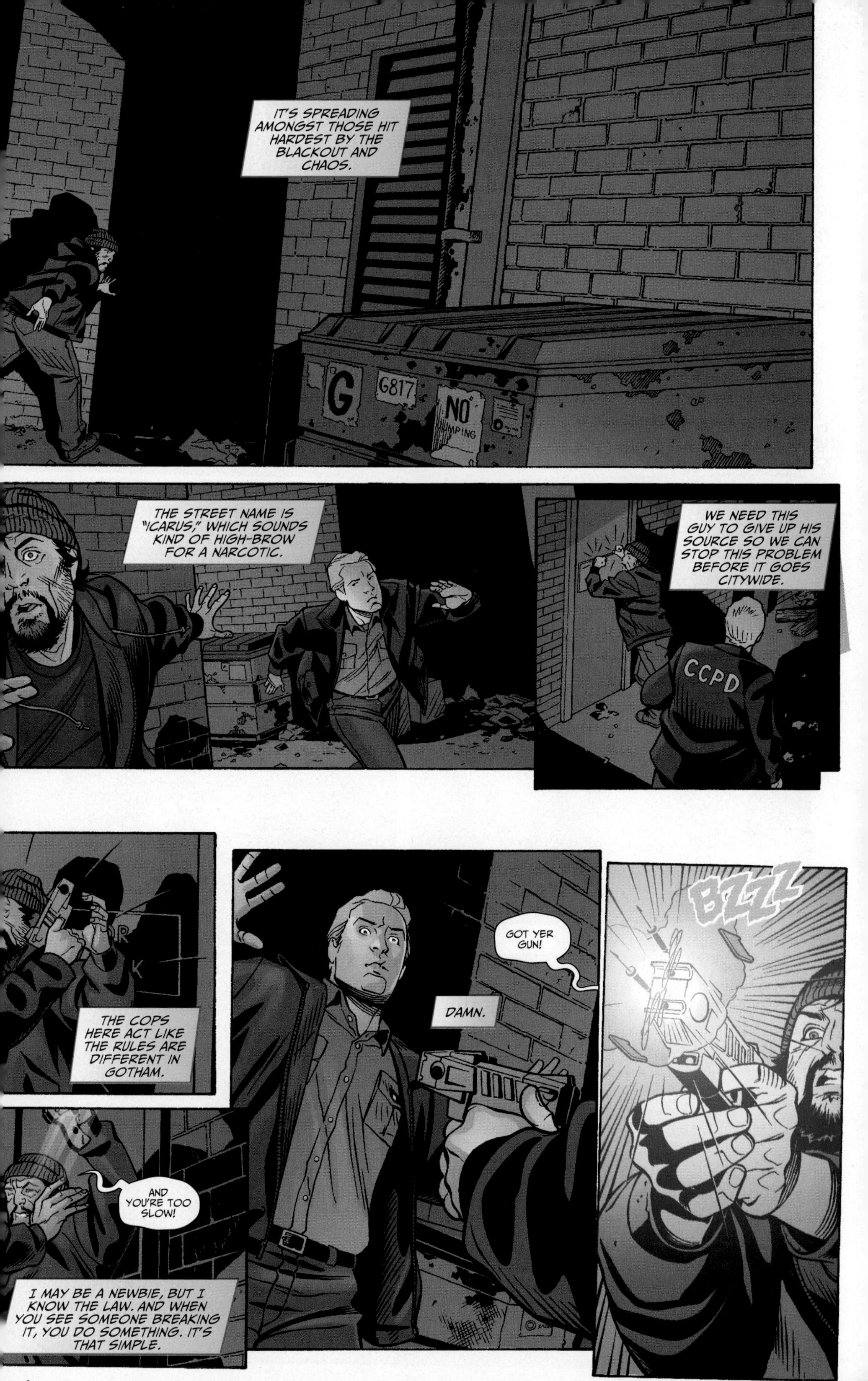

IT'S SPREADING AMONGST THOSE HIT HARDEST BY THE BLACKOUT AND CHAOS.
G
G817
NO DUMPING
THE STREET NAME IS "ICARUS," WHICH SOUNDS KIND OF HIGH-BROW FOR A NARCOTIC.
WE NEED THIS GUY TO GIVE UP HIS SOURCE SO WE CAN STOP THIS PROBLEM BEFORE IT GOES CITYWIDE.
CCPD
THE COPS HERE ACT LIKE THE RULES ARE DIFFERENT IN GOTHAM.
AND YOU'RE TOO SLOW!
I MAY BE A NEWBIE, BUT I KNOW THE LAW. AND WHEN YOU SEE SOMEONE BREAKING IT, YOU DO SOMETHING. IT'S THAT SIMPLE.
GOT YER GUN!
DAMN.
BZZZ

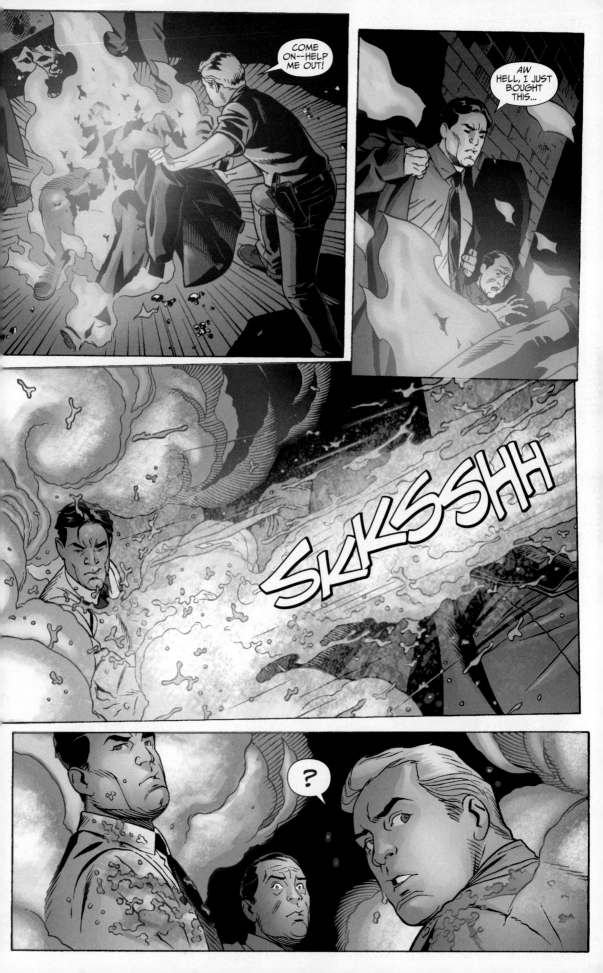

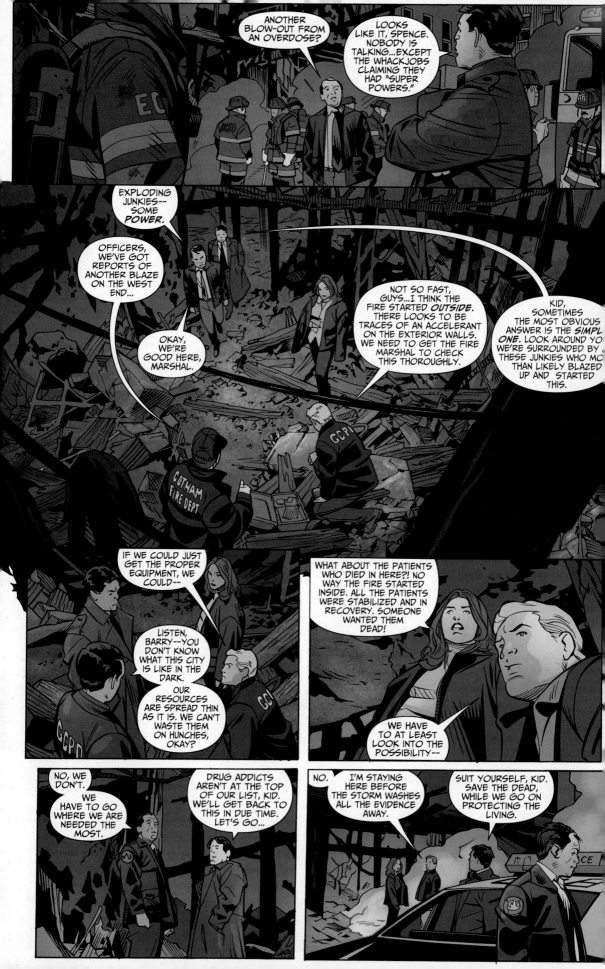

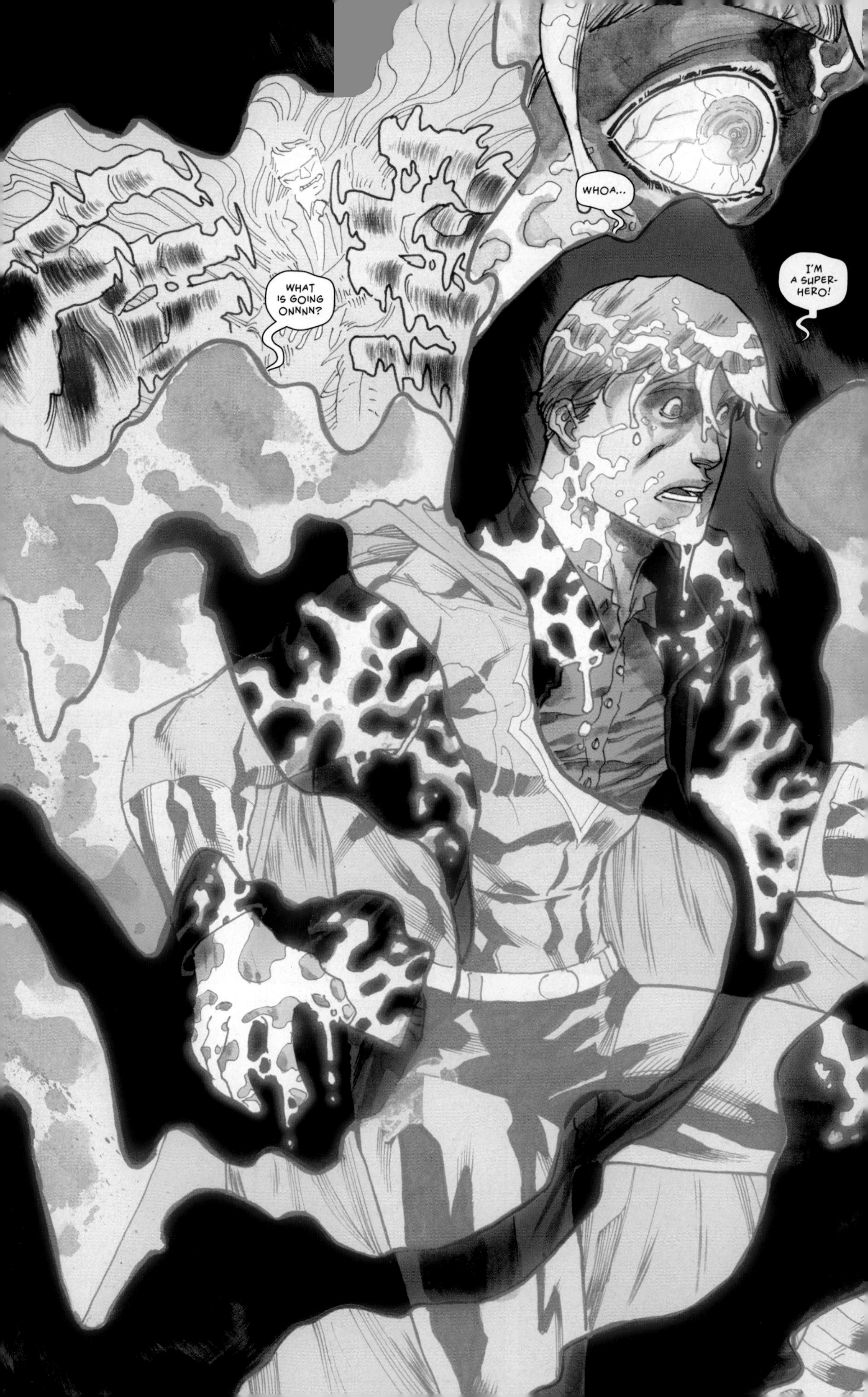
WHOA...
WHAT IS GOING ONNNN?
I'M A SUPER-HERO!

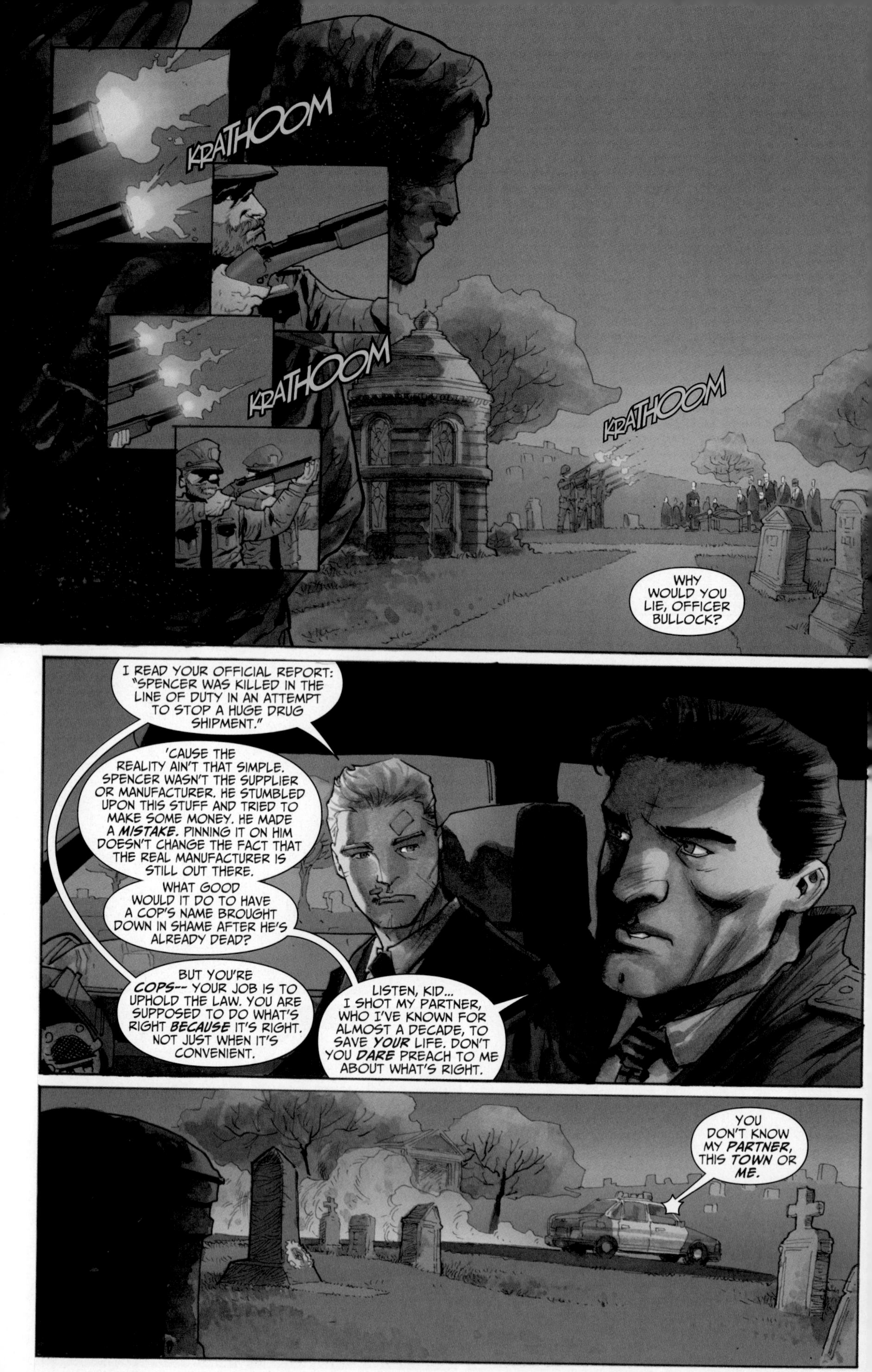
KRATHOOM
KRATHOOM
KRATHOOM
WHY WOULD YOU LIE, OFFICER BULLOCK?
I READ YOUR OFFICIAL REPORT: "SPENCER WAS KILLED IN THE LINE OF DUTY IN AN ATTEMPT TO STOP A HUGE DRUG SHIPMENT."
'CAUSE THE REALITY AIN'T THAT SIMPLE. SPENCER WASN'T THE SUPPLIER OR MANUFACTURER. HE STUMBLED UPON THIS STUFF AND TRIED TO MAKE SOME MONEY. HE MADE A MISTAKE. PINNING IT ON HIM DOESN'T CHANGE THE FACT THAT THE REAL MANUFACTURER IS STILL OUT THERE.
WHAT GOOD WOULD IT DO TO HAVE A COP'S NAME BROUGHT DOWN IN SHAME AFTER HE'S ALREADY DEAD?
BUT YOU'RE COPS-- YOUR JOB IS TO UPHOLD THE LAW. YOU ARE SUPPOSED TO DO WHAT'S RIGHT BECAUSE IT'S RIGHT. NOT JUST WHEN IT'S CONVENIENT.
LISTEN, KID... I SHOT MY PARTNER, WHO I'VE KNOWN FOR ALMOST A DECADE, TO SAVE YOUR LIFE. DON'T YOU DARE PREACH TO ME ABOUT WHAT'S RIGHT.
YOU DON'T KNOW MY PARTNER, THIS TOWN OR ME.

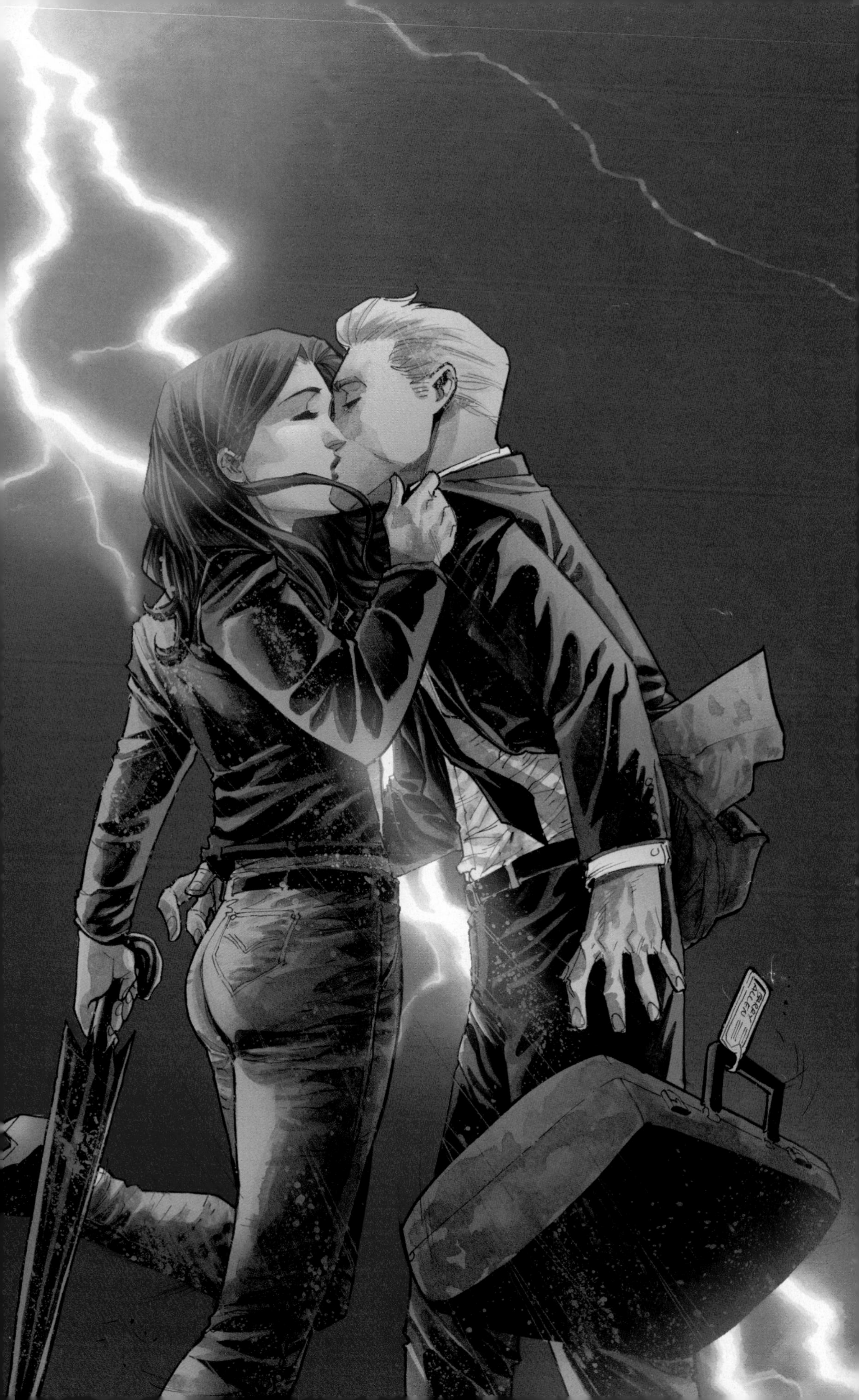
BARRY ALLEN

Pencils for THE FLASH #24 page 20

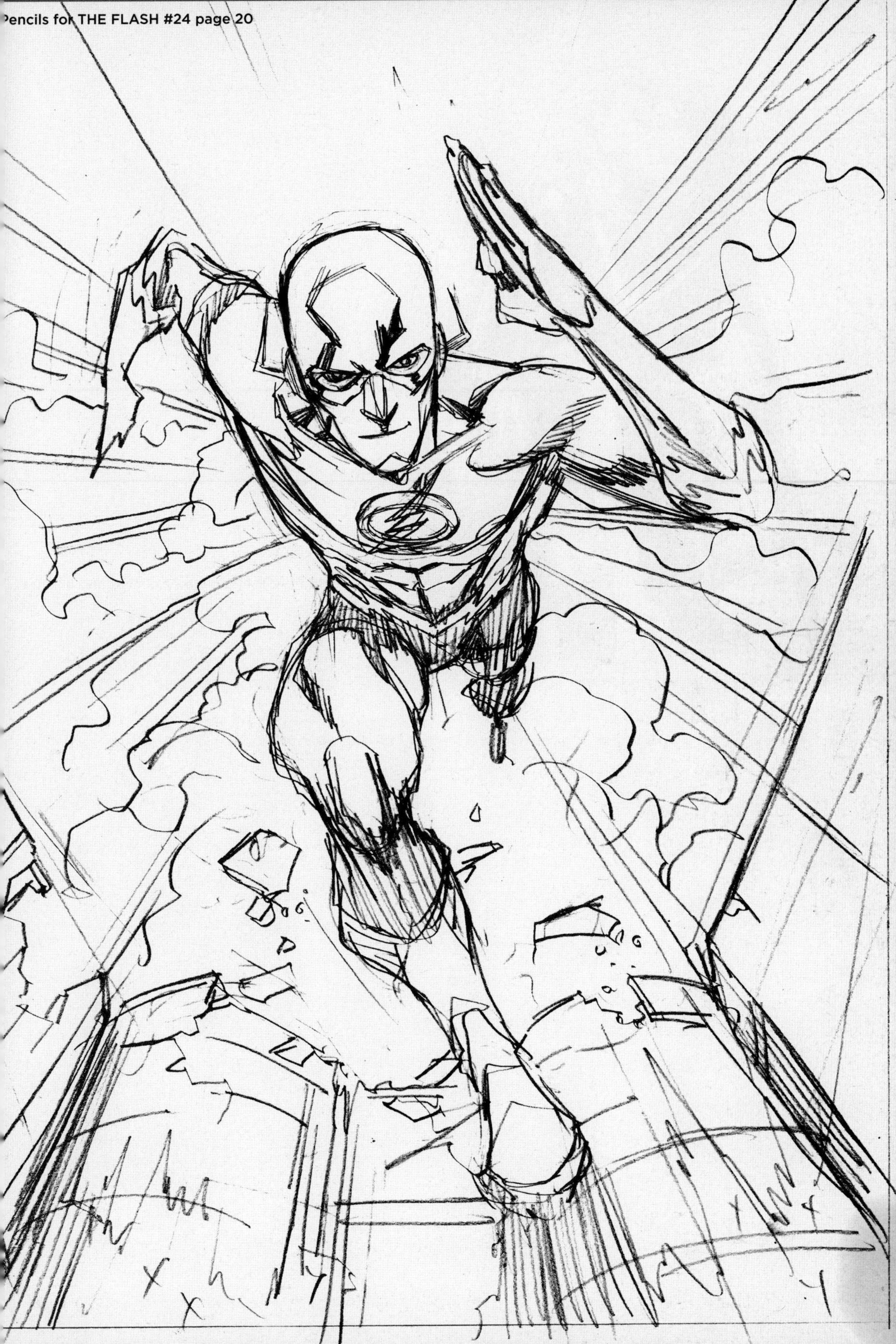

THE FLASH #25 page 27 pencils and finishes

THE FLASH #20 page 20 pencils and finishes

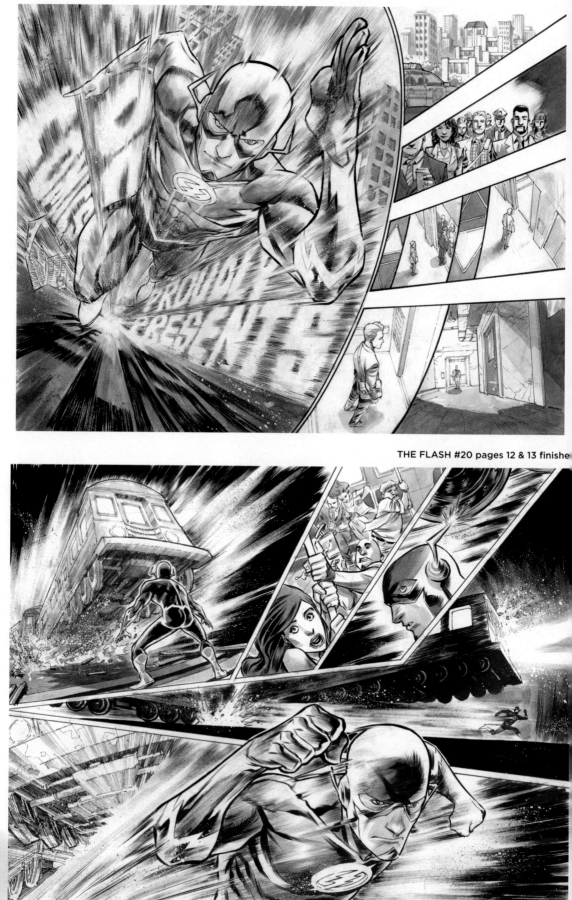

THE FLASH #25 page 28 finishes

THE FLASH #21 page 20 finish

THE FLASH #22 pages 2 & 3 finishes

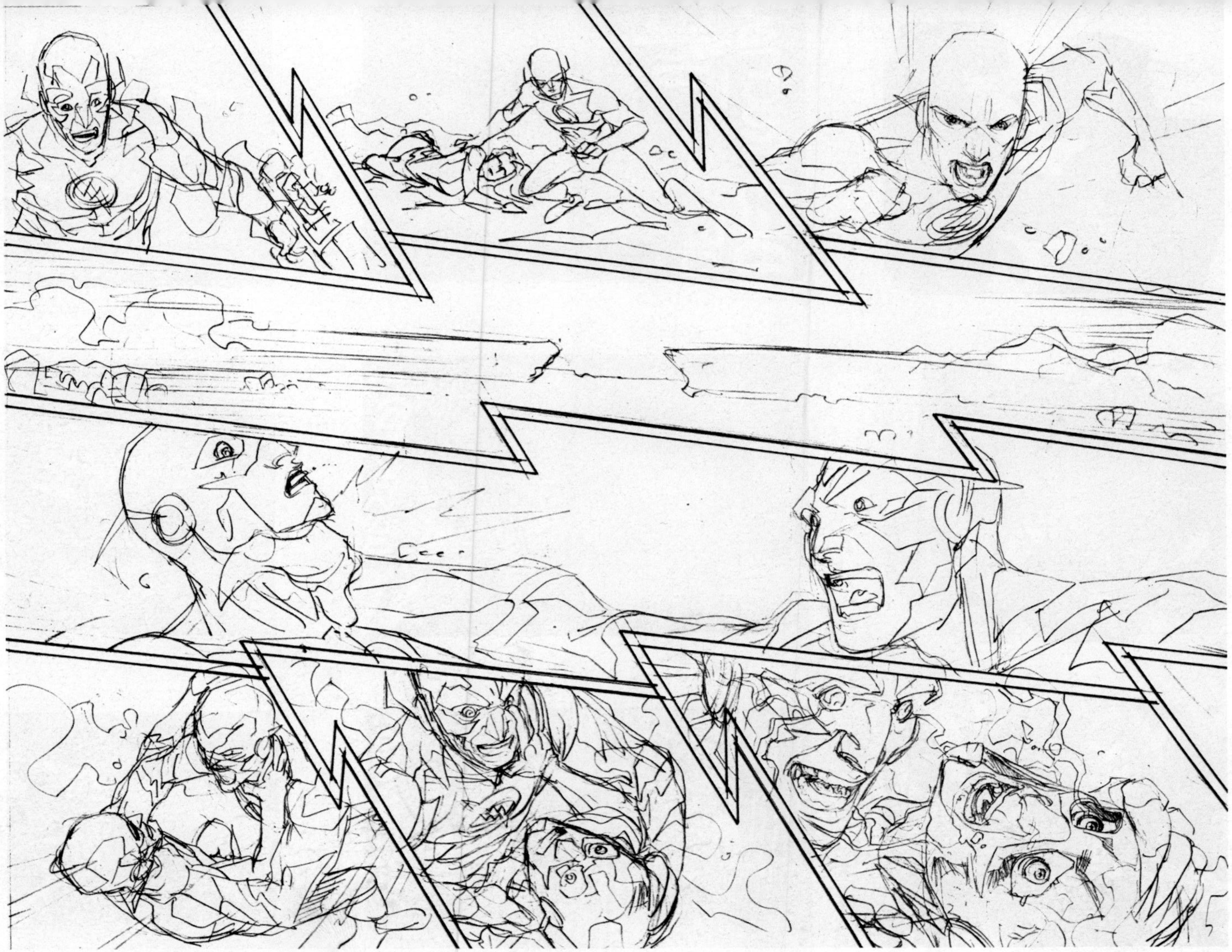

THE FLASH #23 pages 18 & 19 pencils

Cover layouts for THE FLASH #23-25

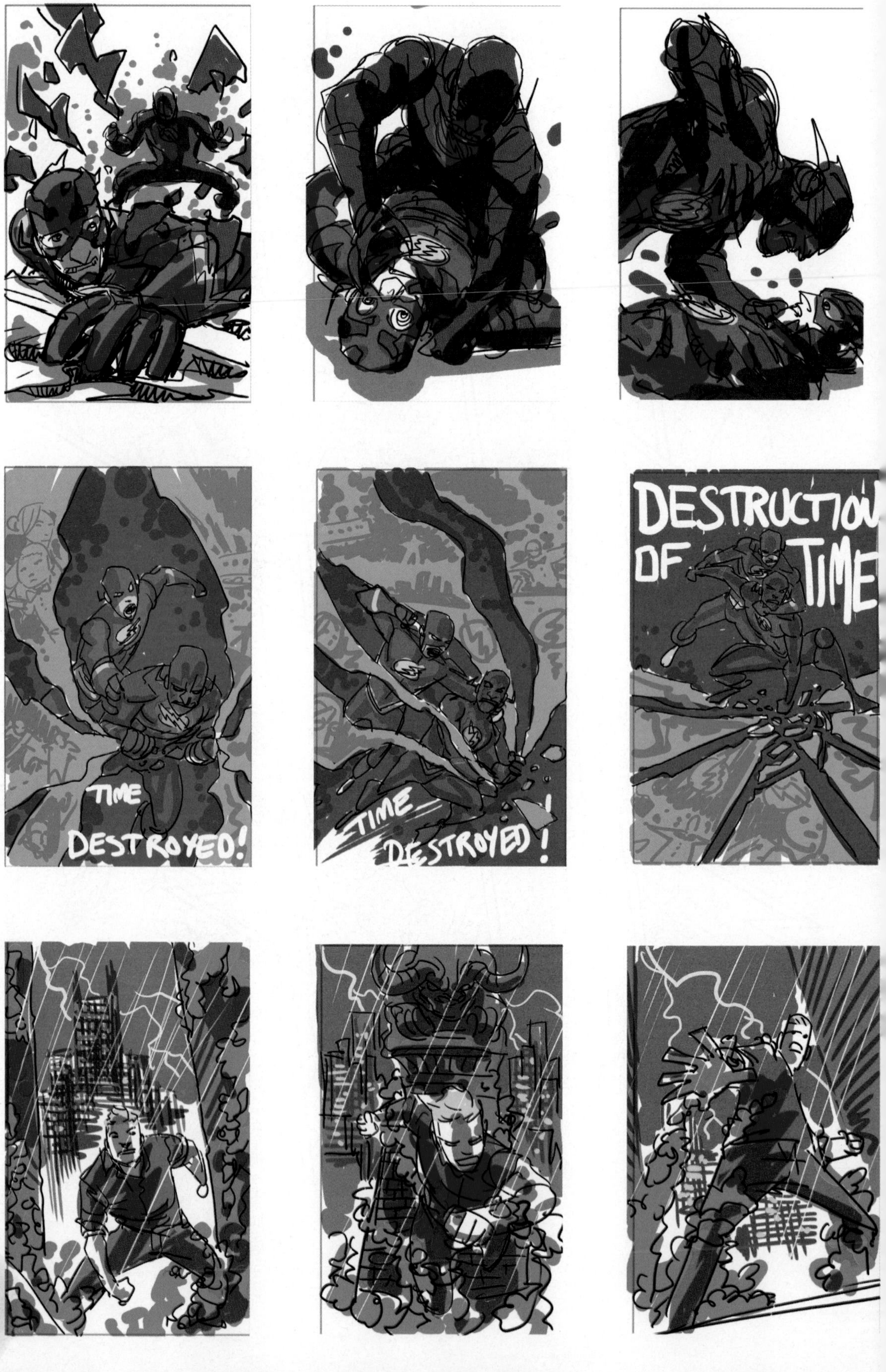
TIME
DESTROYED!
TIME
DESTROYED!
DESTRUCTION
OF TIME